An African Republic

The **John Hope Franklin** Series in

African American History and Culture

Waldo E. Martin Jr. and Patricia Sullivan,

editors

Marie Tyler-McGraw

An African Republic

Black
& White
Virginians
in the
Making of
Liberia

The University of North Carolina Press

Chapel Hill

© 2007
The University of North Carolina Press
All rights reserved
Manufactured in the United States of America
Designed and typeset in New Baskerville and
Clarendon by Eric M. Brooks
The paper in this book meets the guidelines
for permanence and durability of the Committee
on Production Guidelines for Book Longevity of
the Council on Library Resources.

Library of Congress Cataloging-in-Publication Data
Tyler-McGraw, Marie.
An African republic: Black and White Virginians in
the making of Liberia / Marie Tyler-McGraw.
    p. cm. — (The John Hope Franklin series in
African American history and culture)
Includes bibliographical references and index.
ISBN-13: 978-0-8078-3167-0 (cloth: alk. paper)
1. African Americans—Colonization—Liberia.
2. Liberia—History—To 1847. 3. Liberia—
History—1847–1944. 4. African Americans—
Virginia—History—19th century. 5. Free African
Americans—Virginia—History—19th century.
6. Whites—Virginia—History—19th century.
7. Liberia—Emigration and immigration—
History—19th century. 8. Virginia—Emigration
and immigration—History—19th century.
9. Virginia—Race relations—History—19th
century. 10. American Colonization Society—
History. I. Title.
DT633.T95 2007
966.62'004960730767—dc22   2007014848

11 10 09 08 07   5 4 3 2 1

**To the stones
that the builders
rejected**

We are the guardians of a nation
in the bud—a miniature of this
republic, a coloured America on
the shores of Africa.

*C. C. Harper to American
Colonization Society,* African
Repository *3 (January
1828): 325*

Who-so-ever in writing a moderne
Historie, shall follow truth too neare
the heeles, it may haply strike out
his teeth. . . . He that goeth after her
too farre off, looseth her sight, and
looseth himself:

And he that walks after her at a
middle distance; I know not whether
to call that kinde of course Temper
or Basenesse.

Sir Walter Raleigh,
History of the World

Contents

Illustrations

Acknowledgments

Any attempt to acknowledge all the specific and general assistance I have received in writing this book would turn the Acknowledgments into the Personals. I have had perceptive and energetic colleagues, and they have done what they could to encourage me and supply me with both arcane data and grand theories. They have caught many, but certainly not all, of my errors. I am particularly indebted to James O. Horton, who has been a colleague and friend for many years. He steadily supported my efforts to find time from heavy teaching loads and regular employment in public history in order to research and write. Svend Holsoe, now emeritus professor of anthropology at the University of Delaware, has been extremely generous with his time and his unparalleled collection of Liberian materials over many years and queries.

Twice the National Endowment for the Humanities assisted me with Summer Seminar stipends. Directors Larry Levine and Jane DeHart, as well as Donald Mathews, supported my later work, as did Ed Ayers, Suzanne Lebsock, and Phyllis Palmer. A postdoctoral fellowship to the Afro American Communities Project at the Smithsonian Institution's National Museum of American History allowed me to do quantitative studies of the Richmond free black community and to investigate the material culture and folklife of antebellum Virginia's African Americans. A fellowship at the Virginia Foundation for the Humanities gave me access to the rich Virginia history collections of Alderman Library and expanded my list of colonization auxiliary societies as well as my knowledge of their members.

Part of my work as historian at the Valentine Museum, now the Richmond History Center, was to produce a survey history of Richmond, Virginia. This gave me greater context for colonization and helped me to integrate new materials and approaches for explaining the American Colonization Society in Virginia. Staff historians at the Library of Virginia have maintained a professional interest in this enterprise for many years. The friendship and scholarship of Brent Tarter, Sandy Treadway, and John Kneebone, the latter then with the library, and Gregg Kimball, now at the library, have been sustaining. Melvin Ely alerted me to the letters of Ann Rice. A Mellon Fellowship to the Virginia Historical Society gave me access to the papers of Virginia women in the colonization movement. I am indebted to the knowledgeable staff that assisted me, especially Nelson Lankford, Sarah Bearss, now at the Library of Virginia, Janet Schwarz, and Frances Pollard.

A fellowship to the International Center for Jefferson Studies brought me full circle to where I began this study as a political history. My thanks to Zanne McDonald, Gaye Bower, and Rebecca Bowman at the center, and to Peter Onuf for discussions about Jefferson and the American Colonization Society. I shared research with Diane Swann-Wright, then director of African American and Special Programs, and Lucia Stanton, Shannon Senior Research Historian at the International Center for Jefferson Studies, and the greater gain was mine. At the University of Virginia's Alderman Library, Ervin Jordan, curator of special collections, was especially helpful, as was Lucious Edwards at Virginia State University.

Dwight Pitcaithley, chief historian of the National Park Service, indulged and supported my desire for research and writing time, even when it meant more work for him and for the staff of the history section of the National Register, History and Education Office. While I was teaching in the American studies department at George Washington University, Shannon Thomas served as a very competent intern. At the National Park Service, I thank Lois Horton for sending me Sarah Amsler, who worked as an intern in the American Colonization Society records, and I thank the Afro American Communities Project of the Smithsonian Institution for sharing Sarah's time and labors. Laurel Sneed of the Thomas Day Project, Jane Leigh Carter, and Claude Clegg generously shared material on the free black Day family and on North Carolina free blacks.

Readers of certain chapters in various forms include Scott Casper, Doug Egerton, Stanley Harrold, Vivien Hart, Deborah Lee, Randall Miller, Peter Onuf, Phyllis Palmer, Jim Sidbury, Bronwen Souders, Tatiana van Riemsdijk, Brent Tarter, Sandra Treadway, and Trin Yarborough. Brent Tarter read the entire manuscript, and Tatiana and Deborah gave the final drafts much-appreciated close attention. Randall Miller was an engaged, patient, and very helpful reader, and Stanley Harrold showed me where I needed more clarity. My thanks to Charles Grench and Katy O'Brien at the University of North Carolina Press for guiding the manuscript through its many stages. Deborah Lee gave me technical help combined with an informed interest in the topic that made computer issues less daunting than they would have been without her. Howard Wachtel served well as general reader and provided personal support. I hope that this study will motivate related research and, in doing so, correct my inevitable errors and omissions.

An African Republic

At the Library of Congress I first saw some Liberian paper currency from the 1830s—a rooster on one bill and an ox on another. The value of the currency was expressed in dollars. This was my introduction to the American Colonization Society and its colony of Liberia in West Africa, and I wondered if these icons of American agriculture had transplanted as easily to Africa as the decimal-based currency system. As I looked at documents that described the society's founding and its acquisition of land in western Africa, it was unclear to me what the intentions of the society were. Did the African colonization movement hope to end slavery in the early republic by encouraging slave emancipation with African colonization as a catalyst? Or did the society intend simply to send all free blacks to Africa, thus rein-forcing whiteness as a basis for liberty in the United States? Why did any free blacks go there? How could the advocates and emigrants imagine—or dream—that their scheme would work?

T HE AMERICAN COLONIZATION SOCIETY (ACS) has fre-quently been seen as a sideshow in nineteenth-century American history and one in which some of the nation's more bizarre and racist concepts were on display. But the ACS, though seldom in the spotlight, occupied part of the cen-ter ring of the American experience in that century. With racial identities and a national narrative undergoing construction and revision, the ACS fixed on the problem that embedded white prej-udice would severely restrict black achievement for generations. Its solution—an African republic—was problematic in itself. It promised to diminish the free black presence in America while offering a model of black achievement in Africa. Far from being exotic and marginal, the history of the ACS is central to under-standing nineteenth-century American meanings for citizenship in a republic and race as a category.[1]

Formed in December 1816 in Washington, D.C., by white men

who believed that racial prejudice in the United States, which they shared to varying degrees, was an insuperable barrier to black citizenship and freedom, the assumption behind the society's organization was that domestic tranquility required resolution of the "problem" of free African Americans. The society's draft memorial to Congress, seeking funding, said: "This intermediate species of population cannot be incorporated so as to render the Body Politic homogenous and consistent in all its [members] which must be [the] essential consideration of every form of government." The memorial described the free black condition as one of "imperfect connection, just raised from the abyss of slavery, but not to the level of freedom, suspended between degradation and honor."[2]

The "imperfect connection" could not be fixed, in the society's view. Its reasoning reflected the American constructions of race and society as they had evolved to 1816, drawing on arguments that a republic must be homogeneous, on Enlightenment ideas that human achievement is influenced by environment, and on the energetic missionary impulse of Protestant evangelicalism. Most of the founders and early members thought an African republic would demonstrate that the low condition of free blacks in America was based on their historic subjugation and was not a result of lack of ability. Many thought a black republic outside the white republic would encourage gradual emancipation. Some few among them hoped to rid the nation of a destabilizing and troublesome class and to protect slave property. For most, the organization was the logical continuation of earlier emancipation and colonization plans, such as those offered by New England cleric Samuel Hopkins in the 1770s, Virginian Ferdinando Fairfax in the 1790s, black Quaker sea captain Paul Cuffe in the early 1800s, and the example of the British campaign to abolish the slave trade.[3]

The ACS initially attempted to provide a national society so exemplary in its republican rhetoric and so vague as to final outcomes that it could be embraced by both North and South. The vagueness was not entirely a political strategy. The society's definitions of race and nation were as tentative and contingent as were all such theories at the turn of the nineteenth century.[4] All hoped that this project of voluntary free black colonization would be funded by the federal government, and there was good reason to think this—many society founders were influential men in American politics. But the sectional divisions apparent in the congressional debate over the admission of Missouri to the Union as slave or free territory, just as the society began to explore territory near Sierra Leone as a settlement site, doomed the plan for direct federal support. The ACS's historic moment passed, almost before it had well begun, and colonization developed a regional agenda in each state society or local auxiliary. Policies differed significantly, from Connecticut to Virginia to Ohio, and states tended to control their own finances, making generalizations about the ACS difficult.[5]

The ACS plan to colonize American free blacks in West Africa, far from North America's white republic geographically though tied to it in commerce and Christianity, remained the most important part of a project with changing strategies. Between 1820 and the Civil War, the society cooperated in sponsoring the emigration of over eleven thousand African Americans to Liberia. Its major source of alliance and financial support came to be not the federal government but the local auxiliaries established within each state. Increasingly, the society and its auxiliaries employed the tactics of benevolent societies by producing a quarterly journal, the *African Repository and Colonial Journal*; by employing itinerant agents as domestic fundraisers and organizers; and by asking clergymen for sermons in support of African colonization, with the subsequent plate-passing. State societies hived off to control their own funds and sponsor their own settlements in the society's colony of Liberia. In the late 1830s, the society was forced to adopt a new constitution favoring its constituents in Pennsylvania and New York, who at the time were donating much of the money.[6]

Within two decades, although national politicians still attacked or supported African colonization, the transformation from a national political effort to a donations-dependent and locally controlled society was nearly complete. Meanwhile, the national office perched uncomfortably in Washington, reluctant to concede that neither consensus from the states nor cash from Congress would be forthcoming. Despite the fragmentation of its funds and authority, the American Colonization Society established and marginally maintained the colony of Liberia on the western coast of Africa, and that colony became a nation in 1847.

Historians have noted that Virginia was the state in which African colonization might have made a national political difference.[7] Virginia was where emancipation and colonization appeared to be the most beneficial to whites and of the most interest to free blacks and where it appeared the most possible. Proud Virginia extended from the Atlantic Ocean to the Ohio River, and from Williamsburg, dreaming of its brilliant past and inhabited by boisterous students, to Wheeling, glowing with small iron furnaces and increasingly inhabited by German and Irish immigrants. It was the state that produced multiple auxiliary societies, sent the most emigrants to Liberia, and received many small donations and bequests from all over the state.

Virginia had the pivotal geographic position between the emancipation legislation of the North and the increasingly slavery-dependent Lower South. Further progress toward general emancipation would require some action on the part of Virginia with its large black population. The state had nearly half the nation's enslaved and free blacks, with the latter fettered by growing social and legislative restrictions. White Virginians, in harmony with other white Americans, believed that the American republic was a white man's country. Virginians also believed that they were especially well placed to mediate between North and South and to represent the interests of both sections. All these factors led Virginia to establish almost sixty auxiliary colonization societies and to provide prominent leadership and significant donations for the society in its first fifteen years. In the four decades before the Civil War, almost a third of the emigrants to Liberia came from Virginia, and the Chesapeake states of Maryland and Virginia together provided almost half the emigrants and most of the Liberian leadership until the 1870s.[8] The malleable concept of African colonization also attracted, at various times in Virginia, aging Revolutionaries, republican mothers and their daughters, evangelical planters, urban artisans, Whiggish businessmen and their wives, opportunistic politicians, and an intense group of gentlemen novelists.

But the antebellum decades saw the disappearance of the middle ground, the terrain for which Virginians felt they had the best compass. The ACS in Virginia began as essentially antislavery in the older gradual-emancipation tradition but was always monitored from within by proslavery and states' rights persons whose power grew over the decades. The Virginia Colonization Society, organized in 1828, raised little money because its hopes were pinned on the legislature and that assembly always delivered largesse encumbered with so many conditions that the money was scarcely used. Following a dormant period in the late 1830s and most of the 1840s, the state society was revived as a General Assembly–funded enterprise that was part of the apparatus of a growing proslavery orthodoxy. Those Virginia colonizationists who were not part of the Virginia Colonization Society were marginalized but continued to be active in emancipations and donations for an evangelical and domestic African model colony that had long been their personal vision.

One of the needs met by African colonization in Virginia was a vision of domestic utopia shared by a few white men and most white Virginia colonization women, as well as by African American emigrant families from Virginia. Its particulars are apparent in the desire of white women to encourage the formation and recognition of pious African American emigrant families; to construct clean, efficient, and attractive housing; to supply the tools and materials for a dignified life in Liberia; and to make literacy the key to salvation and citizenship. Recognizing the existence and sanctity of the black family was important for the sanctity of the white Virginia family, in the view of Virginia colonization women, who soon encountered resistance to any modification in race or gender statuses. Still, white women used the available gender roles to plead for the black family, complain of male dominance, allude to miscegenation, and advocate for education for black and white women. They carefully nurtured and emancipated selected enslaved men and women to represent their own white evangelical, educational, and domestic values in Liberia.

Virginia's needs and the ACS were also connected by an attempt to compose a suitable Virginia past that was just as much an effort to shape the future. As sectional tensions grew, the rivalry between Virginia and Massachusetts over the origins of American institutions became more heated. Virginia claimed primacy in the creation of representative assemblies, resistance to the British, and Revolutionary leadership. In this core national mythology, the homes and artifacts of the Revolutionary generation, especially Mount Vernon, were the sacred sites of the national narrative the Virginians were composing. But Virginia also had the first large enslaved population and still maintained slavery. Virginia could not construct a national republican narrative with itself at the center while other sections could claim to have cleared themselves of slavery. Virginia had to have at least a visible aspiration to that end. African colonization might answer critics of Virginia's claims and Virginia's free blacks might replicate and verify Virginia's history through the perils of passage, the struggle for survival in a new land, the encounter with "uncivilized" indigenous peoples, and the growth of republican institutions. For prominent Virginia families, such as the Washingtons and the Lees, this was an important part of the appeal of colonization.

Although African colonization never persuaded or engaged significant numbers of free blacks, the enterprise had important symbolic and provocative value for the questions of race and citizenship that it raised. The ACS acted as a catalyst for creating and crystallizing African American positions on those topics. Northern free blacks and their allies grew increasingly vigorous and articulate in their critique of the ACS as a project to transport them from their homes and remove them as advocates for enslaved blacks. Chesapeake free blacks were divided but furnished the majority of emigrants for the decades before the Civil War and articulated their reasons with comparable vigor. In the African American debate over national identity and destiny, northern free blacks had the advantage of black newspapers and black conventions with published proceedings to record their views; emigrants to Liberia frequently had their views filtered through white journals that, although sympathetic to African colonization, were not inclined to print the words of black colonizationists in their full vigor. For this reason, Liberian views on the failings and contradictions of white American society remained muted in public, but not in private, discourse.[9]

Despite the heated rhetoric and invective exchanged between Liberian emigrants and northern free blacks, their means of assessment of their condition were similar. Both tended to measure their status against America's vaunted republican liberty and an emerging, still uncertain, identity with Africa. The Virginia free blacks who constituted most of the leadership class in Liberia for two generations shared all the values and concerns of northern free blacks, except for one. They believed they could not rise to full citizenship in the United States despite their talents, but northern free blacks resisted this conclusion and grew eloquent in defining themselves in opposition. The Liberian enterprise, as colony and as republic, was the emigrants' form of resistance to slavery, but it was one that was denigrated by black and white northern abolitionists and proslavery southerners. Instead, they were described as avaricious, pretentious, and predatory toward the local indigenous population. But, although Liberia offered examples of the usual aggressive ethnocentricities of colonizers, African Americans there sought to avoid the most grievous complaint they had of America: that they were everywhere shut out from improvement or citizenship on the basis of their race. Their constitution made cultural assimilation the standard for citizenship, not descent from Americans.[10]

Free black Virginians of property and local standing felt a need to escape the narrow, restricted lives to which even the most successful of them were consigned but did not believe that moving north would improve their circumstances or resolve their identity problems. Virginia's early free black emigrants were familiar with the work of Paul Cuffe and African American missionaries and saw themselves as constructing their own identities as Americans and Africans without sacrificing their identification with enslaved Africans in the American South, a group that was far more than an abstraction to them. But reversing the transatlantic voyage did not restore these African Americans to their native land because their native land was first Virginia and then the American republic. Their American and Virginian values were the narrative framework on which the Liberian colony was explained to the world and to the settlers. Virginia's history of the Jamestown settlement mirrored Liberia's national origins story, and these recurring themes were celebrated by colonizationists on both sides of the Atlantic as a triumphal narrative. Crossing over from one nation to create another provided abundant opportunities for revising personal and national identity among both emigrants and white advocates of colonization.

Liberians from Virginia dominated public offices in the colony and later in the Republic of Liberia. Their civic and political structures, their religious institutions, and their styles and assumptions reflected Virginia and the Revolutionary generation, nowhere more so than in the Liberian Declaration of Independence and Constitution of 1847. Despite their inevitable cultural biases and personal flaws, these settlers were energetic and imaginative in creating both a republic and a justification for leaving the United States in order to become Americans. They contrasted the dependence of northern free blacks on white benevolence with their own independence and believed that African Americans in the United States who criticized Liberia were deluded as to their own status in that country.

The difficulties encountered by African Americans in Liberia were due in part to their preconceptions of Africans as without knowledge or proper beliefs. But the African American emigrants believed themselves only culturally, not biologically, superior to Africans. The Liberian leadership, although sensitive to class distinctions for their own sake, also understood that Liberia needed trained, literate, and competent emigrants. The lack of a large exodus of talented and solvent free blacks from the United States after the early 1830s added to the lack of financial or military support usually accorded to a colonial outpost by its country of origin, making it very difficult for Liberians to achieve the economic self-sufficiency necessary to function as an independent nation. It was the central tragedy of those in the Virginian leadership that their reproduction of and frequent references to the Virginia colonial experience appeared to work for them in the short term in seeking settler unity and establishing a government, but failed them when issues of economic development and the rights and roles of indigenous people became paramount in the late nineteenth century.

Colonization was a project that could not empty Virginia of free or enslaved African Americans, but African colonization never disappeared from the politics, literature, and religion of antebellum Virginia, and its appearance in other guises signified an underlying anxiety with slavery. Significant for its clustered meanings, African colonization was but one among various theories and practices that permitted white Virginians to live with the intensifying contradictions of slavery and liberty. It was no more fanciful than the "diffusionist" or "safety valve" arguments that promised slavery would weaken and die once it was spread over a greater geographic surface. Black emigration from Virginia to Liberia was simultaneously used as a device for repression of free blacks, a cultural construction employed to explain Virginia and direct its domestic and national future, a religious imperative, a site for African American debate over racial identity and national allegiance, a strategy of black empowerment, and a precursor to general emancipation. Virginia offered a regional stage but the broadest possible cast of characters for interaction, reaction, and the playing out of every contingency, relation, and perspective concerning African colonization, and that kept questions of slavery, race, black identity, and American self-image in play, as venues for such discussion in Virginia grew fewer with each passing decade.

One

A Small Frisson of Fear,
Soon Soothed

THE YOUNGER MEN USUALLY stayed out until well past dark on summer Sundays, but some came back from the fish feast early, complaining that the women had "eat up all the fish." Just about the only thing worth telling about was those big talkers from the Prosser place and their claims about how many guns and swords they got and what they intended doing with them. Brothers Gabriel and Solomon, traveling freely from one gathering of blacks to another, boasted about the swords they had fashioned out of scythes at the blacksmith's forge. Each scythe, broken in the middle, heated and pounded, made two swords, which were hidden away for a bloody uprising against the whites, their masters. These two and the men they recruited met with bondmen and free blacks singly and in groups. Anywhere that black men gathered, Gabriel or one of his followers was likely to be in the summer of 1800.[1]

Throughout the spring and summer of 1800, Gabriel and his fellows organized a wide-ranging and complex conspiracy to invade Richmond, seize the state capitol and the store of arms nearby, hold the governor captive, and negotiate for the release of all slaves. But Gabriel's conspiracy was betrayed by both nature and man, when a heavy rain washed out a bridge on the night planned for moving toward Richmond and two slaves informed their owner of Gabriel's plans. After his arrest, Gabriel said little, but his recruits testified that he had approached free blacks and slaves while they were hoeing corn, fishing under the bridges, working in a blacksmith's shop, at fish feasts and barbeques, after church services, and while playing quoits and cards. Trial depositions referred to secret lists and letters carried from town to town and claimed that Gabriel had been shown every room in the capitol and promised the keys.[2]

Gabriel and his lieutenants constructed their rationale from the world in which they lived and explained themselves and their plans within the familiar political and cultural discourse of the early Republic. Ben Woolfolk testified that he and fellow slave Gilbert intended to purchase a piece of silk for a flag on which they would inscribe "death or Liberty." One witness claimed that if the whites agreed to their freedom, Gabriel would "dine and drink with the merchants of the city on that day." "Outlandish Africans," those born in Africa, were recruited to the conspiracy because "they were supposed to deal with witches and wizards and, of course, [were] useful in armies to tell when any calamity was about to befall them." Although the powers of African magic were respected, the conspirators assumed that none among them still had those powers. In another case, George approached Ben who was chopping wood and asked if he wanted to join a society of Freemasons. No, was the response, based on the contemporary debate over secret societies and their supposed atheism and elitism; "all free masons were going to hell." George then asked directly if Ben was willing to fight the white people for his freedom, and, with the question reformulated, Ben said he would "consider of it."[3]

White Virginians who read the state's evidence printed in the *Virginia Argus* or who heard even more exotic rumors were alarmed. The trial testimony of Gabriel's followers confirmed white fears that black Virginians identified with Virginia's recent Revolutionary past and were conversant with the political debates that animated Richmond. Since the establishment of the American republic, Richmond and Virginia had offered the nation not just the rhetoric of faction, but excellent examples of its fractious formation. Both followers and prosecutors of Gabriel later connected his conspiracy to the fresh memory of the American and French Revolutions, to the complex and ongoing slave rebellion in St. Domingue, and to the charged atmosphere of an American election year.[4] If ever evidence was needed of the discontent of slaves, of their mobility and frequent social interactions, and of their connections with free blacks, it had now been provided.

James Monroe, the state's governor, attempted, with some success, to soothe nervous citizens by presenting Gabriel's plot as an aberration. The fear that was palpable in the aftermath of the rebellion was soothed with time-honored incantations that enslaved Virginians were either content or not capable of sustained rebellion. Most white Virginians were willing publicly to echo these nostrums, but fear continued to flow like a powerful current far beneath the contrived, placid surface of daily life. According to one scenario, blacks were like whites in their needs and desires and would, sooner or later, organize themselves and seek liberty, if necessary through armed struggle. After liberty, they would seek republican citizenship and, perhaps, all the rights of men. Free and enslaved blacks saw themselves as Virginians, not Africans; the rights they sought were the rights of Virginians, not those of a separate people sharing only the same geography.[5]

One important reason for white Virginians to persuade themselves that Gabriel's insurrection was an aberration instead of a harbinger of the future was that such reasoning enabled them to avoid the question of free black status. Virginia's stake in resolving the question of whether black Virginians could ever be citizens was large. It was the question behind the question of emancipation. No scheme or plan of emancipation could be brought forward without addressing the presence of free blacks in the state. After the Virginia Manumission Act of 1782 made it possible for slaveholders to emancipate bondmen, the free black population of Virginia grew rapidly. From 1782 to 1790, the number of free blacks in Virginia rose from fewer than 3,000 to 12,866. Ten years later, the number had increased to 20,000. The state contained some 40 percent of the free black population of the nation at the time of Gabriel's insurrection in 1800, more than all the northern states together. Virginia and Maryland shared a rough parity in the numbers of free blacks by 1820, after which time Maryland surged ahead of Virginia and Pennsylvania and New York came to rank just behind Virginia.[6]

At the same time, the practice of hiring out slaves to domestic labor, merchants, factories, mines, and farms increased in the early nineteenth century. Especially when the hired slave acted as his own agent, this system offered enslaved populations more control over time and space, increasing their sense of autonomy and possibility. White Virginians generally considered hiring out an unwise practice, but its profitability meant that no real effort was made to end it. Hired-out slaves joined growing numbers of free blacks in Virginia's towns and cities, resulting in just the sort of extensive communication networks between free and enslaved, urban and rural black Virginians that white Virginians feared.[7]

Officially presented as an aberration, Gabriel's insurrection was more commonly interpreted as a result of the mobility of free blacks and hired slaves, as well as the lax supervision of slaves and the increased numbers of free blacks. Sentiment grew to repeal the Manumission Act of 1782 that had permitted individual manumissions and to force free blacks to leave the state. Seeking first to rid the state of "persons obnoxious to the laws or dangerous to the peace of society," the Virginia legislature and Governor Monroe, in secret correspondence with President Thomas Jefferson, soon enlarged the discussion to consider the removal of all free and emancipated blacks from Virginia. Removal seemed a desperate measure, fraught with unintended consequences, but Gabriel's web of conspirators put the General Assembly in the proper frame of mind to consider destinations for such an experiment.

Jefferson found nowhere in North America that was acceptable as a site, fearing that American "rapid multiplication" would ultimately reach any such colony and once again disrupt the harmony of "people speaking the same language, governed in similar forms and by similar laws" by the "blot or mixture" of the black presence. He failed to act on a Virginia General Assembly proposal that some portion of the Louisiana Purchase be investigated. At various times in the correspondence, he suggested the West Indies, especially Haiti, or perhaps Sierra Leone, as "a last and undoubted resort, if all others more desirable should fail us."[8] Indeed, no place on earth seemed exactly right for the free blacks of Virginia. After three years, the secret correspondence broke off without conclusion. The most important action concerning free blacks that the Virginia General Assembly took in this period was to pass a law in 1806 ordering all emancipated slaves to leave Virginia within twelve months. Although only sporadically enforced, it remained on the books as a threat to free blacks, discouraging any claims to civic rights. Thus the modest liberalizing tendencies of the 1780s and 1790s were effectively halted in Virginia.

Virginia arrived at Gabriel's insurrection and the secret correspondence over black removal from its long history of laws of bondage, most of which had been straightforward in expressing apprehension about free and enslaved black connections. From the mid-1600s, blackness was a convenient barrier to the extension of English rights of labor, and the temptation to exploit the vulnerable African was too great to resist in Virginia's early labor-hungry economy. Beginning in the 1640s, color began to be associated with lifetime indenture. The court system did not proclaim this; it simply validated it by resolving disputes without questioning the premise of permanent indenture or a separate status for blacks. The system of slavery that developed through custom and usage was supported by court decisions and was finally codified into laws. The fact that this occurred in a piecemeal fashion, characteristic of English case law, does not mean that it was not purposeful. The African's reduction to property happened over generations but was not haphazard.[9]

A few Africans slipped through the tangle of laws and became part of a free black class. White Virginians very soon grew uneasy about the relationship between free blacks and those who were locked into slavery. By 1691, the Virginia legislature was sufficiently apprehensive about the role and status of free blacks to pass legislation restricting manumissions, because "great inconvenience may happen to this country by setting of negroes and mulattoes free by their either entertaining negro slaves or receiving stolen goods or being grown old bringing a charge upon the country." Under this act, no slave was to be set free unless the owner would pay the charge of transporting him from the colony.[10] This concern and this solution were to recur regularly for the next 170 years: manumission must be linked with exile.

Again in the early eighteenth century, the Virginia legislature expressed its concern over "tumultuous and unlawful meetings," "secret plots and conspiracies," and rebellions and insurrections in which free blacks were suspected and accused. The legislative response produced several acts that sharply limited the rights of masters to free their slaves under any circumstances and, in 1723, made manumission an act of the legislature only. The legislative power of manumission was then used largely to reward slaves for informing on conspiracies.[11]

In the Revolutionary Era, Virginians berated the British for imposing the slave trade on their colony, a hapless victim of Britain's mercantile schemes. In 1777, Thomas Jefferson and several colleagues served as a committee to draft a new constitution for the state of Virginia. That constitution included a gradual emancipation clause that provided for colonization of all young adult blacks, but this portion was dropped before the new constitution reached the floor of the assembly for debate. In the next year, the Virginia General Assembly enacted legislation that ended most slave importation and, in 1782, enacted the statute permitting individual manumissions. This was the most significant piece of legislation bearing on slavery passed by the Virginia legislature during the Revolutionary Era, and it marked the farthest point toward loosening the bonds of slavery that the legislature of Virginia would go.[12]

In his *Notes on the State of Virginia*, published a few years after the 1782 law was passed, Jefferson again wanted an end to slavery, but only in conjunction with a plan of removal. He noted the pernicious effect of slavery on whites and assessed blacks as probably inferior to whites "in endowments of both mind and body." Jefferson never deviated from this position in the course of a long public life, several times proposing schemes for emancipation. But these were always coupled with a reference to deportation or emigration, which, near the end of his life, he called "expatriation." Jefferson's writings made him the most selectively quotable founding father used by African colonizationists in Virginia, but in his lifetime he resisted their embrace.[13]

In the early decades of the nineteenth century, the Chesapeake region was the center of black social and cultural life, especially the port cities.[14] Urban free black lives in these areas, although hampered and constrained, appeared enviable to slaves, especially skilled urban slaves such as Gabriel and many of his cohort who worked among them. As explained by one early-twentieth-century historian sympathetic to white unhappiness with this development: "Much difficulty was soon experienced in discriminating between slaves fraudulently passing as free negroes and negroes actually free. . . . Free negroes treated their registers or 'free papers' as if they were transferable and escaping slaves used them to conceal their identity. Enterprising slaves even forged such papers, or secured them from white persons."[15] The "much difficulty" experienced after 1782 in controlling the growing free black population seemed a confirmation of the "great inconvenience" anticipated in 1691 if some "negroes and mulattoes" were set free while others remained enslaved.

Gabriel confirmed fears long held by white Virginians, but his insurrection was just the most visible effort by black Virginians in the Revolutionary Era to turn the American Revolution to their own advantage. The disruption of the American Revolution was itself a profoundly enlightening tutorial for slaves whose knowledge of the geography, society, and politics of their region greatly expanded.[16] During the Revolution's Virginia phases, thousands of slaves ran away or were caught up in the war effort. Black Virginians who fought with Lord Dunmore, the colonial governor of Virginia, in his 1775 campaign to subdue colonial rebels were among the first to think collectively about freedom. These and other enslaved blacks took advantage of the confusions of war in Virginia to escape to the British, and some of them accompanied the British from Virginia to Nova Scotia or to England. In time, and with the aid of an emerging British antislavery movement, some of these ex-slaves eventually traveled to Sierra Leone in 1792 to found a settlement, called Freetown, for free blacks and Africans recaptured from slaving vessels.[17]

David George, once a slave in Virginia, left with the British for Nova Scotia and led the Nova Scotian Baptists to Sierra Leone. Henry Washington, who escaped from Mount Vernon, later took part in an insurrection against the governing agency in Sierra Leone for which he was exiled to a distant farm. Whether these two ex-slaves from Virginia maintained contact with black Virginians is not known, but the effort to establish Freetown was watched carefully by post-Revolutionary abolition societies and by the evangelical and benevolent segments of Protestant churches in Britain and America.[18]

After the upheavals of the Revolution, the Baptist and Methodist churches grew rapidly in numbers, and many of Virginia's slaves were converted to these denominations. Dissenting preachers found an audience among many African Americans, who frequently used Christianity to shape a separate identity that would define them apart from white Virginians' assessments. Evangelical religion also gave black Virginians a separate history that explained, but did not justify, their current oppression and provided members an opportunity to trace their personal histories in the collective memory of congregations.

In 1804, Presbyterian minister John Holt Rice marveled that the black congregation to which he preached at Cub Creek in Charlotte County was formed long before in Hanover County, "when they belonged to Colonel Byrd's estate from which they had been sold and brought into this country." The black congregation on the Byrd plantation in the 1750s was one of the earliest in the British American colonies. It was dispersed with the sale of William Byrd III's estate, but small groups re-formed elsewhere in Virginia, joining existing churches or founding their own. Rice was impressed that "a very large proportion can read and are instructed in religious doctrines and duties" and that "they afford an experiment of sixty to seventy years standing of the effect of this sort of discipline among slaves." The Cub Creek black congregation had a narrative of its personal odyssey in Virginia that was approaching three generations in length.[19]

The Cub Creek congregation was not unique in its long memory. The late eighteenth century in Virginia saw the existence of biracial congregations. Baptist and Methodist camp meetings drew many of Virginia's African Americans, and the two races briefly practiced an approximation of equality in their religious interactions. Black churches were constituted that appeared to scatter, devolve, or die when congregations divided, but they were often resurrected in new places with new names. What remained constant was a core group of black members who brought their institutional memory and spiritual and family histories with them to a new site. From that base arose black churches that survived in some form throughout the antebellum era. Black churches in Petersburg and Richmond were among those with origins in the eighteenth century that survived to consider African colonization in the nineteenth century.

One such church was the Gillfield Church in Petersburg, with its origins in the racially mixed Baptist Davenport Church that existed in rural Prince

George County in 1788. Around 1800, the Davenport Church disbanded and its black members formed the Sandy Beach Church in Petersburg in 1803. In 1818, the church purchased a site called Gill's Field and set up the Gillfield Baptist Church. Not far away, Richmond's black believers in the First Baptist Church organized an African Baptist Missionary Society in 1815 that operated almost independently of the white membership. Another church with its core membership from the dispersed Byrd bondpeople was reconstituted by the white minister John Michaels between 1772 and 1774. By 1820, this church had also moved to Petersburg and become the Petersburg First Colored Church. These and other churches, aware of Sierra Leone and African missionary efforts, provided leadership for the colony of Liberia for the antebellum decades.[20]

Black religious organizations were the one form of potential antislavery organization that survived the generation following the Revolution in Virginia. Chattel slavery in England's North American colonies became a subject for English benevolence in the second half of the eighteenth century when a shift in humanitarian sensibilities and philosophy gradually overtook first the English and then their colonials. Until then, no religious, philosophical, or economic system was incompatible with slavery. Humanitarian objections to slavery, when they arose, were based in scriptural law and republican character, as St. George Tucker, a Virginia writer and judge, identified them in 1796.[21] A gradual and ameliorative antislavery was seen as least disruptive of national unity and most likely to be acceptable to the southern states. This was the dominant form of antislavery sentiment throughout the nation until the late 1820s, and it was the one most congenial to Virginia's politicians and religious antislavery advocates.[22]

✓ Virginians were aware that states to the north ended or began to phase out slavery during and after the Revolution. The Vermont Constitution of 1777 specifically outlawed slavery. In New Hampshire, an assumption that the 1783 Constitution and Bill of Rights outlawed slavery was upheld by the courts. Massachusetts ended slavery through judicial interpretation of the newly enacted Bill of Rights in 1783. Laws for the gradual abolition of slavery were passed by the state legislatures in Pennsylvania, Rhode Island, Connecticut, and New York, although various loopholes kept slavery alive well into the nineteenth century.[23] Those Virginians who believed slavery injurious to the state were encouraged by these developments and, in the same period, produced plans, petitions, philosophies, and court actions that they hoped might bring a similar phased end to slavery in their state.

Near the turn of the nineteenth century, three white Virginians offered plans for gradual emancipation to the larger American public in hope of finding national support not just for emancipation in Virginia but for mediating some larger design that would address the national question of free black status. Ferdinando Fairfax, a wealthy planter from northern Virginia, put forth the first detailed plan for emancipation and colonization in 1790. Fairfax concluded that free blacks could never be the social equals of whites or have all the privileges of citizenship in the United States, and thus it would, he thought, be better to colonize them in Africa with congressional support. The American government could defend and govern the colony until it was well established and could use this success to encourage voluntary compensated manumission to slave owners.

Fairfax expressed sentiments and beliefs common to many Americans of the era: that emancipation was desirable and necessary; that the obstacles to black participation in American society were too great to be overcome; that the United States government should pay for colonization; and that colonization would encourage manumission and lead to an end to slavery. His plan was very similar to that of the American Colonization Society at its founding years later, and Fairfax attended the organizational meeting. Like the later society, Fairfax had no philosophical scruples about allowing the federal government to finance and direct such an enterprise.[24]

St. George Tucker, writing in the mid-1790s, offered a detailed plan in which slaves received their freedom at age twenty-eight, after some years of unpaid labor for the costs of their upbringing, and then entered a serf-like state of freedom with certain civil rights and liberties forever denied them. This emancipation did not include black removal from Virginia, but he anticipated that blacks might disperse on their own, perhaps to the South if Virginia no longer needed such labor. Tucker sent copies of his plan to influential northerners and to the Virginia General Assembly. Although his ideas received a sympathetic hearing in parts of the North, the failure of both the Virginia General Assembly and northern statesmen to consider them meant an end to the potential for dialogue between northern states and Virginia on this central topic even before Gabriel's conspiracy. Shortly after that event, a third Virginian and cousin of St. George Tucker, George Tucker, wrote a brief essay in the form of a letter in which he urged gradual emancipation and the resettlement of freedmen west of the Mississippi River, concluding that African colonization was too expensive and Haiti too undeveloped and culturally different for American blacks.

Each of these Virginia writers, products of planter wealth and education, wrote within a brief post-Revolutionary time period in which a Virginia dialogue with northern states that addressed the consequences of emancipation seemed possible. Although they varied in their postemancipation strategies, all three writers agreed that an end to slavery would force the question of whether free blacks could remain in Virginia with few rights of citizenship or whether that status was untenable. But none of these plans had the public impact for which the authors hoped, and no national or regional political or philosophical discussion or alliance for a general emancipation took place.[25]

Dissenting religions, with very different social origins, ultimately found similar public resistance to their antislavery impulses. New Light Presbyterians and Separate Baptists brought religious dissent to Virginia in the 1750s, creating a groundswell that worked its way upward into the ranks of the elites.[26] The evangelical and dissenting sects that distanced themselves from the official English church measured worth through an individual conversion experience manifested in both personal piety and involvement with the religious community.[27] In 1784, the Baltimore Conference of the Methodist Episcopal Church adopted rules requiring white Methodists to begin manumitting their slaves or face excommunication. In 1785, the General Committee of Virginia Baptists condemned slavery as contrary to the word of God. These pronouncements were short-lived. After only one year, the Methodist Conference suspended the rule requiring gradual emancipation. By 1793, the Baptist General Committee decided that emancipation was a political issue that belonged in the legislature, not in the church. By the end of the eighteenth century, Baptists, as well as Methodists and Presbyterians, moved to place white preachers over black preachers. Baptist and Methodist leaders had come up against the unwillingness of their white members to emancipate their slaves and had to choose between modifying their position on antislavery or losing white members.

In the South, including in Virginia, these denominations appealed most to a striving nouveau gentry, newly possessed of land, slaves, and a little status. Members were receptive to a religious message that promised them the power to save their own souls and to run their own churches, but not to one that asked them to dispose of their newly acquired human property. Even among the dissenting preachers and the evangelicals of the post-Revolutionary generation, few were forthrightly antislavery. The collective evangelical antislavery impulse was never powerful enough to overcome the resistance of its members. When it faltered, evangelicals placed responsibility for slavery inside the household and made it part of household relations with significant consequences. Thereafter, evangelical emancipators would find their arguments for emancipation and colonization inextricably intertwined with their views of domestic relations and Christian community.[28]

The fate of Virginia's abolition societies paralleled that of white corporate religious antislavery. The first such society was formed in Richmond in 1790, at a time when many other abolition societies were being formed throughout the new nation. Although never as strong as their counterparts north of the Potomac, abolition societies in the Upper South, such as those in Richmond and Alexandria, seemed to hold promise as a respectable and sober approach to emancipation based on republican principles, Christian ideals, and the enlightened self-interest of the townsman. Their tactics included legislative petitions urging gradual emancipation, freedom suits in the courts to aid slaves who should have been free under existing law, and greater legal protections for free blacks.

These activities found opposition in the General Assembly, where members passed laws making it almost impossible to win a suit for the freedom of a slave. Legislation in the mid-1790s imposed a penalty of $100 on any person who assisted a slave asserting a claim to freedom if that claim failed and provided that no member of an abolition society could serve on the jury for a freedom suit. Many of the abolitionists were Baptists, Methodists, or Quakers; and the Baptists and the Methodists backed away from the issue in the 1790s. Some abolitionists were urban tradesmen without connections to planter families. They were no match in time, wealth, or influence for the planters who actively opposed them. This response to the mild and legalistic activities of the town-based Virginia abolition societies occurred even before Gabriel's aborted revolt in 1800 and illustrates a deep resistance among Virginia's politicians not just to a change in the status of blacks but also to the exercise of political or legal power by the tradesmen of the abolition societies.[29]

A decade and more into the nineteenth century, it appeared that all antislavery efforts by white Virginians had come to naught. The secret correspondence between the Virginia legislature and President Jefferson after Gabriel's conspiracy remained filed away. The years immediately following the planned insurrection produced a nervous flurry of rumors and arrests in the lower Tidewater counties. In 1809, a general uprising was suspected, and fear of insurrection during the War of 1812 caused the government to move the powder magazine.[30] In the spring of 1816, Charles Fenton Mercer, a Federalist member of the Virginia House of Delegates from Loudoun County who embraced both the economic and the religious arguments against slavery, learned of the secret legislative debate and correspondence. Mercer acquired the journals of the debate and copies of the correspondence and made them known throughout the middle Atlantic states. He determined that the resolutions should be presented to the legislature again, this time without secrecy, and he added a resolution late in 1816 asking the federal government for financial aid in procuring a territory in Africa as an asylum for free blacks.

Mercer met in Washington with Elias B. Caldwell, clerk of the Supreme Court, and Francis Scott Key, a prominent lawyer, and shared his plan for reintroducing the resolutions. Word of their meeting spread among their compatriots in benevolence. Caldwell wrote to colleagues in New Jersey, especially to his brother-in-law, Robert B. Finley. Finley, a Presbyterian minister, had long advocated African missions, and a nationwide colonization effort for free blacks met his standards for collaboration. His enthusiasm was matched by that of an evangelical colleague, the Reverend Samuel Mills. Both men had watched the progress of Sierra Leone with interest and were aware of black shipmaster Paul Cuffe's recent effort to settle American blacks there. The evangelical and political visions of African colonization did not mesh easily at every point, but there was sufficient harmony of interest and enthusiasm to drive the northern ministers and the Upper South men of influence together and to Washington.[31]

As the Virginia legislature reassembled in November 1816, Finley, in New Jersey, disclosed his plan for a national society headquartered in Washington, D.C., to fund free black emigration to Africa. On December 12, Mercer introduced his resolutions in the Virginia House of Delegates. After a day of debate, they were passed and an injunction of secrecy removed. Sent to the Senate, they passed that body on December 23. Two days earlier, a committee orchestrated by Key and Caldwell and meeting in the Morris Hotel in Washington, D.C., began writing a constitution for an American Society for Colonizing the Free People of Colour. They soon moved their labors to the House of Representatives where a draft constitution was adopted at a general meeting of those who had been encouraged to attend by Mercer, Finley, and Key.[32]

It was a propitious and evanescent moment of national unity, favorable for the formation of a national African colonization society and in keeping with the gradualist antislavery approaches that were the national norm for the generation after the Revolution. These practices remained Virginia's approach for another generation. For more than a century after 1690, white Virginia had brooded over "secret plots and conspiracies." Then Gabriel's planned insurrection excited old fears of slave revolt while demonstrating that there was a black perspective running parallel to the white Virginian discourse about slavery. This was enough to doom the already-fragile abolition societies, utopian schemes, and evangelical impulses of the post-Revolutionary era. But, in 1816, the Virginia legislature sought once more to craft a national and international effort for the relocation of emancipated and free blacks. Exactly where that would lead was not clear, but it was the logical outcome of what had gone before in Virginia.

Two

The Alchemy of Colonization

NEAR THE END OF THE eighteenth century there appeared in Virginia a Doctor Perkins who was traveling through the counties and cities of the United States on a self-described mission of mercy. He carried with him "Perkins' Metallic Tractors," two-forked metal instruments about four inches long, flat on one side and rounded on the other, which he claimed to apply scientifically to certain points on the skin. Manipulating them in mysterious patterns, he professed to cure rheumatism, gout, toothache, and headache through the power of the mixture of zinc and silver in the instruments. He illustrated the galvanic effect of this mixture by the sensation produced on the tongue of a volunteer from the audience. Many of those scratched by the tines claimed relief from their symptoms or forgot them with the distraction of skin scraped raw. Perkins sold tractors by the case for $20 each in Virginia. In time, local citizens took to making similar instruments of a variety of materials and claimed equal success, even with a set of wooden tractors painted silver. As the number of homegrown practitioners and concurrent skepticism grew, Perkins moved his enterprise abroad and founded a Perkinean Institution in London.[1]

Dr. Perkins moved through Virginia at a time when enthusiasm for science as an explanation for natural phenomena was growing but, despite experimentation and complex systems of classification, science had not supplanted folk beliefs, which included elements of magical thinking. Perkins had cleverly combined two popular forms of faux science that appealed to the very human desires to make gold from dross and to be healed, especially without pain or effort. One was the medieval belief in alchemy, a science based on the premise that essences of a base nature might be transformed into objects of value by a mixture of elements. Another was an early version of mesmerism that claimed that magnets could create a celestial gravity from the melding of elements that normally resisted blending. Drawn over the limbs of the afflicted, the celestial gravity pulled out illness. For a credulous public eager to believe in marvels, alchemy and magnetism still exerted appeal.

The American Colonization Society (ACS) appeared to undertake a similar experiment in alchemy when it claimed that the free black population of the United States, "base" and "degraded" by a hostile American environment, might be transmuted into an exemplary citizenry by the work of creating an African republic. Although the society emphasized that commerce with Africa and the Christian conversion of that population would be important by-products of any West African colonization project, the avowed goal of the society was limited to founding a colony to which consenting American free blacks could be sent. The ACS was grounded in Enlightenment environmentalism and evangelical zeal for Christian converts, but these concepts were not without difficulties. Enlightenment science was a two-edged sword that could be used to emphasize human capabilities or to categorize and isolate by differences. And evangelical religion in the South had already backed away from the implications of its embarrassing success among slaves.[2] With these competing tendencies within religion and philosophy, colonization would need an alchemical fusion of northern and southern political interests and of black and white perspectives in order to create the envisioned African republic.

Although the new society did not acknowledge the source, the ACS drew a significant portion of the arguments it soon mounted for an African colonization site from a free black New England Quaker shipmaster and merchant, Paul Cuffe. In December 1815, Cuffe had accompanied a band of thirty-eight African Americans to Sierra Leone, where the British had established a colony of recaptured and other diasporic Africans, including some who had escaped Chesapeake slavery in the Revolution and the War of 1812.[3] Cuffe's initial interest had been in the Christian conversion and commercial possibilities of Africa, but he turned his attention to African colonization as a way to deflect what he saw as a coming bloody racial confrontation in the South.

As Cuffe's endeavors suggest, the concept that a colony in Africa might serve as a form of repatriation and empowerment for American free blacks, while also Christianizing Africa and expanding commerce, had a long history before the founding of the ACS. In the early nineteenth century, after the founding of Sierra Leone, the British African Association and African Institution promoted commercial expansion and missionary activity in Africa while the French attempted to place Africans rescued from slavers at

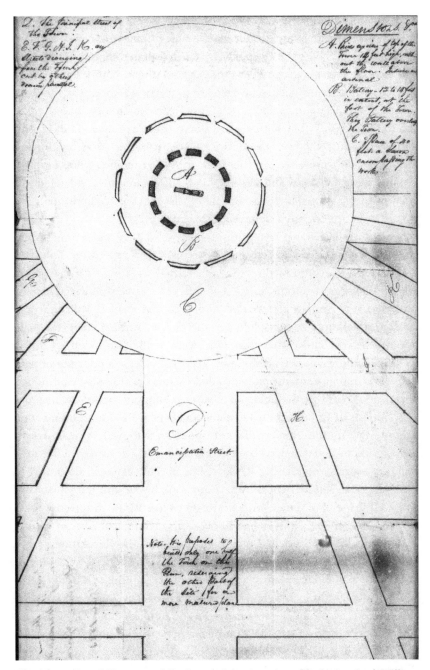

The idea of an African republic founded by American blacks inspired William Thornton, designer of the U.S. Capitol, to produce this urban design for the small settlement at Cape Mesurado, Liberia. Consistent with his vision, he called the "principal street of the town" Emancipation Street. (Library of Congress)

a settlement called Libreville. These efforts assumed that free black settlements could demonstrate the advantages of legitimate trade over the slave trade while spreading the Gospel.[4] This concept had some support among northern free blacks in the United States, and it was of more than passing interest to black and white congregations concerned with African missions. There was hope among some African Americans that the establishment of a settlement run by black Americans would unite all descendants of Africans in America. But even those African American leaders who wanted to establish such a presence in Africa and carry Christianity, civilization, and commerce to that continent still sought equality, autonomy, and a national identity in the United States as well. They viewed African colonization as a pan-African option, not a white American fiat.

Two northern evangelical ministers, Robert Finley and Samuel Mills, had promoted African colonization as a missionary enterprise. They corresponded with Cuffe in the year before the formation of the ACS and sought his support and his African contacts as Cuffe accomplished his first emigrant venture to Sierra Leone. Cuffe warned Samuel Mills that free black leaders must be consulted for any plan of African colonization to succeed. A year later, Mills and Finley were at the first meetings of the ACS in Washington, D.C. Cuffe and other free black supporters of African colonization were at first heartened by this development and hoped that it would provide the financial means for emigration. But the negative descriptions of free blacks from some speakers at the founding meeting and the fact that the society did not intend to work with African American organizations cooled, without extinguishing, Cuffe's interest. He died without entirely repudiating the ACS, but his colleagues in the effort to end slavery and uplift African Americans soon broke with the society and followed the lead of the majority of northern free blacks in rejecting it.[5]

The African American dialogue over the meaning of African colonization for black identity and nationality began in the Revolutionary Era when the concepts of "nation" and "race" were evolving. The meaning of "nation" expanded from groups that shared backgrounds and traditions to a political community that had clear boundaries. The American constitution placed people of color outside those national boundaries and thus tied nation to "race." African Americans struggled to define themselves as a nation and a race without excluding themselves from the evolving American nation from which they drew much of their construction of "nation." Similarly, their vision of themselves as a "race" was to a great extent formed in reaction to their collective experience of systematic oppression in the United States.[6]

The ACS differed from earlier African American or benevolent concerns with African colonization in framing itself as an essentially political organization, concerned with resolving the national question of an "intermediate species of population" in a republic. The ACS draft memorial did not offer any chemistry that could blend free blacks into the American "Body Politic" but instead sought a political alchemy between the white North and the South for resolving the "imperfect connection" between free blacks and citizenship. Unlike other benevolent societies, the ACS anticipated federal and state revenues as its base of support. The all-important political considerations of uniting the states and obtaining federal aid put it in the position of endlessly temporizing about slavery, for fear of offending one or another congressional or popular base. The society inevitably aroused the skepticism of black and white contemporaries and the cynicism of historians by claiming that the colonization of free blacks would both make slave property more secure and tend to encourage emancipation.

William Jay, author of a popular critique of the ACS, claimed: "It is worthy of remark that this constitution has no preamble setting forth the motives which led to its adoption, and the sentiments entertained by its authors. There is no one single principle of duty or policy recognized in it, and the members may, without inconsistency, be Christians or Infidels; they may be the friends or enemies of slavery, and may be activated by kindness or hatred towards the free people of color."[7] This ambiguity meant African colonizationists might be described as a contemporary book described alchemists: "This unprofitable pursuit [attracted] men of all ranks, characters, and conditions: the truth-seeking but erring philosopher; the . . . needy noble, the designing charlatan, . . . [and] the delusion was not altogether without its uses. Many valuable discoveries have been made in that search for the impossible which might otherwise have been hidden for centuries yet to come."[8] In the response to African colonization in Virginia, as in the nation, many valuable discoveries were made about the differences among its white supporters, the diverse assessments of blacks, and the political limits of African colonization.

A first discovery was that the anticipated federal aid to the ACS was almost entirely limited to creative legislation by new congressman Charles Fenton Mercer in 1819. Mercer and the Virginia Episcopal minister William Meade raised money for the first trip to Africa by ACS agents Samuel Mills and Ebenezer Burgess to search for an appropriate site for a colony. Mills, the enthusiastic supporter of Cuffe and of the formation of the ACS, died on the trip. Mercer wrote letters, stuffed envelopes, and used his congressional frank to send out thousands of requests for support. He used the publicity over Africans recaptured from slave ships and about to be sold into Georgia slavery to promote a bill that would have the federal government, not the states, take responsibility for Africans taken from slavers.

To a section of the resulting Slave Trade Act, Mercer attached a colonization agenda, which authorized congressional funds for American efforts to return all recaptive Africans to that continent. President Monroe could usually be persuaded to adopt a view that Mercer proffered, but his secretary of state, John Quincy Adams, could not. Nevertheless Monroe and Adams permitted the Slave Trade Act to subsidize most of the early years of the Liberian colony. Funds from the Slave Trade Act were crucial for the exploration of the western coast of Africa and the establishment of Liberia.[9] Even so, federal funding was inadequate to support any substantial emigration of black Americans to Liberia. This meant that, in a very short time, the society came to depend for financial support on contributions by auxiliary societies, individual members, and interested citizens.

Demographics, geography, and historic preeminence put Virginia at the epicenter of this effort. The ACS at first flourished in Virginia, supplying many auxiliaries and emigrants and possibly more money than any other single state.[10] As the Virginia colonization leadership sought public funding from the Virginia legislature, the ACS was inevitably linked to the state's interconnected questions of political representation and the shifting economic base as well as the question of slavery. Many white Virginians attracted to African colonization imagined, as had earlier Virginia writers, a coming together of North and South on this topic, in a way that could overcome internal Virginia resistance. A colonizationist from Norfolk believed that "southerners and northerners must be reconciled to this work . . . [through a] moral alchemy."[11] That would create a powerful force for African colonization and might, in the view of this colonizationist, provide an opening for ending slavery.

The Virginia ACS political leadership represented a variety of perspectives on African colonization and slave emancipation. Bushrod Washington of Mount Vernon was the national president of the ACS, but it was his position as George Washington's nephew rather than his advocacy of African colonization that made him the president. William Meade, later the Episcopal bishop for Virginia, was a founding member of the society, and he used his organizational skills and evangelical zeal to raise money and found auxiliaries for the ACS. Unlike Bushrod Washington, he freed the slaves that he had inherited and gave much of his personal fortune to the national society. Charles Fenton Mercer, central to the founding of the national society, was a Virginia congressman who was its most assiduous promoter in Congress. Mercer saw slavery as a national moral problem and a deterrent to commerce and industry and approached it that way. He used all the political and legislative devices available to him to get federal support for colonization and Liberia.[12]

The ACS in Virginia also attracted figures prominent in the nation's Revolutionary history. Many of the second generation of Virginia Republicans made their peace with slavery, but one Virginian from the iconic Revolutionary generation, James Madison, and the Supreme Court chief justice, John Marshall, were active advocates of African colonization. Thomas Jefferson considered colonization as a possible solution to the dilemmas of slavery, but he was never a member or supporter of the ACS. Madison and Marshall, however, both joined the ACS and held office at the state and national levels. Madison was the national president for the last three years of his life and, in his retirement, stoked his faith in Revolutionary principles by connecting them with the ACS. John Marshall was president of the Virginia Colonization Society until his death.[13]

Madison developed a "political religion," as Harriett Martineau, an English chronicler of American society, described it. He used his alliance with the ACS in his latter days to sustain his faith in justice and the republic. Colonization, he told an astonished and uncomprehending Martineau in 1835, was a slow process but offered a real possibility for ending slavery. Martineau viewed the scheme as impractical and unnatural but thought it sustained his spirit "through difficulty and change" and left him with no cause for "repentance or even solicitude" at the end of his life. In Madison's conversation with the visiting English woman, he held back some of the doubts he had expressed to Thomas R. Dew in 1832 when he admitted that colonization might prove unworkable but that such "laudable intentions" were the honorable way of keeping faith with Revolutionary ideals. Madison remained a supporter of the ACS until his death.[14]

Jefferson and Madison divided over support for the ACS, but the national society could offer the nephew of the ultimate Revolutionary figure, George Washington. The son of George's brother, John Augustine Washington, Bushrod Washington served in the Continental Army, began a law practice, was elected to the legislature, and voted for ratification of the Constitution as a delegate to the state convention. He prospered in his Richmond law practice where the childless Washington served as a mentor for young law clerks, including Henry Clay and Charles Fenton Mercer. Mercer described Bushrod Washington as a "second father" to him. Washington left his Richmond home, in 1798, for a seat on the U.S. Supreme Court, soon joined there by another lawyer from Richmond, the vigorous and assertive John Marshall, with whom Washington was frequently aligned in court decisions.[15] Washington served on the Court through most of the Marshall years until his death in 1829, while his fellow Virginia Federalist brought the Supreme Court into the center of politics and policy making.[16]

The mild and unremarkable Supreme Court justice, now of Mount Vernon, Virginia, was asked to take the office of president of the new ACS in 1816 and viewed it as one more duty that accompanied being heir to George Washington's estate and to a dim glow from his aura. He understood that he served symbolic functions and performed them, he believed, as well as his circumstances permitted. Bushrod Washington never advocated emancipation. He was, however, concerned with the difficulties of maintaining an enslaved labor force near free black communities in Alexandria and Georgetown, D.C., as well as near the emancipated slaves of George Washington. For this daily problem and for the nation's image, colonization could be an answer, and it was on this basis that it had some appeal to him. He freed no slaves and made no personal sacrifice for colonization. Men like Bushrod Washington made it easier for skeptics to view colonization as a slaveholder's conspiracy or as a painless way to salve one's conscience over slavery while actually doing nothing.

Another perspective was at work in the Reverend William Meade, born near Winchester, Frederick County, Virginia, in 1789, in a modest log dwelling on the plantation called Lucky Hit. Revolutionary Era losses meant that Meade's parents initially lived a frontier existence, although not without the labor of slaves. William Meade's female relatives took an interest in him, especially his cousin Mary Lee Custis, who, with his sister Ann Randolph Page, urged him to study for the ministry and monitored his progress closely. These women were gentry evangelicals and deeply interested in the missionary expeditions to Africa that preceded the formation of the ACS.

Meade's theological studies in Virginia and at Princeton were both broken off before completion, but before returning to Frederick County, he was ordained in Williamsburg. His youth on the Piedmont frontier and the influence of his female relatives tended him toward evangelicalism, rather than the order and orthodoxies of the traditional Episcopal Church. Meade preached against horse racing, card playing, the theater, and other fashionable amusements. This was to his taste, as well as his beliefs, because his talent was for organization and exhortation and not for extended study or spiritual abstractions.[17]

With his zeal for moral improvement through voluntary associations,

Meade was naturally drawn to the formation of the ACS. The project drew his enthusiastic support as a believer in the efficacy of missions and benevolence, as a slaveholder deeply uneasy with slavery, and as a Virginian committed to maintaining that state's place in the republic. He was present at the organizational meetings in Washington in December 1816 and was one of the true organizers and workers, rather than one of the figurehead members. The persons to whom he was closest—Custis cousins and Meade sisters—were among the earliest to inform themselves about African missions, and Meade himself listed the English antislavery leader William Wilberforce as one of his spiritual mentors. Meade was a founder of the Virginia Theological Seminary in 1818. He established Sunday school classes and catechism classes and societies for ministerial education and for missions. In 1829, he performed his last public service for African colonization when, with other prominent colonizationists, he organized the African Education Society in Washington, D.C., as a school for free blacks intending to emigrate to Liberia.[18]

Meade's work for the ACS suggested the flair for drama and organization that he displayed in his church work. In May 1819, Meade was sent by the society to Georgia to try to prevent the sale of the group of Africans taken from a Spanish slaver by the U.S. Navy and surrendered to Georgia. The society first attempted to persuade the federal government to take responsibility for the Africans and return them to Africa. Failing that, it dispatched Meade to Georgia to persuade the governor to hold off the auction while ACS appeals went out for donations to buy the recaptured Africans and return them to Africa. Despite extensive publicity that brought the ACS favorable national attention, too little money and too many legal complications were raised, and it was almost a decade later that the last of those recaptured Africans not dead or sold into Georgia slavery were finally returned to Africa.[19]

Meade used his travels for the society in 1819 to set the standard for organizing auxiliary societies. After personally calling on the most substantial citizens in each area to acquire their endorsement of the society, he published an announcement for an organizational meeting and made certain that a prominent citizen presided. Then he took financial pledges from the officers and members of the new society. He organized auxiliaries in Georgia and North Carolina in this manner and, in South Carolina, got pledges from prominent citizens but organized no auxiliary. Meade did so well that the managers sent him north and east in the fall of 1819. He traveled as far as Maine, acquiring endorsements and pledges from prominent citizens and laying the groundwork for more auxiliaries. His travel to organize auxiliaries was similar to an itinerant preacher's revival circuit, and he understood his work as that of moral alchemy, uniting northern and southern whites for a Christian cause.[20]

Meade took charge of the slaves emancipated by his two deceased sisters and later freed his own bondpersons, all of whom expressed a desire to go to the North rather than to Liberia. "I am heartily sick," he wrote to his cousin, Molly Custis, "of the thousand drawbacks they continually present to my soul's welfare." But it became apparent that northern and western states did not want emancipated slaves. The experience of the emancipated Virginia slaves of John Randolph and Samuel Gist, who emigrated to Ohio and Pennsylvania and were received with hostility, reinforced the belief among Upper South emancipationists that the free states were no more hospitable to free blacks than Virginia was, and this confirmed their sense that African colonization was the only basis for united national action on slavery. Meade was doubtful that his Frederick County ex-bondmen could enjoy any security in the North, but their own preference was for Pennsylvania. Ultimately Meade respected their wishes and helped them move there.[21]

Although successful as an organizer in his two tours, when Meade returned to his parish in 1820 the society did not hire anyone to continue his work. Meade's efforts for the next decade centered in Virginia, where he and his family kept the Frederick County Auxiliary Society in the forefront of donors to the ACS. Meade's contributions, including donations made as the executor of his sisters' wills, were far greater than that of any other individual and represented a significant portion of the ACS budget in those early years. Only the Richmond Auxiliary came close to giving as much as the Frederick County Auxiliary Society.[22]

The founder and most assiduous promoter of the ACS, Charles Fenton Mercer, was born in Fredericksburg, Virginia, in 1778, the youngest son of James Mercer. His mother died in his infancy, and his father, active in the Revolution and in state politics, took the boy with him to Richmond for sessions of the Virginia General Assembly. Introduced early into this intimate masculine world of precarious privilege where most were haunted by debt, the child heard the legislators' boardinghouse oaths and tag-ends of Latin phrases, as they bemoaned the circumstances that, they believed, made them land-poor. When he was fifteen, his father died insolvent, and it was two years before Mercer, although ready for college, could gather enough money to enter Princeton. In several letters written in old age to a cousin, Mercer remembered vividly his grief at his father's death and his fear of the life of poverty that he felt faced him. Mercer worried always about money. He recorded his expenditures until a week before his death and, in every letter to one relative, reviewed his financial situation.[23]

Mercer, who came to Nassau Hall as a scholar of the Age of Reason and left an evangelical Christian, linked "intellectual and moral worth" throughout his life. "I had entered the college a stoic, if indeed I had any settled opinions on the subject of religion. I had derived my principles of action and theory from Plutarch and the then fashionable democratic philosophy of Godwin. . . . Both had taught me that I was to live not for my country, but in a sense more enlarged for mankind. I left Nassau Hall after five years of close application a Christian."[24] Mercer did not find it necessary to abandon the "fashionable democratic" injunction to live for mankind when he embraced the evangelizing theology of the College of New Jersey. In 1799, as a law student, Mercer produced an engraving entitled "The Progress of Reason" for the American Whig Society. In it, a young man with a book is directed upward, through study, to the Temple of Virtue. The achievement of virtue through self-discipline and learning captured elements of both evangelical and Enlightenment thought. Americans would lose their republic to corruption unless education, readily available, taught the republican virtues of civic responsibility and simplicity.[25]

Mercer practiced law in Loudoun County and served as a delegate to the Virginia General Assembly from 1810 until 1817, when he ran successfully for Congress from his Virginia district. Among the last and most energetic of the Federalists, Mercer was an enthusiast for the American System of Henry Clay—expanded commercial banking, industry, and internal improvements.[26] He shared Clay's fears that the Union might fail if slavery continued. His public arguments for African colonization employed the ambiguous modifier "degraded" and described free blacks as trapped at the lowest rung of society and destructive of both economy and society in the American republic. He later feared the influx of German and Irish immigrants in the 1840s in the same way that he earlier feared free blacks, describing them as "rude, illiterate, and degraded," but ultimately he viewed them as candidates for education and citizenship.[27] As salvation was the key to Bishop Meade's colonization work, education was the key to Mercer's, except that his plans were for the education of poor whites and immigrants, in order to make them discerning citizens. In his cosmos, free blacks could not be raised to citizenship because of their color.

His advocacy of public elementary education led him to a significant quarrel with Thomas Jefferson within Virginia. In 1810, the General Assembly established a Literary Fund "for the encouragement of learning," with funding from state liens, confiscations, and forfeitures. Mercer helped to shape this bill even before he was elected to the legislature,[28] but the next legislative session limited the use of such funds to pauper schools. Mercer argued unsuccessfully that all youth had the right to instruction and tried again to find a financial source for public education. In the 1815–16 session, he submitted a plan to put federal repayment for War of 1812 loans into the Literary Fund and to establish a statewide system of public schools without raising taxes.[29]

Joseph Cabell, a legislator working closely with Jefferson to site and fund a university in Charlottesville, misread Mercer's enthusiasm for education. He attempted to enlist Mercer in the scheme to place the proposed university at Charlottesville but failed because Mercer preferred to fund primary education first. Cabell wrote to Jefferson and explained Mercer's educational plan not by its merits or lack of them, but by the machinations of sectional and party factions within Virginia. "I see a scheme already formed to carry the seat of government, sooner or later, *to Staunton* and powerful *private interests* privately preparing and expecting that event." He later noted, "Staunton wants the seat of government[,] and any brilliant establishment at the Eastern foot of the Ridge would shake those claims."[30]

This fueled Jefferson's grandest suspicions, as Cabell must have known it would. Cabell reminded Jefferson to remain aloof from the fray. If not, Cabell warned, the Presbyterians and the Scotch-Irish of Staunton and Lexington and the western delegates would "threaten to divide the state."[31] In an intense struggle at the next session of the General Assembly, Mercer introduced a bill that placed primary education at the forefront of education, but Cabell was successful in detaching that aspect of the bill. Jefferson's allies succeeded in garnering most of the Literary Fund money for the proposed university and in placing it in Charlottesville.

Hoping to exert maximum influence on the course of study, Presbyterian John Holt Rice wrote to Presbyterian William Maxwell at Norfolk: "Now is the time to make a push. The friends of the University are alarmed. They fear a defeat; and dread Presbyterians most of all. I have seized the crisis, gone in among the Monticello-men, and assured them that we are so far from opposition that we rejoice." He hoped that the support of Presbyterian educators for the university would permit their ideas "to be felt in the University and through all its departments."[32]

Both Rice and Maxwell were very soon to be prominent members of the ACS in Virginia, and soon another incident involving Rice reinforced Jefferson's sense that they sought to thwart his most cherished projects. Jefferson planned to install Thomas Cooper, an immigrant British physician and political economist, as the lead professor in a university without a president. Cooper was hostile to all religious tenets, and he was an early theorist of hereditary racial traits that placed African capabilities below European. Although Joseph Cabell warned Jefferson that Cooper "either in point of manners, habits or character, . . . is defective," Jefferson continued to support him. It was left to another member of the university's board of visitors, John Holt Rice, to print, in his *Virginia Evangelical and Literary Magazine*, a selection of quotations from Cooper that were bound to outrage Virginians. Rice editorialized that the "Monticello-men" intended to imbue "atheistical opinions" in Virginia youth. Cooper was forced to withdraw from consideration as lead professor. Jefferson was furious and accused the Presbyterians of wishing to establish a state church and control education in the state.[33]

In the gathering at Washington in late 1816 that formed the ACS, Jefferson saw the names not only of many Federalists but also of many such Presbyterians. The prime founder of the society was Mercer, the Federalist legislator who had, within the year, struggled to keep public monies for education out of his hands in what Jefferson had seen as a Federalist strategy that was attempting to profit from sectional rivalries. The ACS project appeared to be, at least potentially, a cabal of his enemies, inevitably bound to take his thoughts on colonization and use them in a manner he would not approve. In addition, it was Mercer who had recently revealed Jefferson's secret correspondence with the Virginia legislature in 1800–1802. The dissemination of this private correspondence by a Federalist congressman could not have been pleasing to Jefferson, especially since the secret correspondence did not show him to be a staunch opponent of slavery restrained primarily by lack of support in his own state. There was absolutely no reason for Jefferson to wish to advance the career or support the causes of Fenton Mercer and his various allies in western Virginia. He was hardly reassured by the prominence of Virginia clergy, Federalists, and urban merchants in the auxiliaries that sprang up in the last decade of his life.[34]

Late in life, Jefferson gave only abstract intellectual support to emancipation and colonization and in fact discouraged several persons who sought his counsel in support of emancipation. When he retired to Monticello, his daily life became once again attuned to the values, choices, and expectations of the Virginia planter, and he sought to maintain the republic while protecting the interests of his class.[35] There is no indication that the ACS founders sounded him out for a letter of support, although they knew the value of selectively quoting him. They printed, in the ACS Second Annual Report, a letter of Jefferson's, probably without his permission or knowledge, that was in harmony with the philosophy of the ACS.[36]

When Mercer ran for Congress from the Loudoun-Fairfax District in 1817, it was a bitterly fought contest with General Armistead T. Mason, who had resigned from the U.S. Senate to run against him. Mason was a part of the growing conservative faction within the Jeffersonian Republicans, while Mercer was a nominal Federalist and emphatic nationalist. Republicans hoped that the Federalists would be discredited by their lack of enthusiasm for the War of 1812 and dispirited by their inability to mount an opposition to the Virginia Republican presidential dynasty, but Mercer won by a narrow margin and Virginia Federalists held their own in the state.[37]

Mason's loss provoked him to claim that Mercer had made improper personal comments about him during the campaign. When Mercer denied this, Mason claimed that ineligible voters had cast ballots for Mercer. Mercer denied this, too. The entire correspondence was carried on in the Leesburg *Genius of Liberty*, and when Mason subsequently challenged Mercer to a duel, Mercer's refusal was played out before the entire community. Mason then called Mercer "a contemptible coward," and there the matter ended publicly. If Mercer had subscribed to the notion of honor that would not permit a public insult to go unchallenged, he could not have permitted such personal abuse. His commitment to evangelical Christianity supplied an alternate sense of honor that must have resonated in his political district because he continued to be elected to Congress for twenty more years. Mason was killed two years later in a duel with his cousin, John M. McCarty, a candidate for local office who had called him a "disgraceful coward" in the same local paper.[38]

In Congress, Mercer, by his own account, devoted most of the time from 1817 to 1820 to the ACS and was always its best friend in Congress. Some dozen years later, Andrew Jackson's secretary of the treasury came to the not-unreasonable conclusion that the expenditures for Liberian settlement were far beyond the intent of the 1819 act. John Quincy Adams, despite his misgivings about the legality of the ACS acquiring money through the Slave Trade Act, had respect for Mercer, and later, when Adams himself had been sufficiently buffeted and isolated by southerners in Congress, he reflected: "Mercer is one of the most respectable natives of Virginia, and has devoted his life to the internal improvement of the country, and to the gradual extinction of slavery in the state. In both of these . . . purposes his exertions have been abortive. The savage and barbarous genius of slavery has not only baffled them all, but had kindled a flame of popular odium against him. A noble spirit doomed to drudge in the mines."[39]

For almost a decade after the formation of the ACS, its friends rested their hopes on a self-interested unity of North and South that might begin to address a national problem with a national solution. But the moral alchemy of North and South was very quickly diluted by the political realities laid bare by the Missouri statehood bill in 1819. When the Tallmadge Amendment prohibiting slavery in Missouri was attached to the bill, the lengthy and impassioned congressional debate that it provoked worked to the long-term advantage of the conservative Republicans in Virginia and to their principles of strict construction of the Constitution and states' rights. Virginia politicians still formed an elite that permitted the politics of personality, with its informality and minimal party discipline, to continue to dominate Virginia elections. In 1820, that system required Virginia politicians to defend slavery in Congress, limiting their ability to function as national spokesmen. Jefferson himself offered support to the conservatives by proposing that slavery's extension into new territories would dilute and dissolve it. Diffusion, he informed the Marquis de Lafayette, "will dilute the evil [of slavery] everywhere, and facilitate the means of getting finally rid of it." The unified Virginia response to the Missouri controversy caused Mercer to vote reluctantly against the Tallmadge Amendment.[40]

Sectional sensitivities thereafter made any congressional bill for direct funding of the ACS and Liberia impossible of passage and capable of producing significant negative attention. While Virginia continued the shift in its economic base that had begun in the Revolutionary period and that was drawing it closer to its northern and western neighbors, fractious conservative Republicans began a successful march toward control of the state and its congressional delegation. In Jefferson's 1824 letter to Jared Sparks, he reviewed his "post-nati" plan for eventual emancipation of the enslaved, a plan he considered more practical than that of the ACS. This plan would free newborn and thus relatively valueless slaves, bringing them up at state expense until they were old enough to be deported from Virginia. But when it came to a place to send African Americans for what he was beginning to think of as "repatriation," Jefferson equivocated as he had done in his correspondence with the General Assembly. They should be sent to "some country" with a "climate friendly to human life and happiness." But where was that utopia, outside of Virginia? Again, as in 1800, Jefferson could not produce one. But there was now an alternative.[41]

Three

Auxiliary Arms

I N THE FALL OF 1819, the venerable Ludwell Lee and his son, Richard Henry Lee, with a Presbyterian minister, John Mines, put out a call for a meeting in Loudoun County to discuss African colonization. Some seventy local men attended the meeting held in the county seat of Leesburg and organized the Loudoun County Auxiliary to the American Colonization Society (ACS). Ludwell Lee was made president, and the society chose thirteen vice presidents and eight general managers from the county's Quaker farmers, slaveholding planters, and townsmen.[1] The number of such Virginia auxiliary societies would rise and fall in the antebellum decades, but Virginia could initially count more local societies and donors in ACS annual reports than could any other state.[2] Local societies were most frequently formed through a call for a public meeting put forward by one or more esteemed local citizens. Those who answered the call gathered in a county courthouse or church meetinghouse and formed themselves into an auxiliary on the model of the national society, with a prominent name as president and, if attendance justified, multiple vice presidents as well as a board of managers.

Since the 1780s, Virginia had been a southern state moving unevenly away from a tobacco culture dependent upon enslaved labor that marked it as a distinctly southern economy. By the 1820s, the state was a major supplier of corn and wheat for domestic and international markets, with livestock, seafood, and garden crops as other important exports. Virginia was expanding its tobacco-processing industry, and its iron, coal, and salt resources encouraged local manufactures. Colonization came to be of interest first in these urbanizing and industrializing areas of Virginia, especially bay and river port towns such as Richmond, Petersburg, Norfolk, and Fredericksburg, where there were concentrations of free blacks. The most active colonization auxiliaries in Virginia were in these and similar sites such as Lexington, Lynchburg, and Charlottesville. Rural counties with several auxiliaries, such as Loudoun, Frederick, and Jefferson in northern Virginia, had trade connections with Alexandria or other port towns.[3]

A sprinkling of auxiliaries were organized in 1819 in northern Virginia towns and counties by the redoubtable Episcopal minister William Meade. His equally energetic colleague and ACS founder, Charles Fenton Mercer, established one in Fredericksburg. But Richmond was initially resistant to Mercer's efforts. That city was organized in 1823, a time of rapid auxiliary growth in Virginia that was aided by ACS agents in the state.[4] Some sixty or more auxiliaries were formed over a forty-year period in Virginia, but most were organized in the 1820s and a few were exceedingly ephemeral, scarcely surviving the announcement of their existence. Others existed only in the form of an annual meeting with little or no activity between these convocations, but several of these were revived in the late 1840s. Some areas with high concentrations of slaves, such as Amelia, Nottoway, and Powhatan Counties, had colonization benefactors but never developed an auxiliary. Western Virginia beyond the Shenandoah Valley organized auxiliaries in more populous areas such as Wheeling and Charleston and in areas with enslaved labor such as Greenbrier County, but in general transmontane donors operated independently of auxiliaries, writing directly to the ACS from rural Barbour or Hardy Counties.

Most auxiliaries had a few stalwart members as managers, the most important of whom were the corresponding secretary and the treasurer, who did the work of the auxiliary between annual meetings. These men had the task of communicating with the national society about potential emigrants and of assessing the local public mood, white and black, on the subject of African colonization. Local auxiliaries canvassed for members and solicited donations. They inserted the speeches given at annual meetings and other news favorable to African colonization in local newspapers and religious journals, and they sold subscriptions to the society's publication, the *African Repository and Colonial Journal.* Local societies drew queries from free blacks, from those who wanted to emancipate their slaves for Liberia, and from the administrators of wills in which slaves had been emancipated on condition of emigration to Liberia.

The Richmond-Manchester Auxiliary was the largest and most active in Virginia. Predominantly a group of aspiring merchants, the Richmond colonizationists followed the lead of the national society and selected as president John Marshall, chief justice of the U.S. Supreme Court, a prominent national figure and also a local man.[5] Baptists among the founders had already been involved in a colonization venture. The auxiliary secretary in Richmond was William Crane, a New Jersey–born Baptist shoemaker turned shoe merchant, who had since 1815 offered evening classes for blacks in the Baptist meetinghouse. He and his best pupil, Lott Cary, had organized the African Baptist Missionary Society within the Baptist Church in that same year. Between 1819 and 1821, at the behest of Cary, Crane corresponded with the Baptist Board of Missions and the ACS to transport two self-purchased black Baptist ministers, Cary and Colin Teage, with their families to the ACS colony on the West African coast.[6]

The ACS was fortunate to have as managing officers in the Richmond Auxiliary men whose attention to the tedious strategies of the account ledger had advanced their own fortunes and might advance the ACS. Without their patient attention to detail and ability to save pennies, the enterprise would never have survived its first decade. Famous names might lend cachet, ministers hired as traveling agents might exhort, politicians might debate, but it was such men as William Crane, Benjamin Brand, and David Burr in Richmond who carried out the agenda. Benjamin Brand, the treasurer, was a local merchant and prominent member of the Richmond Temperance Society who kept the records not only of the auxiliary's membership but also of the trading company that he formed with Lott Cary and Richmond merchants in the expectation of exchanging ivory, wood, and coffee for tools, flour, molasses, and other staples. Others active on the Richmond Board of Managers were David Burr, a Scotsman and the owner of a small iron foundry in Richmond, and James Heath, state auditor and sometimes secretary of the Richmond-Manchester Auxiliary, who was also a playwright and writer for the *Southern Literary Messenger*. John Rutherfoord, a Scotsman who had established himself in Richmond business, and his brother-in-law, James Blair, a Presbyterian minister, were also members. At the first meeting, the only person to pay $20 for a life membership was William Fitzwhylson, a Welshman who had immigrated to Richmond just after the Revolution.[7]

Such civic-minded merchants were attracted to the cause of African colonization in part due to their status as newcomers to Virginia and their lack of investment in slavery. Most owned no slaves, although they might hire black labor. They were not personally threatened by enslaved skilled labor, as many artisans were, and saw white prejudice as a greater obstacle to Virginia's progress than the presence of free blacks. The Richmond managers tended to judge free blacks by their characters as refracted through the lens of the evangelical small businessman. The letters and actions of the most dedicated agents and officers show their relationships with emigrants to be businesslike, mildly paternal, and premised on shared values and religious beliefs.[8] Treasurer Benjamin Brand struggled with his temperance beliefs and his instincts for the ledger when he learned that Lott Cary was importing liquor as a trade item: "I am sorry to see . . . that *you* intend making ardent spirits an article of trade with the natives . . . as great a curse to them as the slave trade. But if it must be used, [why not] whiskey from our country . . . instead of West India rum."[9]

Virginia's auxiliaries were still being organized when, in 1824, they were given the task of circulating a petition in support of congressional funding for the ACS. In keeping with its sense of national mission and its need for funds, the ACS asked both the auxiliaries and the states to send petitions and resolutions to Congress. In response, the Ohio, New Jersey, and Connecticut legislatures passed resolutions asking Congress to adopt colonization as a step toward general emancipation; Delaware called colonization a "grand scheme of philanthropy." Vigilant against any federal tampering with the rights of individual states, South Carolina declared the resolutions "a very strange and ill-advised communication" and declared that it would not permit meddling with slave property.[10] The Virginia auxiliaries distributed the 1824 ACS memorial request, despite warnings from Charles Fenton Mercer that this would be seen as a political endorsement of Henry Clay or John Quincy Adams. Mercer's caution was well advised. A letter writer in the *Richmond Enquirer* warned that the ACS was the "repository of all the fanatical spirits in the country," claiming that it was an abolition society that encouraged both slave revolt and federal power over the states.[11]

The issue of African colonization, and especially the gathering of signatures for federal aid to the ACS, generated much public discussion in Virginia. Earlier that year, a supporter of colonization wrote in the *Richmond Whig* that a tax on free blacks and slaves would provide enough money each year to transport 2,096 persons to Liberia. In 1825, Virginia congressman George Tucker proposed that the United States examine and purchase Indian lands "lying west of the Rocky Mountains, that may be suitable for colonizing the free people of color." Writing in the *Richmond Enquirer* in late 1825, George Washington Parke Custis of Arlington called for the federal government to "lend us your aid to strike the fetters from the slave," and the secretary of the Norfolk Auxiliary, William Maxwell, signing himself *Liber*, penned an editorial that called slavery an evil and called for emancipation to be Virginia's goal. The Reverend John Paxton in Prince Edward County also published an antislavery tract and freed his slaves for emigration to Liberia.[12]

The response to these outspoken antislavery statements was severe local censure that caused the Virginia auxiliaries to backtrack for the first, but not the last, time. A growing number of ideologically conservative Virginians were alarmed by the potential for federal interference with slavery in the African colonization plans. Paxton was forced to leave his pulpit and the state. Maxwell was condemned in the press and threatened with tar and feathers. Custis's brother-in-law, William Fitzhugh, president of the Fairfax County Colonization Society, quickly defined any federal assistance as for the "common defence and general welfare," not for emancipation, and pressed the national society to declare itself neutral about slavery. Very shortly, Virginia auxiliary spokesmen decided that, although it was still safe to speak of slavery as an evil, it was not politic to declare openly for its demise or to request federal aid for the ACS. But the presumption that the colonization project would encourage emancipation was much slower to lose its power. Most 1820s Virginia colonizationists adhered to the principle that colonization of free blacks would be "an indirect but powerful influence" for emancipation by "keeping the public mind fixed on the subject."[13]

When the national society in 1826 again requested signed appeals for federal funding, gloomy assessments and ominous predictions from Virginia's auxiliaries quickly filled the mailbox of the ACS Washington offices. ACS secretary Ralph Randolph Gurley heard from Richmond: "Our scheme is unpopular with many influential persons because it affects their interests"; "it will not be prudent to apply to our next legislature for assistance to the colony because the enemies of the President of the United States are catching at everything within their reach trying to injure him"; and "I rather fear that your application to Congress may operate to your prejudice in the Legislature as it may be considered a contempt of states rights." From Norfolk: "The state of the public mind forbids anything like pressing the subject." From Petersburg: "If the friends of the society in Washington were distinctly apprized of the state of public feeling here and throughout this region, they too would think it injudicious to attempt to circulate the memorial." From Hanover County: "Even those who have reflected on the subject and are favorably disposed to it are generally opposed to Congress interfering." The *Richmond Whig* carried unsigned articles attacking colonization as a northern and nationalist plot. An offense to states' rights principles meant that "many of the members of our society would withhold their signatures[,] and as to influential names there are not many here on our side."[14]

The Richmond Auxiliary decided that the most politic way to acquire public funds was to approach the Virginia General Assembly. Early in 1825, they asked the conservative Virginia politician and incoming governor, John Tyler, to present their appeal for funds and were encouraged when the legislature appropriated money for farm implements to be made in the state penitentiary and sent to Liberia. In 1827, they again asked Tyler, whom they had made an honorary second vice president, to intercede for them. Tyler preferred to monitor Virginia's ACS auxiliaries from within and was always candid about his surveillance: "The moment in which I discover any improper design on the part of the society will be the date of my opposition to its views."[15] On the society's aspirations to congressional funds, he asserted: "It has no such constitutional power. This matter must be left to the state and to individual exertions." As for free blacks: "I always thought that the northern politicians had gone a bowshot too far when they attempted, as in the discussion of the Missouri question, to elevate to the condition of *citizen* the free blacks." To hear them described as "men and moral agents" provoked, he believed, "a question big with the fate of this union."[16] Tyler's position was clear. Colonization existed to diminish the free black population and the philosophical questions that its presence seemed to inspire.

Despite Tyler's advocacy for state funding, the legislature remained suspicious of the ACS, both for its interest in federal funding of colonization and for its possible role as a wedge toward emancipation. In early 1828, the Richmond Board of Managers began to investigate the practicality of re-forming themselves into an independent state society, and in December the membership voted to become the Virginia Colonization Society (VCS). The new society was now independent of the ACS in the most important aspects.[17] It could control its own money and set its own agenda. This break with the national society in Washington marked the moment when Virginia conservatives began to dominate the formal apparatus of ACS auxiliaries in the state.

The auxiliaries were now subsidiary to the state society and would send representatives to the annual state meeting; the VCS annual meeting would select delegates to the national society in Washington. John Marshall continued as president, and the Board of Managers maintained largely the same personnel, but ten new vice presidents were added, including two ex-presidents, James Monroe and James Madison, and seven members of the Virginia General Assembly. The first general meeting was timed to coincide with the annual meeting of the General Assembly, and the new society presented petitions to the General Assembly asking for state financial aid to circulate information about colonization throughout the state. The petitions were referred to a select committee of the legislature, the members of which were, with one exception, members of the vcs. In reporting out, the committee made a strong formal case for colonization and requested state funding, but the legislature did not vote to authorize this expenditure.[18] Once again, a carefully orchestrated exercise in acquiring conservative spokesmen for state support was unproductive. In establishing a state society, accommodating states' rights sentiment, and acquiring conservative spokesmen, the Richmond group did what seemed tactically necessary but advanced the cause very little.

Less resolute than John Tyler, most Virginia political colonizationists saw themselves, in the early years, as masters of the middle distance, able to unite North and South because they shared the concerns of both. They believed that slavery must be ended in Virginia through persuading slaveholders of its pernicious effects on themselves and their region. It was not hard for them to see themselves as the bulwark of the Union, because, as acs secretary Gurley reasoned, if Virginia could take the lead in adopting colonization as even a token step toward eventual emancipation, it would convince the North that the South was willing to take action. If there was no sign of progress at all in the border region of the South, the Union would be imperiled. A Maryland agent commented that "friends of the cause in the North and the East have heretofore given their money in the hope and confident belief that they were thereby accelerating the period when some one or more of the Southern States would decide in favor of the free labor system, and that, but for this hope, they would have withheld their donations."[19] More pointedly, a colonization stalwart who would soon leave the society wrote, "If Maryland, Virginia, or Kentucky be not detached from the number of slaveholding states, the slavery question must inevitably dissolve the Union and that before very long."[20]

Yet the Virginia argument about its particular fitness for mediation was directed more to the fears of the South than the expectations of the North. Among Virginia colonizationists were those who argued that they understood slaveholders' concerns more than the national society or northern colonizationists could. A clear statement of this position was offered by the Board of Managers of the Lynchburg Auxiliary, who claimed that northern auxiliaries could only offer "a patriotism more vague, and a benevolence less informed by experience than our own." On the other hand, the "hostility to the whole ground of the acs, exhibited by certain writers and speakers in our sister state of South Carolina," was to be regretted, because South Carolina "attribute[s] to the Society objects which are not enumerated in its constitution, and which have, moreover, been repeatedly disavowed by formal resolutions." But no "scheme which was to operate chiefly on the South" could succeed without "SOUTHERN MEN" and the Lynchburg Society, in the center of the largest of the slave-holding states, and composed chiefly of "SLAVEHOLDERS" met that need.[21]

After its organizational meeting and its failure to acquire legislative funds in early 1829, the VCS did not meet again until Benjamin Brand, the treasurer, submitted his resignation in May 1831. In a hastily called general meeting to find a new treasurer, the society determined to have an annual meeting in January 1832. Brand changed his mind about resigning as treasurer, perhaps because the society had at last scheduled a regular meeting.[22] Between that resolution and the meeting fell the shadow of Nat Turner's insurrection in Southampton County in which enslaved men murdered fifty-five white persons. At the January 1832 meeting, there was a sense of renewed possibility and possibly even vindication among the membership. This was despite the fact that Governor Floyd had composed a list of those aiding insurrection, and several categories seemed to describe some Virginia colonizationists. Primary suspects were the "Yankee population" in Virginia, especially peddlers and merchants, who preached equality. Also culpable were evangelicals, especially black preachers, who taught slaves that God was no respecter of persons, and respectable young southern women who believed that "it was piety to teach negroes to read and write."[23] Suspicion of these groups as subversive was not entirely misplaced, but the VCS officers could assure themselves that their official ranks were rapidly clearing of such persons.

In the special session of the legislature that reviewed and debated the issue of slavery in Virginia, the argument for financial support of African colonization was presented by a planter from the southern Piedmont, General William Brodnax, who had been tutored in African colonization by the most active colonizationist in Petersburg, William Mayo Atkinson. Brodnax submitted a bill that would grant $100,000 to the VCS and added restrictive measures against free blacks to the bill to encourage their departure. Atkinson had succeeded in making Brodnax a friend to colonization, but there was no sympathy for the free black or for emancipation in Brodnax. He had taken part in the militia forces in Southampton County after Nat Turner and Brodnax did not share Atkinson's concern for persuasion. He was willing to make deportation mandatory if not enough free blacks volunteered, but this important modification to the state appropriation bill was not adopted.[24]

Virginia colonizationists were stunned when the Senate failed to pass the appropriation bill in March 1832, and the year that followed was the most difficult in their short history. They were attacked by the new abolitionist movement in an influential book by William Lloyd Garrison, *Thoughts on African Colonization,* and by a professor at William and Mary, Thomas R. Dew, in the *American Quarterly Review.* Dew's attack on African colonization was a specific response to the slavery debates in the Virginia legislature. The ACS hurried to have a response by Virginian Jesse Burton Harrison in the next issue, in time to counter Dew's influence with the legislature. William Mayo Atkinson in Petersburg worked diligently to try to separate colonization from the growing Garrisonian abolition movement in the North. He used *Thoughts on African Colonization* and the proceedings of black conventions to demonstrate that the abuse heaped on the ACS in these publications proved that colonization was not a stalking horse for abolition.[25] Edward Colston of Berkeley County worried that abolitionist attacks made it less possible to have a reasoned discussion of slavery. "I am vexed to think that we, who entertain opinions adverse to slavery here . . . should see all our hopes of finally eradicating this evil spoiled & marred by . . . those who are perfectly ignorant of the subject."[26]

In the next legislative session, the General Assembly passed a modified version of the appropriations bill that authorized $18,000 annually for five years for paying the passage of Virginia free blacks to Liberia. The bill permitted an outlay of only $30 per person and applied only to free blacks, not to slaves who had been emancipated for Liberia. It was not an encouragement for emancipation, nor did it cover the costs of an individual passage and six months' support.[27] The General Assembly in 1833 had carved a very narrow channel through which funding for African colonization could flow. On the one hand, the state would not deport unwilling free blacks. On the other hand, it would not provide funding for slaves emancipated for Liberia. These restrictions guaranteed very modest results for state-sponsored emigration to Liberia. The half-measures with which the General Assembly and the VCS ultimately responded to the Nat Turner rebellion made many who had been active inside and outside the state lose hope for any political solution to slavery in Virginia.

William Crane lost hope. After Lott Cary's group left for Africa, Crane was a founder of the Richmond-Manchester Auxiliary Colonization Society in 1823, and he served as a manager in the auxiliary throughout the 1820s. He "earnestly participated in the great scheme of African colonization from its origin, and, along with the friends of that scheme generally, had entertained the HOPE, if not the BELIEF, that our colored population might ALL be separated from the whites, and removed to Africa." More important, he had "for nearly twenty years . . . been on intimate terms with the most respectable, intelligent part of the religious colored people in Richmond." At the end of a decade of ACS auxiliary work, he had to conclude that few free blacks were interested in Liberia and that colonization was "utterly, hopelessly impractical; that the increasing millions of the African race were quite as immovably fixed to the soil of our Southern States as the whites themselves."

Crane ultimately saw African colonization as beneficial only in its demonstration that African Americans could govern themselves and could disrupt the slave trade near them. The ACS could be of aid to the occasional informed and motivated African American who expressed an interest in it, but not to great numbers of slaves or free blacks. Although Crane was antislavery, he did not consider himself a northern-style abolitionist and was frequently critical of them. Blending his Baptist and republican beliefs, he called on "the white man, in this boasted land of liberty, to lay aside his PRIDE OF COLOR, and to admit what was never denied till within the last few centuries, that 'God has made of one blood all nations of men,' that 'all men are born free and equal,' and without any regard to complexion, all naturally possess the same inalienable rights."[28]

Believing that the "friends of the Negro" were politically destroyed and religiously unsupported in Richmond, Crane moved to Baltimore in 1834, where he was active in the formation of both white and black Baptist churches. He continued his connection with Virginia African Americans through his aid in bringing Virginia black preachers to Baltimore churches and through acting as Baltimore agent for Liberia's most prominent newspaper, the *Liberia Herald*.[29] Crane's assessment of Virginia colonization seemed supported by events shortly after his departure from Richmond. The VCS continued briefly under the titular leadership of aged icon John Marshall. After his death, in 1835, John Tyler was elected president. This was sufficiently cheery news to bring politician Henry Wise back to the society—Wise had resigned in 1833, claiming that colonization was too abolitionist in its goals. Upon his return, he triumphantly crowed: "The Colonization Society must now maintain that great original principle upon which it was founded:— 'Friendship to the Slaveholder,' never let it be forgotten or departed from." Wise intended that rallying cry as the counter to the abolitionists' standard: "Philanthropy to the Slave."[30]

In the northern part of Virginia, the history of another auxiliary offered a different set of members and another perspective on colonization. Loudoun County, settled by Tidewater planters, German farmers, and Quakers, had many moderate-sized farms and many landholders without enslaved labor. The county's prosperity was based on diversified farming and numerous villages with their mills and artisans. For a short time in the 1820s, Loudoun County boasted two colonization auxiliaries, the first of which was the one organized in Leesburg in 1819.[31] The president of the auxiliary, Ludwell Lee, carried the most illustrious surname in Loudoun County and perhaps in Virginia. Ludwell Lee was a son of the Revolutionary patriot, Richard Henry Lee I, who had opposed slavery on the grounds that it discouraged "the progress of a thrifty middle class" and "made difficult the way of the small proprietor"[32] Ludwell Lee was the owner of an estate called Belmont on which he kept forty-four slaves at the time the Loudoun Auxiliary was organized. Despite their provenance and property, the Lees were no more protected against bankruptcy and business failure than other local citizens. The economy of Loudoun held no real security for the land-rich planter, and the county's public records note numerous bankruptcies or forced sales spread among famous families, as well as among merchants, farmers, and laborers.

Ludwell Lee's colonization efforts may have been prompted by the rather stark contrast in economic condition between his increasingly debt-ridden family and the more prosperous, nonslaveholding Quaker and German families. The debts of the Lee family of Loudoun County had reached truly embarrassing proportions by the 1820s. In October 1827, Richard Henry Lee II, son of Ludwell Lee and an officer in the Loudoun Auxiliary, wrote to Bushrod Washington to ask him to recommend a gentleman "to teach the *solid* branches of education," because "my sister, Mrs. Love, whose husband has thro' bad management, lost all the property he received with her, intends to open a female academy in Leesburg." A few years later, it would be Richard Henry Lee's turn to be in financial straits, and he left Virginia to become part of the faculty at Washington College in western Pennsylvania. When Ludwell Lee died in 1836, Belmont was sold to Margaret Mercer, a prominent colonizationist, who kept a school for girls there.[33]

There is no indication that Ludwell Lee freed slaves and some evidence that he sold a good percentage of them to pay debts. In the Lee family effort to rid the state of slavery and encourage a spirit of enterprise, it was not their expectation that they would voluntarily and without compensation give up their own most fungible form of capital. Nor did they imagine they would be reduced to selling their land at auction and their furnishings on the courthouse steps. And yet, despite the sale of slaves to stave off disaster, such things happened. The decline and dispersal of this branch of a large Tidewater family was a melancholy history repeated in the early nineteenth century, and the burden of slavery, if not the value of slaves, was often blamed for it. Ludwell Lee and his son, Richard Henry Lee, were sincere in their desire to end slavery for the sake of white Virginians whose financial difficulties they shared.[34]

Matching Ludwell Lee in age, venerability, and community esteem was the Quaker merchant, miller, and farmer, Israel Janney, also an officer in the colonization auxiliary. Janney, part of a Quaker family as numerous and almost as important as the Lees, held no slaves and was known as an entrepreneur and progressive farmer in the county. He introduced merino sheep and developed a system of soil renewal and conservation that was widely imitated throughout the South.[35] Among the other colonization auxiliary officers was Dr. James Heaton from Pennsylvania, who moved to Loudoun County after the Revolution. At his death, he left an estate called Exedra and thirteen slaves, most of them members of the Lucas family, an extended black family almost as large as the Lees in Loudoun County. Two of Heaton's sons, Townsend and Albert, freed five members of the Lucas family and sent them to Liberia. Another officer, Johnson Cleaveland, provided in his will for his slaves to have two years in which to decide whether they wanted to go to Liberia or choose a master from among his relatives. At least four slaveholding officers manumitted slaves, and several auxiliary officers and members were instrumental in helping slaves purchase their own freedom or provided a legal residence for free blacks. Conversely, other officers freed no slaves, and one frequently advertised rewards for runaways.[36]

✓ Members of the Society of Friends, or Quakers, were prominent among the managers of the Loudoun County Auxiliary. They had demonstrated a desire to end slaveholding among the members as early as 1762, and the Virginia Yearly Meeting of Friends had made slaveholding grounds for dismissal from membership in 1784. In 1788, their Yearly Meeting Book of Discipline added that "none among us be concerned in importing, buying, selling, holding or overseeing slaves, and that all bear a faithful testimony against the practice."[37] But the number of Virginia Quakers peaked just a dozen years later, in 1800, and then declined steadily, as many in the Society of Friends moved west to acquire land and to escape the blight of slavery.

The late 1820s were the high-water mark of Virginia Quaker participation in African colonization. Within four years of the formation of the Leesburg Auxiliary, a predominantly Quaker group formed a second colonization society in Loudoun County. The Loudoun Manumission and Emigration Society was dedicated to "expose the evils which result from the existence of African slavery, invite the cooperation of our fellow citizens generally, in order to effect its gradual abolition, consistent with the laws and constitution of our country and to aid and encourage, by voluntary contribution the emigration of our colored population to Hayti, Africa or elsewhere."[38] The new society assured the Washington office of the ACS that they "uniformly acted upon the principle [that] emigration should follow emancipation and that to effect one, there should be a confident assurance of the other."[39]

Quaker Jonathan Taylor was a member of this society and the local agent for Benjamin Lundy's *Genius of Universal Emancipation,* printed in Baltimore. Lundy's paper and the local Leesburg *Genius of Liberty* carried announcements from the Manumission and Emigration Society that attacked slavery as "an atrocious debasement of human nature" and as "inconsistent with the principles of a republican government." Their repudiation of slavery was more vigorous than that of the Leesburg Auxiliary, but they used familiar arguments in saying that slavery was an inefficient system, that Virginia would prosper rapidly without it, and that bloody revolt would always be a possibility in a slave society.[40]

In August 1827, the Loudoun Manumission and Emigration Society hosted an antislavery convention with twenty-one delegates from seven local Virginia societies meeting in the Goose Creek schoolhouse. Adopting a "Constitution of the Virginia Convention for the Abolition of Slavery," they advocated gradual emancipation and colonization, denounced the internal slave trade, and called for a boycott "so far as practicable" of the products of slave labor. Delegates from the convention appointed to attend an ACS convention in Philadelphia in October 1827 included Jonathan Taylor, the local agent for Lundy's *Genius of Universal Emancipation.* The Goose Creek convention confidently resolved to meet annually and chose Winchester in Frederick County as the next site, but the Winchester meeting was apparently the last one.[41]

Membership in the Virginia Yearly Meeting of Friends declined as families moved west, in great part to escape slavery. Reluctantly, in 1844, the Virginians decided to "lay down" the yearly meeting and make their monthly meetings a part of Baltimore Yearly Meeting. The 1828 split within the Society of Friends between evangelical urban Orthodox Friends and the more spirit-centered rural Hicksite Friends had earlier weakened Virginia Friends. William Lloyd Garrison, familiar to Virginia Quakers first through his time on Lundy's newspaper, abandoned gradualism and began to advocate immediate abolition of slavery. The proslavery stance of the post-1832

VCS had no appeal to Quakers. All these centrifugal pulls atomized the remaining Quakers in Virginia, who functioned more as individuals than as a corporate body in the decades after the mid-1830s.[42]

Except for converts such as Nathaniel Crenshaw of Richmond, Virginia Quakers were responsible for few emancipated slaves. Crenshaw was a prominent member of Richmond Meeting, having converted to the Society of Friends in 1826. In 1827, he took sixty-five ex-slaves, freed by himself and a deceased uncle, to York, Pennsylvania. York was a place where runaway slaves from nearby Virginia and Maryland obtained assistance from local free blacks, and he was likely aware of these activities and possibly a participant in them. He is said to have aided in the manumission or emigration of 300 more and affirmed that he had "sent out [to Liberia] three companies of people who were given to me for that purpose by Benjamin C. Coghill, now of Illinois." Crenshaw later bought and distributed a mild antislavery address published by the Philadelphia Yearly Meeting and was indicted for it, although the grand jury dismissed the charge. Nathaniel Crenshaw remembered the emancipationist origins of colonization and did not break with Virginia colonization, but a younger Quaker, Samuel Janney, followed another path.[43]

In the 1820s, as a young merchant, Samuel Janney helped found the Benevolent Society of Alexandria, which was dedicated to rescuing free blacks illegally held in slavery and to exposing the evils of slavery. Arguing that a free labor economy would be better for Virginia and that slavery demeaned republicanism, Janney joined the Alexandria Auxiliary in the 1820s. He favored "immediate and unconditional emancipation . . . but knowing the prejudice against it in the minds of people," he supported free schools to "elevate and enlighten" white children while "promoting the antislavery sentiment which was obstructed by ignorance and prejudice." Janney abandoned the VCS when he came to see it as dominated by proslavery politicians. Yet he remained in the state, proposing education as the first step to emancipation. In 1849, he was twice presented to Loudoun County's grand jury for writing a reply to a proslavery address given by the Methodist president of Randolph-Macon Academy. Indicted the second time, he was prosecuted in 1850. Although he was acquitted, his prosecution marked the change in public sentiment since Crenshaw's indictment was quashed at the grand jury level.[44]

Virginia's increasing suspicion of any activity that disturbed the status quo meant that the VCS had perfunctory annual meetings in the 1830s and failed to hold an annual meeting in the 1840s, until a reorganization in 1849. An exception was the 1837 general meeting, at which attendance was sufficient to allow the society to hope that the legislature might be prevailed upon to modify the impossibly strict terms of the 1833 appropriations and even to advance state funding for a colony in Liberia, which was to be called New Virginia. These efforts failed in the legislature, and the society lapsed into its self-designed function as guardian of the Virginia version of African colonization.[45]

The society's officers began to act as gatekeepers for agents from outside the state, and the national society was warned not to send any into Virginia without the approval of the VCS in Richmond because Virginia was a "jealous jade." In the 1830s, Secretary Gurley found two acceptable men to appoint as Virginia agents, the Episcopal minister Charles Wesley Andrews and Colonel Addison Hall. Hall lasted only a brief time, but Andrews, the antislavery son-in-law of Ann Randolph Page, worked diligently to try to persuade the legislature to modify the 1833 law so that the money allocated for free black emigration might be used for emancipated slaves to go to Liberia. A select committee of the General Assembly was about to approve the modification when Henry Clay's second attempt to secure a congressional charter for the ACS caused Senator John C. Calhoun of South Carolina to declare that the ACS was "calculated to disturb the existing relations between the two races." Those who took their cues from such statements changed their views on modifying the law, and Andrews wrote bitterly, "I regret the time wasted in vain efforts to enlighten the ignorance and awaken a sense of justice in those who for a puff of popularity will betray the best interests of society." Andrews gave up his role as agent but continued to write letters and compose a petition to modify the law to provide compensation for emigration. Nevertheless, the law expired in 1838 without modification.[46]

The VCS was barely functioning in the 1830s, but more vigorous state societies caused the national society to experience first a crisis of meaning and then a financial and organizational crisis. At its sixteenth annual meeting in January 1833, the ACS faced its internal contradictions. "At that meeting, it became apparent that Colonization had two sets of friends, who supported it from motives diametrically opposed to each other," wrote the president of the Maryland Colonization Society. "The north looked to Colonization as the means of *extirpating* slavery — The south as the means of *perpetuating* it. . . . The explosion came at last."

The catalyst for reorganization may have been the financial panic of 1837 that dried up contributions in the Mid-Atlantic and Upper South states. Better-funded state societies in Pennsylvania and New York pulled away from the national society and sought a new constitution that would allow them to maintain control over money donated by their states. The Maryland Colonization Society had long gone an independent way. Under duress, the ACS Board of Managers produced a new constitution in 1838 that reorganized the society as a federation of state societies. The national organization was soon dominated by the northern states, which now donated the majority of the funding; and, under the new national constitution, the Pennsylvania, New York, and Maryland state societies continued to guard their funds for their own colonial projects within Liberia. The Virginia state society raised little money in the 1830s and 1840s. ACS treasurer Philip Fendall complained that wealthy Richmonders no longer donated to the national society, now that they saw that free blacks refused to leave their region. Squabbling became the dominant mode of discourse between the state and national entities as both sought donations from the same pockets.[47]

The ACS contracted with various ministers to canvass Virginia on a commission basis through the late 1830s and the 1840s, but this effort met with little success. When the Board of Managers of the VCS authorized the Reverend T. B. Balch, of New Baltimore in Fauquier County, to work for a year, Balch himself suggested that he work on commission rather than on salary. It was a bad bargain for him. William McLain, a traveling agent who was later secretary of the ACS, had a poor opinion of Balch and thought Virginia hopeless for colonization until the "present society [the VCS] is knocked in the head." According to McLain, the state society did next to nothing under its president, John Tyler, who found it "glory enough to be elected three times." McLain probably understood that this was just the role that Tyler and most of the other officers wanted the society to play. From their vantage point as officers of the society, they could stymie any plans that threatened to subvert their motto: "A Friend to the Slaveholder." In 1842, Benjamin Brand described the state society as "nearly dead."[48]

What then revived the VCS in the late 1840s and brought state attention and funds to the enterprise was initially Virginia's internal politics. Slavery was at the core of the dispute over representation and taxation in Virginia. There had long been agitation west of the Tidewater region for a new state constitution in which voting would be based on the white population only, rather than permitting slaves to be counted for purposes of representation, as was then the case in Virginia and at the national level. A constitutional convention in 1829 to amend the original 1776 document had only partly resolved the several political inequalities and dissatisfactions so irksome to the growing population of the Piedmont and western counties.

Voting rights for all white males would inevitably shift the balance of power in Virginia to regions less invested in slavery, and a more representative General Assembly might remove tax advantages for slaveholders, or might vote to fund emancipated slaves as well as free blacks for emigration to Liberia. Such actions would encourage emancipation, slaveholders feared, and encourage slave resistance. Active promoters of western Virginia saw a revival of African colonization as part of their effort to weaken the power of eastern Virginia and, as Fauquier County colonizationist Robert Scott suggested, their "fearful proclivity to disunion."[49]

The Shenandoah Valley became the center of a colonizationist revival, initially through the efforts of Franklin Knight, hired by the national ACS in the early 1840s, who revived the Lynchburg, Lexington, and Winchester Auxiliaries while founding new ones in Botetourt and Roanoke Counties.[50] William Henry Ruffner published articles in 1845 in support of colonization in the *Kanawha Republican,* in far western Virginia. Two years later his father, the Reverend Henry Ruffner, president of Washington College, advocated a Jeffersonian *post nati* plan in his *Address to the People of West Virginia.* The senior Ruffner's *Address* and his attempt to begin a weekly newspaper in "West Virginia," as well as the younger Ruffner's appointment in 1847 as an ACS agent, showed their intent to further distinguish the region from eastern Virginia by removing free blacks and gradually ending slavery.[51]

In 1847, the Ruffners asked the ACS to appoint a Rockbridge County lawyer as an agent in place of the younger Ruffner. But the society had been approached by a Presbyterian minister, Rufus Bailey, of Staunton, principal of the Augusta Female Academy, and it appointed him.[52] Highly regarded by two other Presbyterian clerics and colonizationists, William Mayo Atkinson and William Maxwell, he was an ambitious agent for the ACS in the Valley of Virginia, where he saw many possibilities for promoting colonization. Thomas Benning of Petersburg was also made an agent at about the same time, but he found the ACS to be "very unpopular" in the Tidewater region. Bailey sought to build support in his region by concentrating on making Rockbridge County, with its reasonably concentrated and town-centered free black population, a model for removing all free blacks from one county.[53]

It was an opportune moment to revive and reorganize the VCS. Nationally, the Mexican War's massive land acquisition engaged Virginians in the debate over slavery's expansion into the West and in the debate that would end in the Compromise of 1850 that temporarily appeased southern fears of slavery's containment. A provision of that act, the Fugitive Slave Law, not only gave slaveholders legal grounds to capture runaway slaves in the northern states but also threatened Upper South free blacks with kidnapping. On the state level, outgoing governor William Smith proposed in December 1848 that all the state's free blacks, a "race of idlers" who were "the ready instruments" of abolitionists, be expelled by law. Some opposition to Governor Smith's proposal coalesced around Bailey's alternate recommendation that the legislature again grant an appropriation for Liberian emigration to the vcs, which was reorganized at Bailey's urging in February 1849. Bailey then helped to guide a colonization funding bill through the legislature in 1850.[54]

The vcs soon appointed the Reverend Philip Slaughter of Fauquier County, a sickly and sycophantic minister without pulpit, as agent. It was a post he would hold until the Civil War. Slaughter's chief goal was always to allay the fears of the conservative Virginia government of the 1850s by aligning colonization with their policies. Slaughter wrote *The Virginian History of African Colonization* in an attempt to reprint relevant documents and stress the central role of slaveholding gentry in the history of Virginia colonization. He revised the historical record to obliterate the era of independent auxiliaries by claiming that the vcs was founded in 1823. Slaughter began a monthly journal entitled *The Virginia Colonizationist* in which he repeatedly declared that African colonization had nothing to do with abolitionism or emancipation in any form. He delighted in republishing Garrison's attacks and agreeing with their view that the ACS saw slaves as property and aimed at free black expulsion.[55]

The revived vcs was even more than before a friend to the slaveholder. At the 1852 annual meeting of the ACS in Washington, vcs agent Slaughter submitted a resolution seeking a ban on any "publication of schemes of emancipation and arguments in their favor in the *African Repository* and other official documents."[56] The passage of this resolution was perhaps indicative of how supine northerners in the ACS had become in their desire to keep Upper South slaveholders in the ACS. One Virginia General Assembly legislative resolution of support for the vcs contained these words: "That considering the principle of African colonization as best responding to the demands of Southern patriotism and benevolence and as offering . . . a common ground of resistance against the mischievous and reckless enterprises of Abolitionists, we regard it as eminently entitled to the support of all parties in Virginia."[57]

The national society sent an agent, Dr. Lugenbeel, to visit eastern Virginia cities with Slaughter, and these gentlemen wrote encouragingly of a

In this fanciful illustration in *The Virginian History of African Colonization* (1855), the president's home in Monrovia is an imposing mansion on a wide-paved and landscaped street in a vaguely tropical setting. The new Liberians canter, booted and spurred, or stroll past immobile Africans who share the street but cannot claim the public space. (Library of Virginia)

change in attitude among "the most intelligent and influential free people of color" in eastern Virginia. But this was more of the polite obfuscation of prominent free blacks, and no upsurge in emigration resulted. Although Rufus Bailey was more successful than Slaughter and Lugenbeel, he still came up against black resistance, especially in the evasive and temporizing responses from free blacks that confounded other white agents. Like the others, Bailey's enthusiasm for the cause long blinded him to the strategies that kept free blacks off ships but still in the good graces of local whites.[58]

In its 1850 session, the Virginia legislature appropriated $30,000 per year for five years for the transportation and maintenance of free blacks emigrating to Liberia—but limited the amount to $25 per person and placed an annual tax of $1 on free black males between the ages of twenty-one and fifty-five to raise the balance.[59] The VCS announced that the state per person appropriation would cover less than half the cost of each emi-

As shown in this photograph of Ashmun Street, the reality of Monrovia's streetscape was much closer to that of a modest antebellum southern town. The town offered substantial and recognizably American-style structures mixed with dilapidated housing, all fronting on wide unpaved streets that hinted of a vast interior landscape untouched by the Liberian presence. (Library of Congress)

grant. Three years later, Philip Slaughter reported to the VCS annual meeting that Virginia had sent 419 emigrants to Liberia since the 1850 act was passed, at a cost of $25,190, of which only $5,715 had come from the state appropriation. The tax on free blacks had brought $18,000 into the state treasury, and that money had met the costs of emigration and maintenance.

Slaughter appeared to see himself as in competition with Bailey, and Slaughter's complaints to the state society apparently led to Bailey's retreat from Richmond and state politics back to the Valley of Virginia and some severe disappointments.[60] The renewed colonization effort already had a history in the Valley of Virginia when Bailey became an agent. George Dabney, a professor at Washington College in Lexington, Virginia, had emancipated Samuel Harris and his family in the early 1840s, and Harris worked at least part-time as a custodian at Washington College with another free black, John V. Henry.[61] With the aid of Rockbridge County colonizationists, Harris and his family left for Liberia in December 1846. Local free blacks intended to watch the Harris family experience closely, and local white colonizationists knew it.[62] To the anger and consternation of the white colonizationists, Harris wrote back from Liberia that his family had experienced illness and that it was difficult to make a living. Quickly, Harris was dismissed as lacking the moral fiber to be a good emigrant. Bailey worked with and encouraged two locally respected free black families, led by Diego Evans and John V. Henry, to lead a group of twenty-nine from Rockbridge and Augusta Counties to Liberia in January 1850.

Diego Evans had studied law in preparation for Liberia but intended to be a trader. Mary J. Henry, daughter of John V. Henry, wrote to friends in Lexington, "We rented a house on Broad Street and Diego rented a house on the water side, which all the old settlers told him not, but he thought he could live there — being a good place to sell his goods. But all his family took the fever. We took the children home and they all got better, but Diego and his wife departed this life."[63] Diego Evans's death, following the difficulties of Samuel Harris, dissuaded several groups that were preparing for emigration and made Bailey despair of finding more emigrant parties from the counties along the Shenandoah River.[64]

In 1853, the General Assembly changed the act of 1850. They raised the per person allotment from $25 to $50 and created a Colonization Board to oversee the "removal of free negroes from the Commonwealth." The Virginia Colonization Board was an arm of the state government. It was necessary to prove, to the board's satisfaction, that the individual had been free before April 6, 1853, the date of the legislation creating the Colonization Board. Once the board was given proof of prior emancipation and emigration, colonization agents could collect up to $50 per person.[65]

A flurry of activity kept the Colonization Board meeting frequently through 1853 and 1854, as Slaughter and the unofficial agent, William Starr of Norfolk, hastened to get $50 each for persons who had committed to Liberia but had not yet left Virginia, or who had left since April 1853. They brought forward the names of 287 emigrants for compensation in those two years. But in 1855, there were only 25 emigrants presented for compensation; there were 9 in 1856, and, in 1857, the settlement of a protracted legal case involving the estate of John Barker of Sussex offered just 41 more. In 1858, its last year of existence, the Colonization Board authorized only 20 persons, two-thirds of them the small children of deceased women who were part of the Barker estate that had provided most of the emigrants from the year before.[66] In addition to the distasteful duty of sending motherless children to a strange and alien environment, the board members may have been motivated to close down operations by the fact that they had exhausted the possibilities, since free blacks failed again to take an interest in the project and newly emancipated ones were ineligible.

When first organized in 1819, and for the next decade, the ACS auxiliaries in the state had attracted a variety of Virginians—cash-strapped planters and Quaker farmers, ambitious or desperate free blacks, artisans and merchants, men who saw the principles of the American Revolution at work, and men and women who watched closely to see that African colonization did not impinge on slavery. For a few years, members who were so inclined spoke freely of their desire for a general emancipation.

But the ACS and its Virginia auxiliaries were initially the product of a political vision and could not be detached from national and state politics. The debate over the admission of Missouri to the union as a slave state occurred just as auxiliaries in Virginia were being formed. Henry Clay's efforts in the 1820s to acquire congressional funding for the ACS deepened political divisions over African colonization. The Lower South forged alliances in eastern Virginia, and this gave proslavery an organizational advantage. The auxiliaries lost their local power to spend money, determine policy, and negotiate with the national organization when the VCS was formed in 1828. Nat Turner's revolt closed the debate on antislavery with an inconclusive special legislative session that failed to take any action but did experiment with a modest level of state funding for colonization, which failed, in three efforts, to attract free black interest.

The moribund state of the VCS and its auxiliaries by the mid-1830s demonstrated that Virginia was neither able to move toward emancipation politically nor accept the fact that it would remain a slave state. And when it was revived, in the late 1840s, its membership was dominated by men whose concerns were, to varying extents, in sympathy with the slaveholder. Although it is not credible that any significant number of Virginia's free blacks would ever have voluntarily emigrated to Liberia or anywhere outside the United States, it was significant that the General Assembly provided so restricted a channel for Liberian emigration. The VCS's 1849 revival was severely hampered by the fact that the Virginia legislature continued to refuse to fund emancipated slaves as emigrants and by the deaths in Liberia of some of the model migrants. In their need to reassure slaveholders and refute southern criticism of African colonization as antislavery, Virginia sent a political message to the northern states that no antislavery legislation could be expected from them.

The perspective of the remaining members of the VCS in January 1861, as the Union divided, probably followed that of William Starr, a Norfolk colonizationist: "These are serious and alarming times now upon us. When will the villainous Black Republicans stop their wicked purposes in the southern states? Virginia will be out of the Union shortly. When things become settled in the state—perhaps Virginia will right upon African colonization—and look toward Liberia, as the home of her free col'd population, and such as may be emancipated. There will then be no more sending freed negroes off to the Northern states—They will be pointed to Liberia and no where else."[67]

Four

Ho, All Ye That Are by the
Pale-Faces' Laws Oppressed
Out of Virginia

I N THE EARLY WINTER OF 1821, a small group of Richmond free blacks gathered in the parlor of William Crane, a white shoe merchant and Baptist, to organize themselves as the Providence Baptist Church. The families of Lott Cary, Colin Teage, and the elderly Joseph Langford were about to embark for Liberia on the *Nautilus*, the second ship to the very new settlement founded by the American Colonization Society (ACS) on the western coast of Africa. As founding members of the Richmond African Baptist Missionary Society, Cary, Teage, and Crane were aware of earlier missionary enterprises and colonizing plans for Africa. Richmond and Petersburg Baptists had sent donations to Baptist missions in the British colony of Sierra Leone and to the black Massachusetts Quaker and African colonizationist, Paul Cuffe.[1]

According to Crane, "Some letters published in No. VI of the [*Latter Day*] *Luminary* (written by Kizell, the Baptist leader in Sherbro Island and by some others) have served to awaken them effectually."[2] The Baptist leader writing in the publication of the Baptist Board of Foreign Missions was John Kizell, once enslaved in South Carolina, who had made his way with the British forces to England and then migrated to Sierra Leone, where he became a merchant and participant in the Friendly Society founded by Paul Cuffe. The promotion of African colonization by such black men carried authority with Cary and Teage. Now the Richmond African Missionary Society awaited news from Nathaniel Brander, a Petersburg free black, who had gone to the settlement on the first ship, the *Elizabeth*. Reliance on assessments of West Africa by fellow African Americans was to be a characteristic of free black emigrants in Virginia, and Brander's positive account motivated his father and two brothers to join the Richmond Baptists on the *Nautilus*.[3]

Despite an early and active role in emigration to Liberia, Richmond free blacks were as cautious as those in other cities. Shortly after the formation of the ACS, a meeting of Richmond free blacks saw some merit in the scheme but emphasized that "we prefer being colonized in the most remote corner of the land of our nativity, to being exiled to a foreign country." Free blacks meeting in Washington, D.C., also suggested a site within American possessions but were more concerned that the scheme was coercive. By far the largest meeting was held in Philadelphia, at which free blacks expressed fear that emigration would become forced deportation and proclaimed it their duty to remain in the United States as long as blacks were enslaved.[4] Yet African colonization was initially attractive to an important and visible segment of urban Virginia free blacks because it was presented to them through missionary societies in which they had some decision-making power.

The formation of the Richmond African Baptist Missionary Society in 1815 preceded by three years the formation of a similar society within the recently established Gillfield Baptist Church in Petersburg. The Richmond Society existed within a predominantly white Baptist Church; Gillfield was predominantly black. Both societies consisted primarily of free blacks for whom African missions had the dual appeal of spreading Christianity and connecting with an African homeland. When those societies learned of the ACS's exploratory expedition to western Africa in 1818, the Petersburg church asked the ACS to sponsor some of its members as colonists and missionaries. Cary and Teage in Richmond sought to be sent to Africa as missionaries under the auspices of the Baptist Board of Foreign Missions. The board agreed to sponsor them as missionaries, and their venture was financed primarily by Richmond's African Baptist Missionary Society which spent almost $700 in outfitting Cary and Teage's group for emigration to Liberia. That society sent $100 a year or more to Liberia for support of Cary's enterprise as long as he lived, a very large sum for a small band of free and enslaved blacks.[5]

The colonizing of West Africa offered an important evangelizing opportunity, but it also offered the prospect of an African settlement where black Americans would exercise political and economic power. In the first decade of emigration, Virginia free blacks held considerable power over whether to emigrate and under what circumstances. After that decade, the "friends of the Negro," as William Crane called them, lost ground before the proslavery forces in the Virginia General Assembly and the Virginia

African American churches offered space for exchange of information and connection with a larger world through traveling ministers and national missionary societies. Virginia's most prominent black churches, such as the First African Baptist Church of Richmond, supported African missions and passage to Liberia. Shared letters from local emigrants gave black churches and communities the opportunity to form independent judgments about Liberia. (Valentine Richmond History Center)

Colonization Society, and free black interest subsided until the 1850s. The General Assembly several times voted money to encourage emigration to Liberia, but the rise and fall of black interest was little affected by Virginia legislative grants. Instead, those who considered emigration gave most weight to accounts from Virginia emigrants, as well as to their own assessment of local and national political conditions.

Blacks, skeptical of white motives, were willing to listen to evidence from other African Americans. Contemplating Goochland County in 1831, a Richmond iron maker urged the society to find a "suitable agent" to be sent among the free blacks, "and he should be a color'd man in whom they have confidence."[6] An ACS agent provided a starkly accurate assessment of black opinion in 1833: "In this place [Lynchburg], the free negroes generally seem to have an unconquerable prejudice against the whole scheme, regarding it as a plot of the whites, whom they look upon as hereditary enemies, to seduce them to a barren soil and sickly climate, anxious only for their departure from among them, and indifferent whether they afterwards prosper, or fall a victim to their credulity." Even so, he reported that "two very intelligent young mechanics" are willing to go to Liberia and return with an account of the region.[7]

The very small percentage of Virginia's African American population that migrated to Liberia is not as significant as the debate among them over their rightful destiny and the roiling of the local waters that the discussion of emigration to Africa caused. Local newspapers, encouraged by ACS agents, almost always published any story of emigration to Liberia, letters from Liberia, and notices of meetings or sermons on the subject. In letters to the ACS, Virginia colonizationists noted that they had to keep their emancipatory plans undiscovered by hostile neighbors, who believed that talk of colonization stirred their slaves to rebellion. Early in the African colonization movement, an Amelia County slave owner wrote, "What are likely to be the horrible consequences upon our slaves by the public discussion of such topics, in sermons and other public harangues?"[8]

Until his death in 1828, Lott Cary was the most vigorous promoter of Liberia among Virginia emigrants, as well as the outstanding example of the self-fashioned and self-made man. His accomplishments made him a model emigrant for the ACS to display, but, as one who felt little obligation to the ACS and answered to the Baptists and his business partners in Richmond, Cary also offered an assertive independence that was appealing to Virginia blacks. Cary was reported to have said, "In this country, however meritorious my conduct and respectable my character, I cannot receive the credit due to either. I wish to go to a country where I shall be esteemed by my merits—not by my complexion."[9]

Cary and Teage were among numerous young enslaved men born on plantations but hired out in towns in the early years of the nineteenth century. Cary rose to foreman in a Richmond tobacco factory, and Teage was a skilled harness and saddle maker. In time, both were able to purchase their freedom and that of their families. Cary's private trade in tobacco and his salary as a factory foreman enabled him to purchase a farm. Both men were members of the Richmond Baptist Church and attended the school held "for the benefit of the leading colored members of the church" by William Crane and David Roper.[10] The white Baptist Crane held Cary in particularly high regard, describing him as "a most extraordinary man—he possessed an energy of thought and a firmness of purpose—combined with the most inflexible integrity, which, without his seeking it, could not fail to command the respect of all around him."[11]

Though Cary was described as of "unmixt African origin," most of the early emigrant families from Richmond, Petersburg, and Norfolk were mulatto. At the turn of the nineteenth century, Virginia's free black population included prosperous free mulattoes whose ancestry was European, African, and, frequently, American Indian. This was a sizable group whose "imperfect connection" with the white "Body Politic," as the ACS described it, was in contrast to their obvious connection to the white body physical. As one white Virginian noted: "It is well enough to remember that Miscegenation is already the irreversible fact of Southern Society in every thing but the recognition of it. . . . Although the marriage ceremonies have been few, the mixture of blood has been very extensive. These Southerners have proved that the repulsion to the alliance of the two bloods extends only to so much of it as the parson and magistrate have any thing to do with."[12] Color was always the essence of the "imperfect connection" of free blacks with full citizenship, but free mulatto families thought, until the end of the Revolutionary Era, that this barrier might be overcome by further admixture, education, piety, commercial success, and exemplary behavior.[13]

The processes by which an entrepreneurial class of mulattoes in Virginia river and coastal cities had evolved, with their own society and commercial specialties, were similar to those of the Atlantic Creoles operating on the African and Caribbean coasts. Mulatto traders in the port cities, a group that once had had high aspirations, saw the first decades of the nineteenth century place increasing limits on them and move the prospect of real citizenship further from view. It was the realization of permanent marginalization, the connection that was not to be made perfect, that caused the exodus of educated and entrepreneurial mulatto families from Virginia to the new colony of Liberia in the 1820s. And Virginia free mulatto merchants quickly saw the possibilities for international trade in the Liberian venture.[14]

The life of Christopher McPherson, born of a white father and enslaved mother in Louisa County, exemplified the petty humiliations and legal restrictions that increasingly thwarted the ambitions of skilled free mulattoes. His career traces the arc of hope felt by free Virginia mulattoes after the Revolution, and his ambitions reflect those of free black Virginians of his generation. McPherson, manumitted in 1792, was the head storekeeper in Richmond for David Ross, whose enterprises included coal mines and iron works. In 1799, he left Richmond for Philadelphia, where he worked as a clerk in the House of Representatives and met Thomas Jefferson and James Madison. Leaving Philadelphia, on his way to new employment in Richmond as clerk in the office of the High Court of Chancery, he stopped in Washington, and there, armed with letters of introduction from George Wythe and Thomas Jefferson, he called on Madison. McPherson recalled with pleasure his social evening in Washington in 1800. "I sat at table evening and morning with Mr. Maddison, his Lady and Company and enjoy[ed] a full share of the conversation."[15]

McPherson thought of himself as an accomplished Virginian. He had acquired property through his diligence and had rendered service to his "Native country." Yet at some point, the trajectory of McPherson's life turned and fell rapidly. In 1810, the Richmond Common Hall Council passed an ordinance restricting free people of color from using hired carriages. When McPherson's petition for relief from this ordinance failed in the General Assembly, he "immediately bought me a hack and a pair of horses and carried my invalid family to [church]." In 1811, he hired a white tutor and advertised "a Night School . . . for male adults of color . . . and with the consent of their owners, Slaves," but a public outcry forced him to cancel his plans. In the same year, McPherson also published a pamphlet in which he called himself the "son of Christ" and predicted an imminent end to the world. He was confined briefly to the Eastern Lunatic Asylum in Williamsburg. By 1815, he had quarreled with Richmond's free blacks, advertised to buy Revolutionary War claims in Ohio in order to wait out the expected end of the world there, and moved to New York City where he died.[16]

McPherson's youthful ambition and descent into delusional prophecy was paralleled by the experience of a contemporary several counties to the south. John Day was a free mulatto cabinetmaker in Dinwiddie and Sussex Counties. His son, the Baptist minister John Day, described him as "the illegitimate grandson of an R. Day of S. Carolina whose daughter humbled herself to her coach driver." The younger Day, an emigrant to Liberia, added, "My mother was the daughter of a colored man of Dinwiddie County Virginia whose name was Thomas Stewart, a medical doctor, but whence he obtained his education in that profession, I know not." The elder John Day saw his initial advantages of complexion, education, and near parity with local white men lose momentum, and, in the early nineteenth century, he fell back among the common lot of free blacks. While the thwarted McPherson proclaimed himself the "son of Christ," the elder John Day took to drink. The father lost his business and property and left the state, leaving his son, who had been schooled and socialized with his white contemporaries, to work off his father's debts in Virginia. The younger John Day became a Baptist minister with a calling to be a missionary in Haiti. But he received little support from Virginia Baptists in this endeavor and turned his attention to the ACS, leaving Hicks Ford, Virginia, for Liberia in 1833.[17]

Such life histories were not uncommon in early nineteenth-century Virginia and provide a context for the appeal of a self-selected migration to Liberia. When Colston Waring, a minister of Petersburg's Gillfield Baptist Church, boarded ship for Liberia in 1823, he was to determine its suitability for thwarted ambitions as well as a missionary field. Waring's positive assessment of the colony upon his return was received in both Petersburg and Richmond, and nearly one hundred Petersburg free blacks, many Gillfield Church members, determined to emigrate with Waring and his family. Waring led an all-Virginia emigrant group that left for Liberia from City Point, near Petersburg, in January 1824.[18] The emigrants on the *Cyrus* represented a cross-section of Virginia free blacks. Among them were John N. Lewis from Petersburg, traveling with his mother and siblings, who were all children of white Adam Naustedler in Petersburg.[19] Reuben Dongey, a free mulatto tanner from Richmond, was part of a family of Dungees who were Upper Mattaponi Indian.[20] From Southampton County came Harris, Page, and Lemuel Clark, free artisans who were over fifty years old and who arrived with their children and grandchildren, in all, thirteen people. The ACS agent in Liberia said the emigrants on the *Cyrus* "had formed in America a worthy and well-compacted neighborhood" and that they "moved together in everything," especially in "aiding one another."[21]

Shortly before the departure of the *Cyrus*, black Richmond Baptists met to determine who among them "were disposed to embark to the American colony in Africa."[22] The Baptist-produced emigrant list contained twenty-seven persons in five families, about half of whom went to Liberia. The brig *Hunter* carried sixty-two persons from Virginia to Liberia in March 1825, among them free blacks from Richmond, Charles City County, and Southampton County. But the next March, a larger vessel, the ship *Indian Chief*, carried only twelve persons from Virginia.[23] Very early on, the white Virginia colonizationists understood that the presence of black men returned from Liberia, such as Colston Waring and Richmond Sampson, was vital to their enterprise. The Richmond Board of Managers asked Lott Cary to write his friends and to visit the United States as the best way to encourage interest in Liberia. Cary answered, "As respects my colored friends in Richmond, I feel for them very much indeed—But what can I do? I wrote to them individually . . . and I found from answers which I received that they had suffered through misinterpretation—I thought therefore that it was best to communicate to them through the Board of Managers of the [Richmond] African Missionary Society."[24]

As for a journey to the United States, Cary believed he could not be spared in Liberia, but he penned a statement defending colonization that he hoped would be published. That essay was so provocative and unflattering of conditions in the United States that the society's journal did not publish it. Answering the claim that colonization would become a deportation scheme, Cary said that the "good people of America" would never banish free blacks because "they have means to punish them without sending them away — [such as] the sweeping of chimneys — Sweeping streets — and representing your nation on coaches and waggons." In defending colonization, Cary returned many times to the intertwined themes of manhood and freedom. "You will never know," he said, "whether you are men or monkies so long as you remain in America," because free blacks were too easily praised for each accomplishment. And "considering the way you were brought up," blacks could never gauge their true level of merit in the United States.

Cary pointedly noted, "I shall believe you to be MEN when I see you conducting the affairs of your own Government; — and not before but so long as you are in your present state of subservience; we cannot view you as on a level with us." To the central objection that "there has been no guarantee given [free blacks] of the Liberation of those who are at present in bondage, I would ask them who they should look to for this guarantee? To the general government or the society? . . . as you have HEARD OF FREEDOM . . . march in pursuit of it . . . — And then and not till then will you be fully able to tell how far your removal will go towards facilitating the liberation of Slaves."[25]

Another circular was published in place of Lott Cary's biting essay. This circular was more decorous in describing the appeal that African colonization had for free blacks in republican America, but it was still pointed: "Forming a community of our own, in the land of our forefathers, having the commerce and soil and resources of the country at our disposal; we know nothing of that debasing inferiority, with which our very colour stamped us in America. Tell us, which is the white man, who, with a prudent regard for his own character, can associate [with] one of you on terms of equality? Ask *us* which is the white man who would decline such association with one of our number."[26]

Cary's death in a gunpowder explosion late in 1828 was a considerable blow to the Virginia prospects for free black emigration, although one important group departure was already being planned when he died. The *Harriet* left Hampton Roads on February 9, 1829, with the highest hopes of Virginia colonizationists and 155 passengers, of whom more than 100 were free blacks from Richmond and Petersburg. On board were nineteen

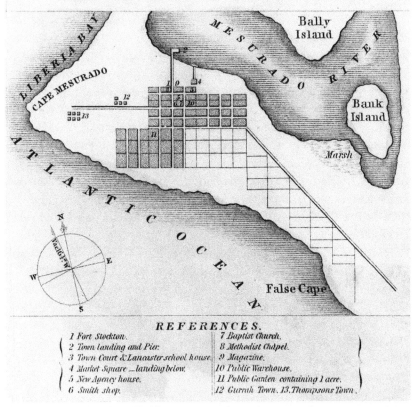

REFERENCES.

1 Fort Stockton.
2 Town landing and Pier.
3 Town Court & Lancaster school house.
4 Market Square — landing below.
5 New Agency house.
6 Smith shop.

7 Baptist Church.
8 Methodist Chapel.
9 Magazine.
10 Public Warehouse.
11 Public Garden containing 1 acre.
12 Gurrah Town. 13. Thompsons Town.

Built on a high promontory, Monrovia was the first and primary town in Liberia. Early settlers received five acres of farmland and a lot in the town, which was laid out in a standard grid pattern, as shown in this town plan from an 1828 map by Jehudi Ashmon. The town depended on trade for its modest prosperity. (Virginia Historical Society)

members of the David and Eleanor Sprigg Payne family from Richmond, including Nancy Sprigg, apparently the 80-year-old mother of Eleanor Sprigg Payne, and another relative, Beverly Page Yates.[27] On the same ship were nine members of the Amelia Roberts family from Norfolk and Petersburg, which was to provide Liberia's first president, Joseph Jenkins Roberts. Both the Roberts and the Payne families were comparatively well educated, practiced in commercial enterprises or trained in the ministry, and propertied. As a member of those interconnected families and later a vice president of the republic of Liberia, Beverly Page Yates explained, "Liberia is an offshoot from the United States, primarily from the *Southern states* and three-fourths of the people who laid the foundation of the Republic were from Virginia."[28]

After the *Harriett*, four vessels carried almost two hundred Virginians to Liberia. The last of these was the brig *Valador*, which carried some forty skilled free blacks from Southampton County to Liberia in February 1831. Three months later, an ACS agent traveling through Southampton County was told that an ACS auxiliary in Elizabeth City had been disbanded because members no longer supported the cause. Near Jerusalem he was told that no more free blacks were willing to go to Liberia until they received letters or information from the passengers on the *Valador*.[29] That summer, David Burr in Richmond reflected on the whole state: "From the inquiries I have made, there does not appear to be any probability of a single emigrant from the city or vicinity. [In other counties] I apprehend there is little more spirit among them for the cause than here and the free colored here seem to be at a dead stand."[30]

Shortly after Burr's glum assessment, Nat Turner's Southampton County insurrection murdered some fifty-five white persons over a two-day period in August and created a counter reign of terror against free blacks in Southampton and neighboring counties. The region witnessed the maiming and murder of blacks in the area. Levels of achievement or respectability meant nothing. No family, no person, was safe. In this environment, many of Southampton's free blacks decided to delay no longer and arranged through sympathetic white persons, some with ACS connections, for the ACS to assist their emigration to Liberia.[31] For some, their departure was part of a long-planned exodus; others had not considered emigration until the terror of the reprisals.

Free blacks sold their property quickly and left the area for Norfolk and Washington, where they waited for a ship to be chartered and fitted out. The *James Perkins* left Norfolk in December 1831 with a good portion of the free black Virginians from Southampton and surrounding counties. Of the 338 passengers on the *James Perkins*, 245 were from Southampton County and 281 were from Virginia. Many of the family names of those who left Southampton before 1831 recur on this ship. The dramatic free black exodus that was a result of Nat Turner's insurrection continued on a reduced level after the *James Perkins*, as four more vessels carried 250 more Virginian emigrants to Liberia over the next fifteen months. Southampton County emigration in total, both before and after Nat Turner, was as important to Liberia's early history as was the emigration from Richmond, Petersburg, and Norfolk.

Still, just a year after Nat Turner's insurrection, free blacks in Albemarle

County were canvassed as to their willingness to emigrate to Liberia. None expressed an interest.[32] Questions about Liberia persisted. The question most frequently asked by African Americans concerned the death rate, which hovered around 25 percent for emigrants in their first year, due mostly to what was called the acclimating fever, a form of West African malaria. Some emigrant groups were particularly hard hit and lost more than half of their number in a short period.[33] When this happened, black Virginians heard about it. Although Liberians from Virginia wrote claiming that many deaths could have been avoided by more cautious behavior on the part of emigrants, free blacks tended to be most influenced by the stark basic statistics, especially those for persons from their region. "I have seen all them books and maps and information about going to Liberia," wrote one free black Lynchburg man, James Wynn, "and I destribeted them among the free people and tha done grete good, but sir a leetle while and thay [free blacks] received letters to here from Liberia informing us that a great many of the people that went through Lynchburg from Lexington on way to Liberia was dead and some 12 or 15 others had fell with this Africa fever." Wynn went on to ask if it were true that one-third of the emigrants died of the acclimating fever and said that fear of it prevented many from emigrating.[34]

Emigration shifted toward emancipated slaves after 1832. Despite the fact that the Virginia General Assembly in early 1833 authorized money for free black emigration to Liberia and pointedly excluded money for emancipated slaves, the next two decades of emigration consisted predominantly of emancipated slaves who were sent to Liberia with ACS and private funds. These emancipations were primarily by will for emigration to Liberia and were done by men and women who referred to the rights of man or God-given rights in justifying their acts. The largest emancipation of the decade was that of Dr. Aylett Hawes, whose firsthand experience of slavery's brutalizing effect on the slaveholder was noted by an escaped slave.[35]

Hawes appears in the slave narrative of William Grimes, a runaway who wrote of his life as a slave in Virginia. As a young boy, Grimes was favored to make and serve coffee in the dining room of his master's plantation. A jealous cook put an evil-tasting substance in the coffee, causing Grimes to be blamed and severely beaten. It was the master's son-in-law, Dr. Aylett Hawes, present for the coffee incident, who told the master to stop beating the boy. Some years later, when Grimes ran away for the first time and was caught, it was again Hawes who drew on his status as a doctor to advise that the boy should not be beaten. Grimes eventually ran away successfully, and Hawes's aversion to the daily cruelties of slavery was channeled into an interest in the ACS that drew the suspicion of his neighbors. Hawes was a major donor to the ACS and also supported the Female Colonization Auxiliary in Fredericksburg. He subscribed to the *African Repository*, until his neighbors threatened, in 1831, to take him to court for bringing such incendiary material into the community. At his death a few years later, he freed over one hundred slaves for emigration to Liberia and provided money for each to be settled at Bassa Cove, an experimental settlement structured on pacifist and temperance principles.[36]

Another Virginia doctor, who had been schooled in late-eighteenth-century Edinburgh, also emancipated his slaves by will and directed them toward the Bassa Cove settlement. As a medical student in Edinburgh, Dr. James Jones had become a religious skeptic. On his return to Lynchburg, he joined the local philosophers in the Infidel Club that met at Painesville, allegedly named for Tom Paine. Age and experience modified his youthful enthusiasm for Enlightenment skepticism but did not change his belief that the degradation of blacks was to be found in the environment. Both Jones and Hawes, products of late-eighteenth-century Enlightenment educations, were particular in their preference that the emancipated people should settle in Bassa Cove, under the direction of the New York and Pennsylvania Young Men's Colonization Societies. Corresponding with northern colonizationist Elliott Cresson, Jones undertook to persuade the enslaved persons in his household to emigrate to Liberia. Jones's will instructed that "the whole subject is to be fully and intelligently presented to their minds, so that they may have the option of going to the Colony or remaining in bondage." His wife, as executor, softened the options by offering either migration to Liberia or emancipation with the right to remain in Virginia.[37]

Emancipation by design and by degrees, rather than wholesale emancipation by final testament, was another approach to colonization in the 1830s and 1840s. John Hartwell Cocke was the Virginia colonizationist best known for an elaborate system by which his slaves both earned their freedom and became, in his view, competent to handle freedom. Cocke and his second wife, Louisa, exemplified the early-nineteenth-century evangelical reformer family, with their dedication to temperance, agricultural reform, and African colonization. Cocke's long career as a colonizationist also exemplifies the gradual shift from an optimistic belief in a program of emancipation for emigration to an acknowledgment that such schemes would not convert most Virginians to antislavery or provide a satisfactory freedom for enslaved blacks.[38]

Cocke is an exception. Carefully nurtured and emancipated men and women sent to Liberia were generally the province of Virginia women. Prominent among these women were Mary Blackford of Fredericksburg and her mother, Mary Minor. Among the slaves emancipated by them was James Cephas Minor, trained as a printer by Mary Blackford's brother, John Minor, owner of the *Fredericksburg Political Arena* until its sale to William Blackford. James Cephas Minor arrived in the Liberian colony as a self-confident eighteen-year-old in 1829, where he was to work at the *Liberia Herald*.[39]

The young printer wrote back exultantly to William Blackford, "Ho! All ye that are by the pale-faces laws oppressed, come over to the above-mentioned destiny!" He complained, "Nothing do I hear of the coloured inhabitants of the town of Fredericksburg migrating to Liberia. . . . Will they still lay down in Turkish apathy? Africa is a land of freedom; where else can the man of color enjoy temporal freedom but in Africa? They may flee to Hayti or Canada, but it will not do; they must fulfill the sayings of Thomas Jefferson, 'Let an ocean divide the white man from the man of color.'"[40] But the white ACS agent in Liberia grumbled, "The printer Minor has become or always has been lazy and insolent."[41] Again, as was the case with Lott Cary, the ACS exalted the Liberian experiment as the forge in which free blacks would be remolded as men, but many white officials had initial difficulty reconciling themselves to verbal and political assertiveness by black men.

The Lucas brothers received admonitions to manhood in rural Loudoun County, Virginia, in 1829. Albert and Townsend Heaton emancipated Mars and Jesse Lucas and seven other members of the extensive Lucas family of slaves and free blacks. In January 1830, the Lucas brothers left Norfolk for Liberia, and the two sets of brothers exchanged letters. Letters from the Lucas brothers asserted their eagerness to become "true men" by becoming landholders and local officeholders on the models they had seen in Loudoun County. They saw themselves as pioneers on a new frontier, clearing the land and facing hostile natives. A letter from their former master, Albert Heaton, recites what they must do to become both manly and free: "Few indeed of the free blacks have done well here [in Virginia] & Never Can—But you have gone to a Country where the No'blest feelings of Liberty will spring up. . . . Liberty [is] the dearest right of man, the strongest passion of the soul, you have shewed the true dignity of man by imigrating to Liberia. . . . It is well to show feeling and mourn the loss of friends, but to distress yourselves about them over-much is unmanly and you ought not to do so. . . . You are now your own Masters and it depends greatly on your own conduct whether you will do well and prosper. . . . No Man can expect to do much for himself or others unless he is industrious, saving and correct and fair in his conduct."[42]

While stressing the connection between liberty and freedom, Heaton hit upon most of the socially approved models of manliness available: a mix of respectability, gentility, Christian self-control, and the self-made economic man. These models were adapted by both northern and Upper South free black leaders, whether they favored emigration or not. Manliness was sometimes referred to as a generic human dignity that included men and women, but it often meant exclusively male political and economic prerogatives. Perhaps the struggle to gain acknowledgment and respect for the black family and the precariousness of the southern black female's control over her body made it necessary to stress conventional gender roles among emigrants. Equally likely, it was an internalization of American gender conventions that made antebellum black colonizationists much like their northern black counterparts in defining manliness.[43]

The emphasis on manliness as Christian self-discipline and economic enterprise could be used to deflect criticism of Liberia. In 1847, the family of Samuel Harris, a black man freed by a professor at Washington College in Lexington, was sent to Liberia as a bellwether for the region. If free blacks and emancipated slaves in Rockbridge County heard nothing bad in a year, perhaps they would migrate. But Harris wrote back that he and his family were having a very hard time. Colonizationists were furious and described him as "babyish." Local free blacks lost heart for the enterprise, but Diego Evans, a free black barber reading to become a lawyer in Liberia, called Harris "weak-minded" and rallied the potential emigrants. Rufus W. Bailey, the colonization agent, urged free blacks to show as much initiative in considering Liberia as local white families were showing in moving to California. He assessed their hesitation more realistically in a letter to the ACS: "These people are the sport of circumstances. . . . They have been taught by experience that they can depend on nobody."[44]

Norfolk was the primary point of departure for Virginia emigrants, who often arrived there after long journeys by cart, train, and boat. The emancipated family of Jacob Snyder traveled by train from their home in Harpers Ferry to Baltimore, and then by ship to Norfolk to embark for Liberia.[45] In Norfolk, Virginia, emigrants were likely to meet emigrants from Tennessee or Kentucky and be housed, awaiting passage, in the homes of free blacks or white colonizationists. John McPhail, acting as an ACS agent, was often called upon to put up emigrants in a house he owned. Although there was frequently a national agent in the town, the Norfolk managers took responsibility for accommodations, checking supplies, and storing luggage.[46] They were also responsible for making sure that emigrants were not persuaded to change their minds or slip away from the ACS. Many of Norfolk's free blacks and urban slaves distrusted the motives of the ACS and were more than willing to share their suspicions with emigrants waiting for passage.

The ACS and its Virginia agents frequently attempted to orchestrate the scene of departure for maximum sentiment, with speeches, specially composed hymns, and prayers. Genuine feeling sometimes broke through the sentimental and scripted leave-takings. Thaddeus Herndon's extemporaneous remarks to his emancipated slaves showed a desire, common among emancipators, to maintain connection. "And now may God bless you. I can never forget you. Write to me, Washington, you can write: I have provided you with paper. Keep a journal, put all your names down, even the children, and write opposite to each one everything that happens concerning you."[47] Although most emancipators were concerned about emigrants, few came to the water's edge for such emotional scenes. Ship departures were more commonly the sites of tensions based on the fear that emigrants would disappear into Norfolk's free black community or, more likely, that the emigrants would use this opportunity as leverage to alter or adjust their circumstances.

One example of opportunistic resistance to ACS plans played out when Willis Cowling, a member of the Board of Managers of the Richmond Auxiliary, decided to free fifty slaves and hoped to persuade them to go to Liberia by sending one well-equipped artisan, whose success would lead the others to emigration. Cowling, a furniture maker and secondhand furniture dealer, chose Jack, a carpenter married to free black Agnes Byrd, and equipped him with a chest of tools and enough supplies to maintain him in Liberia with his wife for six months. But when the *Norfolk*, bound for Liberia, stopped in Savannah, Jack Cowling and his wife went ashore and boarded another ship bound for New York City, where he loudly spread erroneous stories that the ship's captain had sold two young women back into slavery in Savannah. This caused the Richmond Auxiliary to change the terms of emancipation. Benjamin Brand informed the national office that henceforth "slaves from this place will not be liberated until they arrive in the colony."[48]

Jack Cowling's claim was given credence among black Virginians because many took seriously the argument that the ACS simply wanted to rid Virginia of free blacks and did not care what happened to them once they were gone. Such maladroit functionaries as Rev. William Starr in Norfolk confirmed such suspicions—he created an uproar among free blacks when he confiscated emigrant papers identifying them as free and sent the papers to Richmond several weeks before ship departure. Despite his protests that he was only trying to certify their departure in order to claim the money promised by the state legislature for free black emigration, he was forced to retrieve and redistribute the free papers among the emigrants waiting to embark for Liberia.[49]

While rumors circulated among blacks about reenslavement or death among emigrants, some white Virginians worried that their runaway slaves would slip on board and escape to Liberia. A well-known case in Maryland, in which a slave disguised himself as aged "Aunt Lotsie" in order to go to Liberia with his wife's free black family, provided another source of anxiety for Virginia colonization agents who checked embarkation lists against passengers. Local slaveholders petitioned colonization agents to be alert for such runaways as Willis Smith, a well-dressed young mulatto with pleasing manners who had run away from the dry goods firm of T. R. Crouch and Co. in Richmond.[50]

Embarkation did provide occasional opportunities for leaving a vessel or stowing aboard, but more emigrants used their passage to leverage the emancipation of family members. Efforts to use African colonization as a ruse to free family members were not uncommon. A Hampshire County white man responded to the society's inquiry about one free black woman, asserting: "Sir I have been and am yet of the opinion that the woman does not intend to go to Africa but that her views are that she will manage in such a way as to get her husband with her and then to continue within the United States."[51] Another slaveholder found his efforts to emancipate his rural slaves and send them to Liberia more subject to negotiation than he had imagined. A troubled conscience persuaded Colonel David Bullock to send twenty-two of his slaves to Liberia. As they prepared to leave, Patrick, the left-behind father of four-year-old Mary Ann, became distraught and persuaded Colonel Bullock to write the agent at Norfolk to send the child back. Bullock did so, promising to educate the child for several years and then send her, with her father, on to Liberia. In the next mail, Bullock reversed himself and consented to let Patrick take passage in the *Doris* with his wife, Judy, and daughter, Mary Ann. It appears that Patrick had prevailed, and, despite Bullock's willingness to educate the child in order to keep Patrick, he had finally acceded to the departure of all the small family.[52]

It was not unusual for members of an African American family to be divided among themselves about emigration to Liberia. And it was not unusual for members of a colonization auxiliary to use the willing emigrants to pressure the unwilling ones. Auxiliary members viewed this emotional manipulation as in the true interests of the family involved. David Burr, the owner of a Richmond iron works, sponsored a free black wheelwright named John (Jack) Brisbane, who had "served a regular apprenticeship with a good mechanic of this city" and had worked in David Ross's foundry for five or six years. Burr was surprised to discover that Brisbane's wife and children, who lived with him, were still enslaved, despite the fact that the wife had been given her freedom in her late master's will.

The necessity for leaving the state if emancipated had kept the wife from registering as free, in collusion with the will's executor, John Gamble, another auxiliary member. Jack Brisbane was reluctant to commit to going to Liberia, but Burr and Gamble now legally freed his wife on the understanding that she would emigrate or be forced to petition the state to remain. Four days before his family was to leave on the *Nautilus* in late 1827, Brisbane came forward to register for emigration. Burr expressed much of the evangelical family- and nation-building aspect of African colonization in his assessment of Brisbane as "improvident" and "rather intemperate, but with due encouragement & restraint will make a useful man in the colony as a mechanic," adding "it is chiefly on acc't of his wife and children that I have promoted his removal as they have everything to gain by the changes."[53]

The 1850s saw a renewal of interest in emigration on the part of free blacks, northern and southern. The passage of the Fugitive Slave Act in 1850 affected both regions, making every state less safe for free blacks. Though not as well documented as in the North, kidnappings and claims to the "ownership" of free blacks were common in the Upper South. But in the North, even those now willing to consider emigration to Africa, as well as to Canada and Haiti, were still reluctant to consider the new republic of Liberia. Decades of denouncing the Liberians as dupes meant that northern blacks preferred to set up their own emigrant companies rather than merge with the Liberian effort.[54] Free black Virginians were more willing to consider Liberia. Its familiarity to black Virginians and its emergence as an independent nation with most of its public offices held by Virginia emigrants were factors. But the threat that long-ignored restrictions on free black residency were to be enforced and the reactivation of the vcs, combined with the Fugitive Slave Act, also prompted new free black emigration from Virginia.

Much of the discussion of African colonization among Virginia's African Americans continued to focus on the Liberian death rate and the motives of white colonizationists, but black colonizationists from Virginia continued to defend their choices. Twenty years after leaving Hicks Ford, Virginia, Baptist minister John Day, of Bexley, Liberia, wrote an open letter to free blacks in the United States that stressed their subjugation within the American nation. This concept was always an important part of the rhetoric concerning Liberia, and it had more strength in the 1850s than it had had in the 1820s, as the legal status of free blacks deteriorated in the United States. Day's arguments renewed the themes of manliness and liberty: "I have wept and wondered whether every manly aspiration of soul had been crushed in the colored man, or does he pander to the notion that he belongs to an inferior race?" Day had rejoinders to the argument that free blacks must remain in America out of loyalty to the enslaved and had a practical response to criticisms of the ACS that did not absolve the society of its frequent negative assessments of free blacks: "What good has your continuance there done them [enslaved African Americans]? None, nor ever will. Some have objected to coming to Liberia on account of their dislike of the Colonization Society. I dislike as much as you unkind, and in some instances, unjust remarks of many who have written and spoken on the subject of colonization. The Colonization Society is, however, one in which more elements combine in working out a good than any other I know on earth."[55]

Day, aware of anti-immigrant tensions in 1850s America and speaking as an American evangelical, imagined with a grim satisfaction that Roman Catholicism would spread "its baneful influence over that apparent garden of the Lord," the United States. He predicted the imminent fall of the American republic if black laborers were replaced by "herds of poor, infatuated Romanists from Europe," who answered to the pope before the president. The nation, he predicted, will wish its fellow Protestants back when they have gone to Africa. "May not a reversion take place and Africa again be the garden of the earth?"

In the fall of 1860, Washington Copeland, another defender of Liberia and an elderly black man only recently freed by his own exertions, wrote familiarly from Circleville, Ohio, to the ACS in Washington. He was now ready to go to Liberia but he did not want the society to pay his way, "as the Colinisationest Society was under a great many expences." Instead, he promised to "do all that I can to put the expense on Mr. Samuel Miller and not on you." Samuel Miller was a Presbyterian minister and colonizationist in Lynchburg, where Washington Copeland had once been a preacher. Copeland thanked the ACS for sending on to him letters from John Henry Lynch in Liberia, and he noted that Lynch was "one of the ten boys . . .

from Lynchburg that went through my influence some 17 or 18 years ago
. . . part of the 48 that I have been the cause of going."

From the vantage point of 1860 and Ohio, Copeland still believed that
"this is not the place for the colored man. . . . I hope I shall see the promise
land of my forefathers yet for I am confident you [the ACS] are worth to
the colored people five hundred abolitionists for they say abolish slavery
and after they get us leave they will not do any thing for us except Rob us
of everything."[56] Copeland's comments were a latter-day and somewhat de-
based version of the arguments made earlier by Cary and Day and the exu-
berant printer, Minor, that American freedom would mean little to those
who had neither the franchise nor the finances to protect themselves from
becoming a permanent and exploited laboring caste.

Washington Copeland in 1860 engaged themes that Gabriel's followers would have recognized in 1800. What were the motives of whites and
to what extent were alliances with them possible? What was the basis for
black freedom and on what terms was it possible in America? From Gabriel's conspiracy to Virginia's secession from the Union, free and enslaved
blacks in Virginia left evidence that they had absorbed Revolutionary and
Enlightenment values and applied them to their own conditions. No less
than northern free blacks, they sought to find a national identity. Free
blacks and many of their enslaved kin and neighbors used African colonization to debate their connection with Africa and America. Most remained
suspicious and rejected emigration, but the existence of Liberia affected
their arguments and their perspectives on Africa.

Just before the clash at Fort Sumter that began the Civil War, James
H. Jones wrote from Petersburg, "I am one of the sons of Africa and I am
desirous to go to my native land," echoing Lott Cary's declaration forty
years earlier and perhaps telling the ACS what he thought they wanted to
hear. Those free black Virginians who first made an argument for Liberia
did so on the basis of their bitter perception that America would never
return their embrace of its institutions. On the eve of the Civil War, little
seemed changed. Northern free blacks may have been justified in scoff-
ing, as James Forten of Philadelphia once did, that, after four generations
in America, he could hardly be expected to find his way back to "the old
hut."[57] At the same time, some Upper South free and emancipated blacks
found African colonization to be an alternative that might offer true citizenship. Their vision was as American as Forten's, but those who thought
Liberia offered more possibilities than Philadelphia were not so dismissive
of Africa as a homeland.

Five

My Old Mistress Promise Me

I N THE WINTER OF 1817, a young woman living near Annapolis wrote a chatty letter, full of gossip from the national capital, to her brother in Liverpool. "There is a glorious scheme in contemplation and indeed going into execution to make a colony of the free blacks in Africa. It originated with Fenton Mercer. . . . It is intended to induce so many as can be persuaded to go voluntarily and join the establishment of Sierra Leone from where it is hoped good accounts will soon attract followers. It will also be a great inducement to slave holders to emancipate. Oh, it is glorious. Our national sun will yet attain its zenith freed from the foul blot which Britain left upon it. It has been the fondest of my dreams since infancy."

In the same letter, Margaret Mercer referred to the new British ambassador, Mr. Bagot, as so "handsome and charming" that he might have been able to avert the American Revolution. The Russian ambassador, however, was a "bear" and a "brute," and she wished that the Emperor Alexander knew how he treated his poor wife. Miss Mercer was certain, she confided to her brother, that he "carries one of those Russian shilelaghs [cudgels] over his shoulder."[1] Elsewhere, Margaret Mercer sighed over the fate of Mary, Queen of Scots: "If only she had been firm about marrying Bothwell." And she hoped to be relieved at the backgammon table by visitors to her family home.[2]

The romantic and perhaps slightly frivolous young woman in these letters became the most prominent woman in the African colonization movement, a woman for whom the national sun would rise in proportion to the numbers of slaves emancipated and colonized. African Americans frequently maintained a certain skepticism about white women's good intentions, partly expressed in the black folk rhyme: "My old mistress promise me, when she die she set me free. She live so long her head git bald; she give out'n the notion of dyin' a-tall."[3] In Margaret Mercer's case, emancipation was accomplished, but it had to be joined to African colonization, a dubious prospect to many of those asked to undertake it. The folk rhyme offers a sharp contrast to the hagiographic biographies published of Mercer and other Virginia colonization women after their deaths. Those slender didactic volumes portray the women as so saintly as to be one-dimensional.[4] But their commitment to African colonization was the stuff of real world vexations, frustrations, personal risk, and frequent disappointment.

Coming primarily from Virginia gentry families prominent in the American Revolution and from the evangelical movement within the Episcopal and Presbyterian Churches, they were a generation of women who were collectively the most active female advocates of African colonization. Their lives exposed them to public affairs. A sense of Revolutionary heritage—passed on as a prized possession in these Virginia families—kept alive their sense that they had roles to play in the republic.[5] This small cohort of educated gentry women saw the pernicious effect of slavery on their families and their society, as much as they saw the injustice and inhumanity of slavery to African Americans. Domestically, that pernicious effect included the moral corruption that human bondage produced in the souls of masters and slaves. It included the habits of tyranny encouraged in their children and the sexual license granted their male relatives. It included their own households, in which they were the frontline troops in confronting indirect and constant slave resistance. It included their fear of slave rebellion and of mulatto progeny. When they considered Virginia and its place in the nation, slavery appeared a fatal corruption of the promises of republicanism and salvation. In its degradation of master and slave, in its inefficiency and recalcitrance, in its thwarting of moral and intellectual improvement, slavery in Virginia was an evil that had to be ended by voluntary and gradual emancipation.[6]

African colonization appeared to remove the one obstacle—the presence of a large and unassimilated free black class—that prevented greater voluntary emancipations. These Virginia women saw themselves as in the tradition of gradual emancipation. Their emancipation advocacy was not derived from a desire to make slave property more secure or to make Virginia more economically competitive. Their insistence that the black family, enslaved and free, be recognized as inviolate—with gender roles distributed as they were among white families—reflected their belief that encouraging respectability, piety, and education in black families would enhance those qualities in their own white families. African colonization offered them their best opportunity to carry these convictions into the

Margaret Mercer, shown in this portrait by Thomas Sully, was the most prominent woman advocate of African colonization in both her native Maryland and Virginia, where she lived during her last busy decade. She differed from most other Virginia colonization women in remaining unmarried, and thus she was able to control her estate and emancipate for emigration to Liberia. Other women typically emancipated for Liberia when widowed or after raising the money to purchase the freedom of an enslaved person known to them. (Atwater Kent Museum, Philadelphia)

larger world. It was self-serving in its desire to remake the white family, but it also emphasized natural rights, expressed as civil rights such as binding marriage, for enslaved blacks.

Benevolent societies flourished in the early American republic, and women used them both to advance their visions of national reform through amelioration and to extend their own influence in society. Women's advocacy of antislavery, more than any other benevolence or reform, was highly politicized, and women were frequently censured for entering such a rancorous and unsuitable public arena. Most of the national censure was directed at northern women who spoke to public audiences, organized antislavery societies, or worked directly with African Americans. It can be argued that northern and Virginia women who wanted to end slavery were not that far apart. Virginia women who advocated gradual emancipation as supporters of African colonization, organized auxiliaries, and worked directly with African Americans were visible and numerous enough to attract similar negative attention. But Virginia women lived in a slave society that grew increasingly hostile to criticism or deviance, and the roles and duties of the southern woman were more intertwined with a rationalization for African slavery that viewed women as similarly dependent on men. The experience of Virginia colonization women provides a vivid illustration that educated Virginia women had concerns similar to their northern counterparts, but the presence and later justification of slavery more effectively limited their voices and activities.[7]

The leaders among Virginia colonization women promoted in their own families what they saw as the true Revolutionary ideals of benevolence and civic-mindedness. They made the domestic world the proper center of education and salvation. In the early days of the republic, the development of the idealized republican mother, the upright and patriotic matron who educated her sons for citizenship, was a consolation prize awarded by women to themselves, and evangelical Protestantism provided a voluntary self-discipline and a belief system with which to structure and justify their benevolence. Virginia republican mothers and evangelical women concerned about slavery found a natural home in the American Colonization Society (ACS). More than a year before the formation of the ACS, the devoutly evangelical Ann Page read of Samuel Mills's efforts to found a colony on the west coast of Africa, and this appeared to her as "the light of a taper at a great distance in a dark passage."[8]

Colonization gave these and other women an opportunity to engage the world of ideas and action and to demonstrate their abilities. It appealed to women already connected with temperance and religious tract societies, Sunday schools, and missionary work. They subscribed to such religious journals as the *American Baptist* and the *Latter-Day Luminary* or the Richmond-based *Family Visitor*. They found missions and missionaries well represented in the ACS journal, the *African Repository*, and they bought subscriptions for their ministers and family members. They asked for special collections at churches and sponsored Liberian Fairs in order to support schools and missionaries.[9] Typical of their busy benevolence was Louisa Maxwell Holmes of Norfolk, who was converted to evangelical Presbyterianism by her brother, William Maxwell, and joined the Juvenile Mite Society, the Board of Commissioners for Foreign Missions, and the Orphan Society, as well as forming a Sabbath school in Norfolk. She was already a member of the ACS when she married colonizationist John Hartwell Cocke.[10]

The most active generational cohort of Virginia women colonizationists was born between 1780 and 1800. Among them, Margaret Mercer was the first and most singularly dedicated. She was the product of an unusually rigorous and thorough late-eighteenth-century education and was unimpeded later by the responsibilities of a husband and children. In an age when most women received, at best, a smattering of education from wandering tutors, ill-prepared widows in financial distress, or distracted mothers, she had been instructed in her Maryland home by her father in all the branches of learning offered to boys. At the completion of her education, she experienced a sense of futility and initially felt, as she wrote a cousin, "cut off from every means of usefulness and could not find anything on earth to do that might not as well remain undone."[11] With female Hunter and Garnett cousins in Essex County, Virginia, she founded Sunday schools that taught the rudiments of reading and writing as well as religious instruction to enslaved children. She took up the cause of Greek independence but found her calling at home, in African colonization, where her cousins, Charles Fenton Mercer and John H. B. Latrobe, were central figures. The Essex County cousins founded a girls' school at the Garnett home in 1821 and made raising funds for colonization an integral part of the curriculum.[12]

In that year, Margaret Mercer inherited sixteen slaves as her share of her father's estate and began to correspond with the ACS about sending them to Liberia.[13] This was a double burden, because most estates paid debts by selling slaves and she intended to send all of them to Liberia. "I think every day that I am certainly possessed with madness to be making preparations to go on with so painful and so precarious and ungrateful a task. However my motive must carry me through. I must pay my father's debts and then I will be free again."[14] Mercer used "free" in the same way that other slave-owning Virginia women involved in African colonization did—and in a different way from white men who spoke of freedom and liberty. For Virginia colonization women, freedom from the responsibilities of slaves was less a political abstraction than an imagined domestic utopia.

For slave emancipation was seen as their own emancipation. It would allow them to escape the daily domestic chaos of slavery and the enforced sociability of the Virginia gentry that they believed shackled them to the household. Women colonizationists complained to their diaries and to each other of the "numerous duties" and "one thousand vexations which daily annoy me."[15] Ann Page proclaimed to her cousin, Mary Lee Fitzhugh Custis: "My days are an unceasing round of *dying peace-meal* [underlined twice] in the service of this family."[16] She described the moment at which she first began to carry into practice her growing religious convictions. "The practice of dining [out after church] was at that time carried to a great extent in our neighborhood," but she began to feel she should come home after church and be "among my fellow creatures in bondage on the plantation." At first she lacked the courage to tell her neighbors why she refused invitations to dinner. But "fear of God enabled me to overcome the fear of man," and she withdrew from society, fixing on emancipation and colonization as her Christian duty.[17]

As the prospect of federal funding for colonization faded and factionalism beset the ACS, Margaret Mercer's cousin, John Latrobe, of the Maryland Colonization Society, wrote to ACS corresponding secretary Gurley, suggesting that Gurley encourage the formation of female auxiliaries. "By getting the women enlisted for us, we may move the men who may ultimately move the government." Put out a circular, Latrobe urged Gurley, "prefaced by some general remarks [on] female sensibility—sympathy, & etc."[18] Latrobe's tone was patronizing and his knowledge limited. Women had already organized in Virginia through money-raising activities for African colonization and Sabbath schools for enslaved children. Women in Virginia had taught black children to read in Sabbath schools, despite the law and the hostility of neighbors. Only their status as gentry women protected them from arrest or at least the closure of their schools. As one noted, "I have been myself twice threatened by the grand jury for teaching on Sunday a few colored children to read their Bibles. I know they cannot get any white witnesses . . . against me." These benevolent societies, Sabbath schools, and girls' boarding schools frequently formed the core of a local auxiliary. In Charlottesville, the Albemarle Female Colonization Society was organized two years after local women had sponsored a Liberian Fair. The Essex County Society, it was reported, "consists entirely of ladies, principally the family of Mrs. James M. Garnett, and includes the greater part of her pupils."[19]

Female auxiliaries organized with high hopes and the tactics of female benevolence. An Albemarle County correspondent wrote to the national society that she believed that almost every woman in the county would join the society if she knew about it. In Essex County, "it is confidently believed that everyone in the county would do so [become members] if it were practicable to attend the meetings."[20] Female money-raising activities and women's donations and bequests became an important part of the ACS budget. Women held fairs and sold handiwork, such as embroidery and weaving, and they made clothes and collected books for emigrants. "The [students] are laboring hard at the Fair, all our neighbors indiscriminately are to be bidders so if you are minded for a bustle, just step in on the first of May, provided it be a good day," was the jaunty invitation from Margaret Mercer's school.[21] At Mrs. Garnett's school, the meetings took place every Saturday, "the whole of which is devoted to the making of various little articles, both for ornament and use. . . . The entire proceeds go . . . to the colonization society."[22] They acknowledged that "our own exertions . . . must be within a contracted sphere," but their subtext was that women could and should "set the first example to our sex of an association of females engaged" in public causes.[23]

Female auxiliaries were active and visible in Virginia for roughly the decade between 1826 and 1836. The most active were those of Fredericksburg and Falmouth, Richmond and Manchester, and Albemarle County. The best-known and most active woman in the work of African colonization in Virginia was Mary Berkeley Blackford of Fredericksburg. A married woman with five sons, she believed that slavery would destroy the nation and the state by undermining its moral fiber. Mrs. Blackford had no slaves whose future was legally hers to design, but she did have an antislavery history in her family. Her father, General John Minor, had introduced an emancipation bill into the House of Delegates in 1773, and her mother, Lucy Landon Minor, had emancipated approximately a dozen persons with the intention of sending them to Liberia. Her brother, Lancelot Minor, went to Liberia as a minister in 1837 and died there in 1843. Family legends abounded with tales of financial sacrifices made by the children of both Mrs. Minor and her daughter for the sake of African colonization.[24] But the Blackfords, husband and wife, both active in African colonization, disagreed over tactics and goals. William Blackford was a lawyer, editor of the *Fredericksburg Arena*, and leader of the Virginia Whig Party.[25] Mary Blackford hoped that colonization would pave the way for the gradual emancipation of the slaves, but her husband saw the scheme primarily as a means to remove the degraded free black population.[26]

In 1829, she founded the Fredericksburg and Falmouth Female Auxiliary. The auxiliary used the tactics of other benevolent societies and the web of kinship to form colonization networks. An 1833 letter from a woman in Fredericksburg to her sister in King and Queen County suggested how ideas and materials circulated among women who were scattered over several Virginia counties: "Mrs. Blackford has been to see me lately to endeavor to interest me in the Colonization Society. Mrs. Grinnan has sent me several copies of the last Annual Report . . . and I shall send you one by this mail, begging you at the same time to read and circulate those pamphlets on the subject which I carried you last spring and the one which you purchased here in the summer. I am very anxious that something may be done . . . in your neighborhood." The writer judged that the women might have to wait before forming another society since they had just formed a religious tract society that was engaging the energies of the "ladies in the church." In the meantime, "there is a great deal of prejudice to subdue and ignorance to enlighten . . . which may pave the way for [colonization]."[27]

Their work was carried on, Mary Blackford assured ACS secretary Ralph Gurley, "in the domestic circle, around our own or the firesides of our neighbors, without the sacrifice of time or the proprieties of our sex."[28] Women like Mrs. Blackford hoped to make the domestic work of fireside, classroom, and chapel as important in antislavery as the pulpit and legislative hall. Her examples of the evils of slavery were also domestic and came from vivid personal experiences that described such ruptures of black domestic life as the sudden sale of her cook's husband and the sale, in batches, of small motherless children. Such family-destroying sales, Mrs. Blackford and others knew, were often a result of the chronic debt common to Virginia's slave-based economy. Women felt very uneasy that carefully tended black families, intended for emigration, might be sold for debt. Debt, as women knew, meant that the market prevailed over the domestic fireside in all cases.

With these realities in mind, women hoped to maintain control of the money they raised for the ACS cause. They focused on projects that emphasized the centrality of female education to the success of any colonizing or state-making venture. In Virginia they provided primary schools in the guise of Sabbath schools, and in Liberia they provided teachers and money, especially for girls' schools. In 1826, a letter from the treasurer of the Richmond auxiliary accompanied one trunk of clothing being sent by the women of Richmond to Liberia: "The ladies, I believe, wish the girls' dresses to be kept for such native African girls as may be educated. It is now understood that the best way to civilize a nation is to educate the girls." The word "understood" was scratched out, and the word "said" was written above it, indicating the ambivalence with which the treasurer passed on this bit of received wisdom.[29] The women of the Female Colonization Society of Richmond and Manchester later forcefully expressed their sentiments when they claimed that they were "extremely anxious that in the infant state of your [Liberian] Colony, your daughters should possess the advantages for obtaining it [education]: it is the *Females* who will exert an influence over the rising generation. . . . Besides *this*, Education will most effectively tend to preserve to you, your civil rights and liberties as a colony."[30]

These female auxiliaries soon learned that any effort to affect policy through the use of their money would bring them rebukes. The Fredericksburg and Falmouth Female Auxiliary asked a friend in the Virginia Colonization Society (VCS) in Richmond to inquire about hiring an ACS agent to canvas the state to raise money, noting privately that the "female society must not appear too much in it. There is a considerable objection to our sex interfering in a subject that they say is purely political and that we have no business with." In Richmond, William Crane wrote them that the state society was "very lukewarm" on the subject of hiring an agent, and the VCS soon rejected their offer and their money. Mrs. Blackford found that "chilling." She returned to her auxiliary's original plan, asking the national society to send them an agent and declaring, "women . . . I hope may love their country almost as well as men."[31]

In 1833, the Female Colonization Society of Richmond and Manchester received a similar tutelage in the limits of female good works. The Richmond women had raised money for a "female free school in the Colony, for the purpose of supplying the lamentable deficiency which exists there in this department of education." They "resolved to invite a coloured woman, residing in Princeton, New Jersey, to come to Richmond" to qualify herself as a teacher; but "it was subsequently ascertained that it was unlawful to introduce a coloured person from another state into this Commonwealth," and "it was deemed expedient that this plan should be dropped." Apparently the Richmond women had not given prior thought to the laws that forbade free blacks from entering Virginia. They then contracted for and paid the salary of a free black woman, already trained, from Charleston, South Carolina.[32]

When it became clear that women would not be permitted to make policy or personnel decisions, the Richmond Female Auxiliary changed its name to the Ladies' Society for Promoting Female Education in the Colony of Liberia.[33] The Fredericksburg and Falmouth Female Auxiliary also reorganized as an educational society, and its founder, Mary Blackford, cited the "great objection made by the gentlemen to anything that can in the remotest degree draw the attention of the Negroes to a society they cannot understand."[34] But simply by conducting benevolent and educational business with free black men and women, white women disrupted decorum. Responding to a letter from the Richmond women about supplying a teacher, Colston Waring and Elijah Johnson wrote from Liberia: "We take it a great blessing that you have conferred upon us by preparing a 'Lady' who is qualified for this great task. . . . We hope the Ladies will lose no time in sending her out—we intend to prepare for her."[35]

The reference to a black woman as a lady had to have the tentativeness of quotation marks, unlike the reference to white women in the same paragraph. Once slavery was removed as the defining difference, how were Liberian men to address Virginia women? Ladies were a class within the category of women. Not even all white women were ladies, and antebellum Virginia society permitted nothing approaching such deference for black women. But courteous exchanges prevailed between Liberians and Virginia colonizationists, even though they seemed subversive of the good social order necessary to maintain race and gender hierarchies. To conservative Virginians, especially after Nat Turner's insurrection, these sorts of exchanges confirmed their worst fears of the potential disorder of such experiments.[36]

Nat Turner's insurrection provoked a special session of the legislature to consider the future of slavery in Virginia. Three petitions to this legislative session from women asserted female concern for domestic safety in the aftermath of the slave revolt. The documents did not challenge gender relations, but the petitions used the argument of women's domestic primacy to influence public policy. All three petitions originated in Virginia's African colonization movement, but their histories suggest that Virginia women were not to follow northern women from antislavery into women's rights. One woman colonizationist withdrew her petition before seeking signatures, one was written by a man, and one was commissioned by a male colonization stalwart. Mary Minor Blackford, writing for the women of Fredericksburg, withdrew her petition. She wrote on her copy: "I could have gotten more [signatures] if I had persevered, but I had not support and I was weak and timid." John Hartwell Cocke was asked by Charles

Augustus Stuart to work with him to write a women's petition for Augusta County. For Fluvanna County, Cocke asked Virginia Randolph Cary, the conservative author of a well-known advice book for young women and not a colonizationist, to write a petition.[37] This lack of an authentic antislavery female petition, despite the novelty of women's petitions in 1831, was a sign of the coming difficulties that Virginia women would experience in maintaining gradual emancipation as a part of African colonization in the coming decade.

Margaret Mercer's life demonstrated the growing constraints, both social and financial, on women who carried their colonization principles into action. After the emigration to Liberia of her former slaves in 1829, she was financially dependent on the school that she had started in 1824 in her Cedar Park, Maryland, home. She often pled lack of funds to her Hunter and Garnett cousins in Essex County as the reason she could not pay them a visit. "I need not tell you what my situation is—I have exactly the same cares to contend with except that I have to pay more to servants and masters and for provisions [I must] see to that. While my nominal income is large, my profits are almost nothing." In 1836, she moved the school to Belmont, the Loudoun County, Virginia, estate of Ludwell Lee, a former local colonization auxiliary officer. The house and outbuildings were in deep disrepair, and the rooms were described as "spartan in their plainness."

The school at Belmont had high academic standards and a strong religious and moral tone. "It is the land of spinsters," one young woman assessed approvingly. "I would advise all who entertain any prejudice against elderly young ladies (as Mrs. Bankson calls them) to suspend their opinion until they have visited this region." The continued existence of her school at Belmont was precarious.[38] "I have been in such a state of absolute starvation that I had not the means of getting a dinner for my family for one week except as I killed the old hens and the old geese. When that was done I had to send a cart down to Washington begging. My situation is not much better now with a school not sufficient to pay my teachers."[39]

Mercer had a wide correspondence with other colonizationists, including Gerrit Smith, whose apostasy in leaving colonization for abolitionism provoked a sharp critique from Mercer. "I am grieved," she wrote, "that my poor friend Gerrit Smith has put himself at the head of the incendiaries: but he is a noble-spirited fanatic—not very strong in the attic."[40] In leaving the society, Smith accused colonization of being more interested in attacking abolitionists and colonizing free blacks than in fighting slavery. The offended Margaret Mercer responded, "This very morning I have prayed that your dogmatical, opinionated, persecuting spirit might be changed for one more calculated to do good. . . . Sir, from the bottom of my heart, I believe that I am *more* opposed to slavery *than you are.*!!! I believe that I would do more, if personal sacrifice would avail, to put an end to African slavery. *But neither you nor I are God* . . . and I am, and always shall be of the opinion that you want that humility which trusts to the mild prevailing effect of Christian doctrine to work a *gradual* change."[41]

Such gradual change was anathema to another southern woman from a slaveholding family. Angelina Grimké, with her sister Catherine, left her South Carolina home and moved to Philadelphia. From there, she addressed letters and essays to her "Southern sisters."[42] Grimké, in a vigorous and plainspoken representation of the abolitionist position, dismissed the idea that "when a colored republic is built up on the coast of Africa, then we shall respect that republic, and acknowledge that the character of the colored man can be elevated: . . . Miserable sophistry! deceitful apology for present indulgence in sin! . . . These professions of a wish to plant the tree of liberty on the shores of Africa, in order to convince our Republican Despotism of the high moral and intellectual worth of the colored man, are perfectly absurd."[43]

Grimké's argument against African colonization was stronger than her ability to suggest an alternate plan of action for southern women. Even if they accepted her criticism of the ACS, Virginia women were not reassured by her "Appeal to the Christian Women of the South," in which she counseled them that immediate emancipation would not lead to uprisings and social dislocation. Nor did they feel she could advise them to do what she herself had failed to do—persevere in speaking and acting for immediate emancipation in their southern homes and communities. Grimké asked for the most basic civil disobedience from women—do not respect those laws of your state that sustain slavery; they are immoral and therefore null and void.[44] Virginia women had already broken or argued against several of the laws Grimké cited, including those that denied slaves the right of marriage, the right to their children, and the right to education. But although they were eager to ameliorate the condition of the slaves and end slavery, they shared the dominant American beliefs expressed in Ann Page's admonitions to her slaves as her first group of emigrants prepared to leave:

> I have used chiefly this language to induce them to go—Altho' it is a fine country, and you will if industrious, obtain good property and many advantages, yet much as I wish you to have comfort in your life,

these are not the objects I send you for—my heart is set on your being in a situation to live an upright life before God. . . . I yearn to have you in a situation where your children cannot be sold from you[,] *that* bitter woe to my view—your children will receive *education* there. . . . You will be as a light set on a hill—the eyes of the world will be upon you to see if you walk worthily—I cannot set you free here, you would be in obscure places where I should never know whether you were doing good or ill. . . . You cannot expect that as white people have taken the trouble to settle this country they will give it up to you, so as that you could have sufficient advantages here to become an independent people—that will not be—to continue together must be to continue in bondage, and of course liable to be sold at the will and for the debt of white people. I cannot die in peace without using all the means in my power to place you safe from that dire anguish, giving up your children for sale.[45]

This reasoning saw African Americans as a "people" who could never be an "independent people" in the United States. Mrs. Page and other colonization women accepted the nationally pervasive belief that African American history was not part of the national history under construction. Page wrote to Gerrit Smith, "I think that their Race will more surely arrive at a just and advantageous estimate in [the] view of our country there than they ever can here. There *would* continue some idea of superiority and rule among us, for ages to come."[46] But what really fired the imagination of Mrs. Page—her repeated concern in her admonition to her emancipated slaves—was the family and the individual soul, not the impossibility of black citizenship. Family nurture and education, the essentials for an "upright life," were most conducive to salvation. As she reviewed all the evils of slavery, the paramount one—to which Page alluded twice—was the sale of children away from their families. Fear of family separation was a powerful argument "to induce them to go," and she was convinced that children could be raised "for God and glory" more surely in Liberia than in the "obscure places" of the American nation, where brutalizing prejudice made a slide into "shame and disgrace" all too easy.

When Grimké made her 1837 appeal to her sisters in the South to attack slavery on their home grounds, Virginia women active in colonization had already had some experience in the reproofs and repression that followed even a gradualist approach to antislavery. Although they were thought to have "indulgent" husbands and ACS support, that indulgence only extended to certain forms of female benevolence. Remonstrances and criticisms from Virginia men who were political colonizationists made

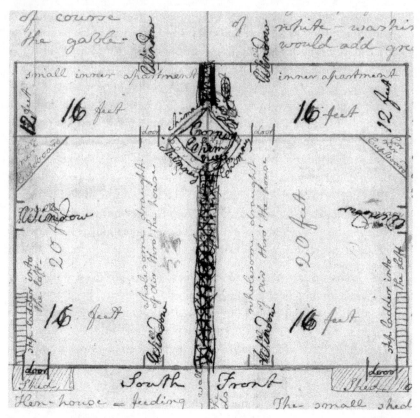

Ann Page, of Clarke County, Virginia, designed this model duplex slave quarter in 1814 with attention to every detail of daily life, believing that "decency, cleanliness, and good order" would prepare enslaved families for freedom. Virginia colonization women, such as Page, believed that domestic design, moral instruction, and education for women were necessary for the success of Liberia and would elevate the condition of women in both Virginia and Liberia. (Annfield Collection, Clarke County Historical Association, Berryville, Virginia)

the limits clear. John Randolph, present at the founding of the ACS and ever one to point out deviance or irregularity in others, noted in 1828 that "our women . . . to the neglect of their domestic duties and many to the injury of their reputations . . . are running mad after popular preachers or forming themselves into clubs of one sort or another that only serve to gratify the love of selfishness and notoriety."[47] William Blackford was for several years a U.S. diplomat in Bogota, Colombia, and considered having Mary Blackford join him there from Virginia. "You will have no benevolent societies here to occupy your thoughts . . . no . . . wearing out body and soul in Negrophilism or other philanthropic schemes."[48]

John Hartwell Cocke, perhaps Virginia's leading colonizationist, wrote to George Fitzhugh, "You have doubtless seen in the newspapers the struggle we had with the strong-minded women . . . in the World Temperance Convention. . . . We gained a perfect triumph and I believe have given a rebuke to this most impudent clique of unsexed females and rampant abolitionists. . . . [We] must put down the petticoats—at least as far as their claim to take the platform of public debate and enter into all the rough and tumble of the war of words." Fitzhugh replied, "I most heartily rejoice with you in the defeat of those shameless Amazons."[49] An "unsexed female," as General Cocke called them, could not rely on men to protect her. White women who behaved as Amazons would be seen as Amazons—to be treated as men, much the way black women were treated in the law and in their labor as black men. Black women had no social or legal protection—and white women who claimed male prerogatives might find themselves suspected of sharing traits often assigned to black women.

An example of what might happen to "unsexed" white women occurred when ex-president John Quincy Adams, now a congressman from Massachusetts, was presented with a Fredericksburg petition in support of the abolition of slavery in the District of Columbia. It was signed by nine black women. A congressman from Richmond, John Patton, who had long resided in Fredericksburg, came to the congressional clerk's desk to read the names and then announced that none of the women were of "decent respectability." He recognized one free mulatto woman "of the worst fame and reputation," and he was sure the others were the same. The Virginia congressman said that Adams should not refer to these women as "ladies." Adams asked, in mock innocence, how Patton knew them if they were infamous. Was it, he asked, because as mulattoes they bore the countenances of their masters? There the political badinage ended, but even a hint of such public abuse would have driven a white Virginia woman beyond the pale of society.[50]

The rebuffs experienced by female auxiliaries in Virginia preceded national economic and ideological shifts in the 1830s and 1840s, in which Virginia's continued commitment to enslaved labor exacerbated its differences with the northern states and put Virginia women in a political climate that viewed an expansion of gender roles with even more suspicion and hostility than northern women experienced. Colonization women who had sought or assumed the support of their ministers and churches found the major Protestant denominations split over slavery from the mid-1840s forward and their own churches developing a proslavery doctrine.[51]

There are few records of women's auxiliaries or Liberian educational societies meeting after 1836. Those women who remained dedicated redoubled efforts in household discipline to construct model families that could not only manage without enslaved labor but could save money for African colonization and save their own souls. Mary Blackford proclaimed, "I want to turn out a noble set of Spartan boys, inured to hardship and fatigue, afraid of nothing but God, despising luxury." She added, "I want to pay my debts, to give my children the very best education, to be independent." "Make not provision, then, for the unnecessary indulgence of the flesh," advised Ann Randolph Page. "What charges did I receive on this subject from my mother? She would say, 'Your guests see your well-spread table, but God sees in the negro's cabin.'"[52]

With their domestic and personalized perspective on colonization, Virginia women had an interest in the survival and prosperity of emigrants that went far beyond the standard practiced by the ACS.[53] Their desires for the emigrant families reflected their own values—with religion, family, and literacy a permanently linked triad of prerequisites. Highly preferred was a man with a skilled trade to act as head of household in Liberia. Virginia women urged and exhorted the male emigrants, whose preparation for emancipation they had carefully fostered, to be the kind of Christian men who placed family and community above profit and display.[54] For the black women who emigrated, white colonization women appeared to desire a version of themselves: educated, religious, devoted to family, and able to prosper in a new republic. If emigrants did not prosper in Liberia, some Virginia women emancipators were willing to consider that they would return to Virginia.

Elizabeth Van Lew of Richmond sent at least one emancipated slave, a young mulatto woman born into the Van Lew household and educated near Philadelphia, to Liberia. Although of northern parents and excellent education, Van Lew had learned the lessons of flattery and deference by which Virginia women persuaded men against their will. In this case, the man she sought to flatter out of his bad humor was a black shoemaker and minister from Petersburg, now a Liberian official annoyed at Van Lew's protégée, Mary Jane Richards.[55] When Richards expressed her dissatisfaction with Liberia, Van Lew wrote a conciliatory letter to Anthony Williams, saying that she would pay for Mary Jane's return to the United States: "If anything should happen to her or in case of her death we should feel very badly on account of keeping her in Africa when so much against her will—I am sure the climate does not agree with her—that may be the reason for her irritability and ill conduct."[56]

Richards's return demonstrated that even carefully fostered emigrants might resist the roles that well-meaning white women had created for them. Sometimes a tug-of-war was in evidence between those women who were designing model Liberians and the recipients of their ministrations. One of the pupils of Mary Blackford was Abram Blackford, on whom Mrs. Blackford focused her hopes.[57] He was sent to live with Mrs. Blackford's brother, Lucius Minor, for a year to learn farming before he went to Africa, but that agricultural tutorial was interrupted because Abram paid a long visit to his mother.[58] When he left Norfolk, Mrs. Blackford continued to smooth his path: "I wish him to go under the best auspices, will you recommend him to the special kindness of the governor . . . ? Tell me if he went off in good spirits."[59]

When Abram Blackford left Virginia for Liberia, he described himself not as a farmer but as a teacher with a good education. When the ship's list was published in the *African Repository*, Mrs. Blackford was upset for two reasons. First, she wanted her husband to be credited as the emancipator, and, second, she thought Abram had overreached in his self-description: "You are mistaken in thinking Abram calculated. He would not learn [to do calculations] when he was a boy although I tried hard to teach him. Now he is anxious to learn and hopes to do so in the colony."[60] This was Mrs. Blackford's last effort to be the expert on Abram. By the time he reached Liberia, Abram was the expert on himself. He did not become a farmer. By 1852, he was a part owner and operator of the sloop *Mary Ann* and had a factory at Cape Mount.[61] The self-described teacher boarding a vessel for Liberia and the later successful Liberian merchant bore little resemblance to the modestly literate farmer Mary Blackford had intended to send out.

Rewriting the scripts for their lives did not alienate emigrants from the Virginia colonization matriarchy that had nurtured them. They continued to exchange letters for many years. But, for the women, writing to Liberia or to the national ACS office or to each other after the mid-1830s became the most important means of connection to the cause as disapproval in the local community and in the press grew. In their long letters to the various ministers who were the secretaries of the ACS in Washington, the women described their sense of isolation and their need for connection to others in the enterprise of colonization. "I feel so alone in this region that the kindness of my distant friends, is very soothing and encouraging. Those around me are very kind and affectionate. But they frown on this enterprise and fear I may make other negroes discontented." The distant friends to whom Anne Rice of Prince Edward County referred included the secretary of the ACS, to whom she was writing. Slave-owning families in the neighborhood, alarmed by the emancipation and impending departure of Mrs. Rice's slaves, refused to allow their own enslaved people to come into contact with them.[62] Because Mrs. Rice had inherited status and important kinship ties, her activities were criticized and her neighbors would not speak to her on the subject of colonization, but she was not interfered with or completely cut off from the community. She turned frequently to the ACS office in Washington for a sympathetic reader.

The enterprise to which Mrs. Rice, widow of Presbyterian minister John Holt Rice, referred was the gathering together of two families of slaves and their removal to Liberia, "the grand object before me ever since they were subject to my control."[63] Although slave marriage was not legally binding in Virginia, women colonizationists honored it as if it were. The gathering of a dispersed enslaved family was difficult and expensive, and, even if it had not been an article of faith among most women colonizationists, it was frequently insisted upon as a condition of their emigration by emancipated slaves themselves. Since Rice spent "every cent I had" to purchase the wife of Anderson Brown and Brown also had "a very smart young daughter by a former wife," Rice suggested that donations to purchase the daughter would be welcomed by the "divided, but still united and covenanted family."[64] Such solicitations divided northern antislavery advocates over whether it was ever good practice to pay for freedom.

But Virginia women continued to emancipate for freedom and for African colonization through the 1840s and 1850s, with little remaining hope for general emancipation but with a sense of personal duty and responsibility. At the same time, as political sectionalism intensified in Virginia and the generation of republican mothers and their daughters aged, a new image of the republican woman patriot emerged. Her self-sacrificing devotion to the republic was more to be trusted and honored than that of ambitious men.[65] But in the 1840s, the patriotic emphasis in Virginia shifted from the nation to the state. The role of patriotic woman was one for which Margaret Mercer was well qualified, but her antislavery views would not fit into this construction when it was reduced to Virginia.

After ten difficult years at Belmont, Mercer died of tuberculosis in 1846, leaving only the school library and science laboratory to which any value could be attached.[66] Whether "the mild prevailing effect of Christian doctrine" had had any effect on her Maryland and Virginia neighborhoods appeared doubtful. Even her beloved Virginia cousins, the Hunters and the Garnetts, who had founded a Liberian Society in the 1820s and had sold handmade items to raise money for Africa, became a family of states' rights advocates. Martha Fenton Hunter, of Essex County, one of Margaret

Mercer's frequent correspondents and a cousin, wrote a fictional defense of slavery that appeared in the *Southern Literary Messenger* in 1848. Her theme was that the North was uninformed about the South and that the plantation was a model of order and morality.[67] Hunter's life among relatives who were prominent proslavery politicians in Essex County made her perspective inevitable. But Mercer had found northern Virginia and an isolated girls' school more congenial as a female space — one in which she could maintain an antislavery position.

Female auxiliaries appear to have stopped meeting by the late 1830s, although correspondence between the national society's secretary and Virginia colonization women continued. In 1840, there was one effort made to rally the state's women under the banner of the vcs. A group of women in Richmond organized the Female Colonization Society of Virginia and urged the state's women to "form a Society in your neighborhood auxiliary to us and thus make the Female Colonization Society of Virginia the medium through which your contributions shall be remitted to the parent society."[68] Few of the women still active in African colonization were interested in funneling their money through Richmond, and other women were generally unenthusiastic about organizing new auxiliaries in the 1840s.

The resurrection of the vcs in 1849 and a modest revival of debate among Virginia free blacks as to the merits of Liberia had slight effect on women colonizationists. But the publication of Harriet Beecher Stowe's *Uncle Tom's Cabin* brought to light the reality that the women active in colonization in the 1820s and 1830s had been replaced by a younger and smaller generation. Many of these women were familiar with African colonization from their families' long involvement — but that they thought about it differently was evident in their responses to Stowe. Stowe's novel portrayed vividly all the evils of slavery from the perspective of a middle-class Christian American woman of the North, concluding with the murder of the sainted Uncle Tom and the emigration of the mulatto George Selby to Liberia. Stowe gave Selby a long speech in which he praised the Liberian republic as the only home for ambitious and educated African Americans. Even artless and manic Topsy was sent to Africa, after training as a missionary.[69]

Southern women's tracts, novels, and letters defending southern institutions included writings by Virginia women who moved from the earlier theme of understanding and reconciliation among the states to a defense of slavery and Virginia. These literary works of the 1850s fit seamlessly into the construction of a southern national identity, and African colonization was still frequently seen as a resolution of the problem of slavery. But it was no longer a step toward emancipation and national reconciliation — it was the guarantor of a system in which all blacks were enslaved.[70]

No one was more emphatic in making this point than Julia Gardiner Tyler, the wife of ex-president John Tyler, who had succeeded in his efforts to monitor and guide the policies of the VCS from its origins to the Civil War. The northern-born Julia Tyler, in her essay "To the Dutchess of Sutherland and the Ladies of England," which was published in the *Southern Literary Messenger* in 1853, defended slavery in response to an English critique and maintained that African colonization was the best answer for the question of free blacks. But the first and best-known response to Stowe's novel was another novel, Mary Eastman's *Aunt Phyllis's Cabin: Or, Southern Life as It Is.* Although a transplanted Virginian and not a colonizationist, Eastman carried forward the argument that the state would be better off with free labor and that ex-slaves would have to go to Liberia.[71]

Other women with ACS family connections emerged as writers in the 1850s. Judith Walker Page Rives's husband was a vice president of the Albemarle auxiliary of the ACS, as well as a U.S. senator. Deeply interested in politics, she was an officer in the Mount Vernon Association, formed in the 1850s to preserve the home of George Washington. She shared this interest in preserving and interpreting Mount Vernon with Julia Gardner Tyler and Margaret Junkin Preston, women long associated with colonization through male members of their families. The Rives family participated in sending a number of emancipated families to Liberia in the 1850s, the same decade in which Judith Rives published a sentimental novel of idealized plantation life, *Home and the World.* Although a Unionist, Judith Rives felt that it was necessary to defend Virginia and slavery in the face of literary and political attacks in the 1850s.[72]

Margaret Junkin Preston, of Lexington, daughter of the president of Washington College and wife of a professor, was part of a family and college deeply involved in African colonization. Her husband's first wife was the niece of colonizationist Archibald Alexander, now president of Princeton University, and the Junkin family had come from Lafayette College, Pennsylvania, where they had known two students who were emancipated by John McDonogh of New Orleans for eventual emigration to Liberia. Her contribution to antebellum African colonization in the Shenandoah Valley was to write poems and hymns such as those celebrating the departure of emigrant families for their "native shore." Her hymn to Africa sang of Liberia as a replication of the American republic and of the value of slavery as a tutorial for African Americans. After the Civil War, Preston wrote poetry for southern magazines and Confederate memorial dedications. The work of these women in idealizing the plantation and master/ slave relationship while promoting African colonization provided the base for the rise of a Lost Cause legend after the Civil War.[73]

But the redoubtable Mary Blackford was still alive at the beginning of the Civil War and pointed out the true cause of southern secession: "All the quarrels that have shaken the country to its foundations have grown out of this fatal cause [slavery] and now it is destroying us as a great people."[74] Reflecting on the antebellum decades a year after the Civil War ended, Blackford repeated the creed of her generation: "But had gradual emancipation been then adopted, connected with colonization in Africa, what an amount of good might have been done!! The preventing of this terrific war would have been one item, beside the benefit to the poor negroes, and to Africa."[75]

The initial cohort of colonization women in Virginia believed that "decency, cleanliness, and good order" among slave families was a prerequisite for gradual emancipation and that the same qualities would strengthen the white household. But the sources of their power—spartan household discipline, an evangelical worldview, the advancement of female education, and the careful nurturing of model citizens for Liberia—were domestic and private and were unable to resist a political metamorphosis into a defense of the Virginia household and, by extension, slavery in that household. Their initial acceptance of the belief that the United States was a "white man's country" aided the shift from an effort to unite the North and South through understanding Virginia's realities to defending Virginia as it was. This was more easily done because the women were consistently marginalized by the increasingly conservative VCS. They lacked sanction and any public venue for their concerns, energies, and abilities until they abandoned gradual emancipation. The more public women among the next generation overcame that difficulty and participated in African colonization as proslavery advocates, or, at least, they accepted the prevailing comfortable notion that slaves would be free in God's own time.

Six

Revising the Future in Virginia

I N 1827, JESSE BURTON HARRISON declaimed, "Nothing is more frequent than to hear . . . lamentations over the departing greatness of our commonwealth. . . . But the most pointed complaint is of the disappearance of the old Virginia character. The mistake appears to me to consist in *regretting* it. Do you want the old Virginia character back? It can be done; it is the easiest of political problems. You must repeal the statute of distributions and introduce hereditary wealth; then check the spirit of commerce by abolishing the banks, bringing back all wealth to consist in land and slaves; and then you will have it restored in two generations: but for how many generations it would last, I cannot say."[1]

For Harrison, the old Virginia character based on land and slaves was outdated and an obstruction to Virginia's prosperity. He did not want it back, but others did—or insisted that it had never departed. Harrison saw himself as a progressive Virginian in this speech before college students in 1827, as he did five years later when he defended the American Colonization Society in response to William and Mary professor Thomas R. Dew's attack on it in the *American Quarterly Review*. Assessing the 1832 Virginia special legislative session called to consider Virginia's response to Nat Turner's insurrection, Dew attempted to consolidate his reputation among states' rights southerners by refuting any plan to end slavery in Virginia. He carefully explained that the entire structure of Virginia prosperity and social order would collapse with any plan for general emancipation. As part of his argument for the necessity and essential rightness of slavery, he calculated the financial and demographic impossibility of colonizing Virginia's black population in Africa. He reasserted the popular view that Virginians had been compelled by the British to adopt slavery, corrupting their Atlantic Eden, and the equally self-serving fantasy that the passage of time might somehow rectify this error. Inexorable economic forces might, Dew suggested, eventually drive free blacks and slaves to the Lower South and out of Virginia.[2]

Harrison, in response, argued that white Virginians must now face their "sacred duty" to blacks. "Either their condition must be radically bettered by the grant of such privileges as would make them useful citizens" or they "must accept a home elsewhere." The South, he thought, would not accept the first option, so African colonization was necessary to break Virginia of its injurious dependence upon slavery. Despite Virginia's "moral duty" to blacks, Harrison said candidly that he directed his comments "almost exclusively to the injuries that slavery inflicts on the whites," and he emphasized, with underlining, his intent "*to show the necessity of her [Virginia] promptly doing something to check the palpable mischiefs her prosperity is suffering from slavery.*" Harrison made the familiar argument that slavery kept white farmers and artisans from migrating to Virginia and drove out her own white youth. Virginia, now less dependent upon the tobacco economy that had encouraged slave labor, might be reduced to acquiring capital through the shameful sale of excess slaves out of the state. Emancipation and transportation were both necessities and had to happen soon, he concluded, despite Dew's financial calculations and his vague reassurances of a faraway happy Virginia Eden without slaves.[3]

Thoughtful Virginians, reading the essays of Dew and Harrison, might have felt they were being offered a choice of fantasy futures—one grounded in the absolute necessity of maintaining slavery for Virginia's current economy and republican liberty and the other grounded in the absolute necessity of combining emancipation and emigration for the same economy and liberty. For both men, and for most Virginians, the key to imagining Virginia's future was always in imagining the future of bonded labor in the state. There was a general and self-serving agreement among most white Virginians that the burden of slavery fell primarily on whites and that emancipated blacks could not remain in the state without retarding its progress. Just exactly how and under what circumstances some 40 percent of the state's population would be moved beyond its borders gave rise to speculative scenarios that generally entailed more social and political change than most citizens thought possible or bearable. Yet such speculations arose, often in a form too removed from politics to cause censure but revealing the deep anxiety of Virginians over slavery and the continuing role of African colonization in Virginia's construction of its future.

In imagining Virginia without slavery or without black Virginians, white Virginians expressed their own deep yearnings to be rid of all of the Nat

Turners—the proximate cause of the Harrison-Dew debate—but more centrally to halt Virginia's slipping status in the nation, a condition that many considered to be tied to slavery. Early nineteenth-century Virginia had experienced a relative loss of population and economic power and a real loss of national political power. In the political debate on the causes and cures of this decline, African colonization was sporadically invoked as part of a litany of reforms that included equalization in state taxation and representation and the advance of industry and commerce.[4]

Political rhetoric was only one way of debating African colonization. African colonization in some form, whether acknowledged or not, was central to the interpretation of Virginia's patriotic past, its domestic and political present, and its future tranquility. It appeared in novels and religious tracts, as well as in politics, and it was also part of a patriotic narrative under construction in the state. Emotive sermons, sensationalist newspaper articles, patriotic orations, sentimental fiction, and hagiographic biographies that reached a growing reading public were popular in Virginia and central to public opinion. References to African colonization were found in all of these forms. Although novels were seen as inferior to writings in law or philosophy, Virginia men attempted them in the 1820s and 1830s in order to reach a larger audience and perhaps to pursue their visions of the future without the constraints of law or scholarship. These varied literary productions were examples of the ways in which Virginians speculated about themselves, framed issues, and proposed solutions at the margins of political debate. To anticipate their future, Virginians had to review their past and reinterpret it to meet new narrative and theoretical needs. Already burdened with dense layers of earlier interpretations, the state had a supply of utopian symbols and images that writers were quick to employ and develop.[5]

Historians have generally viewed Virginia as untroubled by utopian longings or experiments. Vernon Parrington's early assessment remained little altered: "Virginia had no share in the Revolutionary enthusiasms of the Utopian 1830s and 1840s. . . . Plantation society was static and social speculation was unwelcome. . . . Utopian experiments were untried." In truth, social speculation and utopian thinking were attenuated but hardly extinguished, and African colonization was an impetus to thinking about a new and improved Virginia in literary forms.[6] For young men such as Harrison, colonization was part of a forward-thinking agenda that would leave behind any nostalgia for an earlier state, modernize the political structure, and put Virginia in the front ranks of commerce and industry. For others, the colony in Liberia fulfilled the symbolic function of reenacting the founding of the American republic. African colonization was also a strategy to re-create the perceived glory days of Virginia and revitalize a group of traditionally powerful families.

There was also an ominous dystopian side to Virginia prophecies of the future. William Byrd II described a future Virginia in which Ethiopians in rebellion would "tinge our rivers as wide as they are with blood." Reversing the hopes of early promoters who saw the Virginian environment as transforming idle beggars into sturdy yeomen, Byrd's vision saw slavery as the evil in Eden that would cause the commonwealth to swarm with "idle poor whites who would rather steal than work" and masters who would be constantly wielding the lash in order to control the ever-bigger population of slaves.[7]

When Gabriel's conspiracy in 1800 threatened to fulfill Byrd's prophecy, George Tucker, a young cousin of St. George Tucker, responded by writing a pamphlet that proposed that slaves be freed and colonized on western lands. When he next published on the topic of Virginia slavery, a generation had passed and his critique of slavery was more muted but still present. His novel, *The Valley of the Shenandoah*, written in 1824, was the first novel to use a southern plantation setting and the only one of that genre to describe a slave sale. Tucker traced the moral and economic decline of a Virginia planter family through their overweening pride, extravagance, and lack of concern for practical matters. Slavery, the novel suggested, made pompous petty tyrants of white Virginians, but emancipation would be disastrous for enslavers and the enslaved without emigration.[8]

Years later, Tucker tried a political economy approach to the same topic, investigating the Malthusian fear that blacks would increase and multiply so prolifically that they would destroy Virginia's prosperity and drive both white and black to starvation and warfare. But Tucker's own use of Thomas Malthus's gloomy predictions caused him to predict that slavery would disappear in sixty to eighty years as population increased on limited soil. Slavery, no longer profitable, would end, and free blacks would decline in numbers due to their demonstrated lower fertility rates. If slaveholders believed that "the number of their slaves is too great for them to quietly remain, when the period of natural liberation arrives, as an inferior caste, or with a qualified freedom," then they ought to emancipate and colonize them in the present.[9]

George Tucker made three attempts at a critique of slavery in Virginia. In his literary efforts, his antislavery perspective was shared by his contemporary, James Ewell Heath. Both men were affected by the growing restraints on antislavery sentiments in Virginia in the 1830s and by their own sense of the importance of gradualism. Heath was a founder and officer in the Richmond Auxiliary of the ACS—he was appointed secretary of the Board of Managers in 1823. In 1828, Heath published anonymously a two-volume romance of plantation life called *Edge Hill, or the Family of the Fitzroyals*. Set in Virginia during the Revolution, the novel portrays a heroic slave who spied for the Continental forces, a character based on the exploits of a Richmond-area slave freed for his services to the American cause. In 1839, Heath published *Whigs and Democrats, or Love of No Politics*, a comedy staged in Philadelphia in 1844 that featured, in place of a resourceful black spy, a pompous old slave who basks in his master's reflected glory.[10]

In just over a decade, the cultural climate had shifted, and Heath joined other writers of the late 1830s in portraying only happy slaves. As early as 1831, John Pendleton Kennedy's popular *Swallow Barn* acknowledged the possibility of some distant African homeland while praising the civilizing nature of slavery. "I am quite sure they [slaves] could never become a happier people than I find them here. Perhaps they are destined ultimately to that national existence in the clime from which they derive their origin. . . . If it be so, no tribe of people have ever passed from barbarism to civilization . . . better supplied with mild and beneficial guardianship, adapted to the actual state of their intellectual feebleness."[11] Popular novels, such as Alexander Caruthers's *The Cavaliers of Virginia*, created a past that justified a Virginia hierarchy dominated by a mythic hereditary aristocracy of English Cavaliers that called itself the "Chivalry." After 1835, no Virginia literature could criticize slavery. By 1845, the aging Tucker, who had been offering up both economic and literary commentaries on the evils of slavery for more than forty years, acknowledged that there was little audience for his theories and moved to Philadelphia.[12]

James Heath was also the first editorial advisor to Thomas Willis White, publisher of the *Southern Literary Messenger*, the Richmond-based literary quarterly that was an effort to counter northern literary production and to present southern perspectives to a popular audience. In the first issue, Heath called for support for southern literature and for comprehensive education for women. Unhappy with the South's limited literary production and readership, he asked, "Are we doomed forever to a kind of vassalage to our northern neighbors?" In a later issue, he responded to an essay in which Beverley Tucker praised domestic slavery as the guarantor of white freedom. Slavery was evil, Heath wrote, and, because of property rights, Southerners were the ones who must abolish it.[13]

Southern religious periodicals shared the problem of being overwhelmed by northern literary production and northern antislavery perspectives. Northern evangelical publications that condemned American corruption and materialism frequently cited plantation wealth and slavery as examples. One response of southern writers was to produce their own religious journals that promoted a more conservative religious culture and, at the same time, met the popular tastes of a growing reading public for a variety of themes in evangelical and other journals. A transitional figure in this effort was John Holt Rice, the Presbyterian minister and early supporter of African colonization, who initiated and edited a monthly Presbyterian magazine called the *Virginia Evangelical and Literary Magazine and Missionary Chronicle*, beginning in 1818. Later southern religious journals, such as the *Family Visitor*, edited by Nathaniel Pollard, evolved toward a larger popular audience, becoming smaller and cheaper and containing more accessible literary pieces than Rice had offered.

Editor Pollard was a man whose favor the Virginia colonizationists regularly sought in order to place ACS reports and letters in his publication. The early evangelical imprints in Virginia, as in the nation, were interested in African colonization as a mission field and understood that Africa offered an exotic setting from which to publish missionary letters and attract readers. Liberia offered the added drama of battling the slave trade and providing letters from emigrants. Widely read and aimed toward an ambitious evangelical middle class, religious publications were an important source of financial support for African colonization, and Virginia colonizationists always tried to insert promotional material of any sort in them.[14]

At least one person who perused the *African Repository* for letters from Liberia did not intend to use them as propaganda for Liberia. By the 1840s, Virginia agriculturalist and writer Edmund Ruffin was a foe of African colonization, as was that other highly idiosyncratic Virginian, Beverley Tucker, whom James Heath had disputed in the pages of the *Southern Literary Messenger*. Jesse Burton Harrison seemed to anticipate both men when he addressed a colonization meeting in Lynchburg in 1828. Harrison predicted that in ten years proslavery men would either be those "pirates by nature" who still saw slaves chiefly as commodities or those "men of respectable age, of strong peculiarities of mind, often of considerable ability, accompanied by invincible prejudices among which is foremost a prejudice against every plan not originating with themselves. . . . Spleen drives the business with some; nerve with others."[15]

Spleen and nerve were among the driving forces for Tucker and Ruffin, possibly the most public and dramatic of slavery's Virginia defenders and part of a proslavery southern attack on African colonization.[16] Tucker, a son of St. George Tucker and a cousin of George Tucker, was briefly a planter and judge in Missouri and later a professor of law at William and Mary until his death in 1852. His novel, *The Partisan Leader: A Tale of the Future,* described an ideal patriarchal Virginia family and created a great stir, as he wished it to, when it was published anonymously in 1836. Written to promote his secessionist views, the novel is set thirteen years in the future and describes Virginia "patriots" scheming to carry the Virginia Commonwealth into a southern confederacy already organized. This was Beverley Tucker's Virginia utopia. At the 1850 Nashville southern-rights convention, Tucker called the ACS "premature" and predicted that sometime later the "race of Ham" might be ready for colonization but that they were not ready now.[17]

Edmund Ruffin agreed that enslaved Virginians were not ready for colonization, but he believed they never would be. Ruffin had not always been a secessionist with a concurrent belief in Africans as a separate species. In the 1820s and early 1830s, his calculations had proved, to his own satisfaction, that slavery was unprofitable unless the natural increase in slaves was sold. He was disturbed by this, and it drove his experiments to increase productivity on his Virginia land. In 1833, Ruffin was still willing to consider African colonization and published both sides of the Dew and Harrison debate in his journal, the *Farmer's Register.* But in the 1840s, his belief that slaves would not work unless forced, combined with his earlier reading of Malthus, turned him toward the southern defenders of states' rights, and he began to imagine a different future for Virginia. In his new perspective, Virginia needed more, not fewer, slaves for its envisioned new agricultural prosperity. Slave labor, as he stressed in his presidential address to the Virginia State Agricultural Society in Richmond in 1852, could be profitable. It was also at this moment that he began to articulate his theory of black inferiority.[18]

Ruffin's argument against the ACS followed that of Thomas Dew but, reflecting the changing times, made stronger arguments against African American abilities and achievements in Virginia and the North, as well as in Liberia, Haiti, and Jamaica. By the late 1850s, Ruffin's solution for free blacks in Virginia was to reenslave them or "colonize" them in the North. He saw it as particularly important to prove that Liberia was a failure, because Virginia colonizationists had claimed much success for black Virginians there.[19] In 1859 he published "African Colonization Unveiled," a pamphlet that denied all the claims made by the ACS for the success of Liberia. Carefully parsing all the promotional literature from Liberia, Ruffin refuted it with his own clippings of statistics and his own interpretation of Virginia emancipators and emigrants that he believed showed the colony to be a great failure in every regard, especially that of black ability. The only good that he saw coming from the Liberian experiment was evidence of "the great truth (until recently admitted but by few, and still denied and resisted by many) that the negro race is greatly inferior to the white, in natural capacity—and is incapable of self-government, and of improvement . . . except under the direction and control of a superior race."[20]

Earlier Virginia efforts to dismiss colonization as physically and financially impossible or to condemn it as a death trap for emigrants had not addressed the central question of black ability, as Ruffin was now doing. Virginia colonization had stressed that the successful establishment of Liberia demonstrated the portability of republican principles and Christian religion from Virginia, the intellectual ability of blacks, and the long-range intention of Virginia to end slavery. Ruffin's task was to demolish that argument. His delighted fellow believers wrote to congratulate him for the pamphlet. One, in fervent agreement, added, "And can anything, short of the wildest fanaticism, lead men to expect those, whom God physically, mentally and morally has degraded with his curse, shall triumphantly erect a glorious republic on the shores of benighted Africa?"[21]

Among the advocates of African colonization who countered Ruffin's arguments were a cluster of Virginia families involved in an effort to reestablish Virginia's preeminence in the republic. Most visible were the families at Mount Vernon and Arlington House, where various collateral descendants of George Washington participated in the African colonization project. George Washington had early been appropriated by all Americans as the model republican citizen in both his domestic and public roles. Washington's willingness to free his slaves raised the question of why other patriotic Virginians, especially his relatives, did not do the same. Colonization, as an active project that promised to end slavery, could remove the greatest obstacle to giving Virginians pride of place in the republic. Beyond this sectional rivalry and its political considerations, there were domestic reasons for seeking to end slavery at these estates.

Mount Vernon, in the possession of Bushrod Washington, was in the process of becoming a national shrine. To a lesser extent, Arlington, the manor house of George Washington Parke Custis, had also become a site for Washington's apotheosis. Both Mount Vernon and the more recently built Arlington House represented the proud Virginia estate in decline and disarray. There were no better examples of the difference between the idealized Virginia plantation of emerging fiction and the painful realities of daily domestic experience than Arlington and Mount Vernon. Both sites were close to the urban life of Alexandria and Washington, D.C., a constant temptation to escape for slaves, and a constant source of visitors for the resident owners. Home to Washington descendants, both seemed pulled toward some vortex of disorder and unmanageability.

Arlington House, with its imposing hilltop site and grand ceremonial approach and entrance, met the standards for planter residences but was not a working farm or plantation as was Mount Vernon. The Custis family made most of its living from the work of slaves on their plantations deeper into Virginia, where most of the slaves lived. Arlington House and its grounds were maintained by slaves, but no cash crop was produced. It lacked the order and discipline of a working plantation, a sense of order that Mount Vernon had once had but was now losing.[22] As Mount Vernon declined in appearance and productivity, it increased in symbolic value. After the death of Martha Washington, Justice Bushrod Washington, Washington's nephew and executor, moved in. The estate caused Bushrod Washington much difficulty. He did not enjoy farming as George Washington had and felt harassed by the presence of so many free blacks, who had been liberated by his uncle and who were so near to his own slaves.

In a spontaneous acting out of the republican meanings of the Revolutionary War, Mount Vernon had been visited by the curious and the patriotic since George Washington was in retirement there. After his death, the estate was overrun with strangers, who wanted to see the home of the Father of his Country. Bushrod and Anne Blackburn Washington entertained guests regularly and, at first, received many visitors cordially, despite the expense. Bushrod sought "what would make the hours flow smoothly, rather than what would give them a keen relish," and was inclined to the "disengaged talk of a club supper table and the circulation of a temperate glass."[23] Mount Vernon was itself a considerable expense. Bushrod Washington used his Supreme Court salary to maintain the estate, yet the buildings and landscape appeared more shabby each year. As president of the ACS, he purchased a life membership in the society in 1819, but when he was later asked to pledge $100 per year to the society, he replied that southerners who were completely dependent on the profits of agriculture could never match the rich northern philanthropists whose wealth came from more certain sources.[24]

The ACS was only four years old when the combination of Mount Vernon, slavery, and African colonization brought public shame on Bushrod Washington. In August 1821, the Leesburg, Virginia, *Genius of Liberty* reported that about one hundred slaves had passed through Leesburg on their way south and that about fifty of them were "unhappy wretches [who] had been sold by Judge Washington, of Mount Vernon, President of the

George Washington Parke Custis, the adopted son of George Washington, collected Washington artifacts, wrote patriotic plays and essays, and promoted African colonization as an aspect of Virginia's claims to being first among the states. At his death, he willed his slaves' freedom, but by the time his son-in-law, Robert E. Lee, could emancipate them, the Civil War had essentially done so. (Mount Vernon Ladies' Association)

Mother Colonization Society." The article was picked up by the *Baltimore Morning Chronicle* and by *Niles' Weekly Register.* Niles editorialized that there was "something excessively revolting in the fact that a herd of them should be driven from MOUNT VERNON, sold by the nephew and principal heir of George Washington."

Editor Niles's comments and those of other editors were made for a national audience, which was already attuned to think of Mount Vernon as a national shrine and George Washington as the exemplar of what southerners should do with their slaves. The Leesburg, Virginia, *Genius of Liberty*, in the home district of ACS founder Charles Fenton Mercer, focused on Washington's hypocrisy as the ACS president. Various northern newspapers published a letter written by a man who said he had spoken with the remaining Mount Vernon slaves, asking an old man if he had been living there when George Washington died. "No, sir. Not so lucky—I should not have been a slave now if I had" was the response.[25]

Stung with anger and propelled to an uncharacteristically rapid response, Washington wrote to *Niles' Weekly Register* that he had indeed sold the slaves and that he had every right to do so. He went on to unburden himself in a general complaint about conditions at Mount Vernon. He had, he said, sold fifty-four of his ninety slaves to two New Orleans planters because for years he had suffered insubordination among them that rendered them worse than useless. They were near to and often related to George Washington's free blacks and did not understand why they were not free. The best laborers ran away to the north and could not be recaptured. Further, northerners visiting Mount Vernon spoke with his slaves without his permission and often told them that they should be free or would be soon, since their master was president of the ACS. Worst of all, sightseers had told the slaves that they would be free at his death, giving them every reason to want to hasten that event. He added that some families were separated, although he had tried to keep them together. Shortly after this episode, Bushrod Washington addressed the problem of intrusive and mischief-making sightseers in a public notice: "Notice—The feelings of Mrs. Washington and myself have been so much wounded by some late occurrences at this place, that I am compelled to give this public notice, that permission will not, in future, be granted to Steam Boat parties to enter the gardens or to walk over the grounds; nor will I consent that Mount Vernon, much less the lawn, shall be the place at which eating, drinking and dancing parties may assemble."[26]

The visitors, who continued to descend upon Mount Vernon, were not deterred by the withdrawal of the welcome mat. Lafayette's triumphal tour of the United States in 1824 and 1825, widely covered in the American press, included an affecting and dramatic visit to the tomb of Washington at Mount Vernon that confirmed Mount Vernon as a sacred space and site of pilgrimage, to the ever-greater unhappiness of Bushrod Washington.[27] The deaths of Bushrod and Anne Blackburn Washington in 1829 marked a significant shift in Mount Vernon's management. It became the property of Bushrod's nephew, John Augustine Washington, an agriculturalist from nearby Jefferson County. This Washington tried to make the estate a profitable enterprise but found himself coping with the question of where George Washington should be laid to rest.

Early in 1832, Washington Custis rejoiced to Charles Fenton Mercer that Congress planned to exhume the body of "my venerable Grandparent" and rebury him "beneath the dome of the Senate house,"[28] but longtime plans for a national commemoration of the centennial of Washington's 1732 birth had become ominously divisive. States' rights intruded on the message advanced by honoring Washington through a national burial site. The Nullification Controversy in Congress, in which South Carolina threatened to leave the Union, increased sectional tensions to such an extent that the Washington relatives grew less willing to let the first president's body be given to the nation. John Augustine Washington hoped that the national government would buy Mount Vernon at his death, but he was not inclined to allow the removal of Washington's body from his tomb in order for him to be reburied at the capitol.[29]

John Augustine Washington lived only three years at Mount Vernon before his death, at which time it became the property of his widow, Jane Charlotte Washington. Her concern was to keep Mount Vernon and restore it, in part by making the uninvited guests pay for their visits. She opened Mount Vernon to visitors but regularized their access to both the interior household and the exterior buildings and grounds. She saw the visitors as a source of cash for upkeep of the estate, a source more certain than agriculture, and she enlisted the help of the slaves, who expected tips for their service as tour guides. As participants in the first heritage tourism industry, the slaves soon learned how to enhance their narratives, sell souvenirs, and charge money for such courtesies as a glass of water or buttermilk. A decade and more later, souvenir canes, supposedly carved from trees near Washington's tomb, were a popular item for sale. No one questioned Jane Charlotte Washington as she capitalized on Mount Vernon's sacred status in order to save it.[30]

In nearby Charles Town, Jefferson County, the sisters of Jane Charlotte Washington were busy with a different project to burnish Virginia's image and restore her soul.[31] Judith and Christian Blackburn were committed to adequately outfitting several recently emancipated families bound for Liberia. Lacking sufficient funds themselves, they canvassed the neighborhood and their many local relatives for a complicated mix of donations and supplies. This emigrant group carried high hopes with it. Christian

By the late 1850s, Mount Vernon was in serious decline. The Washington families that inherited the estate from George Washington found it difficult to farm the estate profitably. They complained that the most skilled workers among the slaves sought freedom in the North and that the enslaved population heard antislavery ideas from northern visitors, causing them to resist direction. (Mount Vernon Ladies' Association)

Blackburn "suffered from much anxiety of mind" over the welfare of Eliza Hatter, whom she had "raised with great tenderness" and equipped to be a teacher in Liberia. Eliza Hatter was also equipped with her husband, Reuben Hatter, who had been purchased by Christian Blackburn from Walter Washington. Others in the emigrant company included Lydia Carroll, a woman in her fifties, and her daughter and son-in-law, Andrew and Priscilla Green, and their four children, the youngest of whom was Lott Cary Green. Another was George Washington Green.[32]

The women revealed deep concern for the health and education of individual emigrants and the unification of families, and the emigrants reciprocated in their efforts to be model citizens. Eliza Hatter carried the burdens and benefits of her upbringing to Liberia. She wrote to her sister, "I never was better satisfied in my life, if I had only my dear relations and friends with me. We enjoy the same liberty here our masters and mistresses do in America." She wrote to her former mistress, thanking her for buying her husband, Reuben Hatter: "When Mr. Hatter returns, he intends to build us a stone house." Andrew Green wrote proudly, "It gives me great satisfaction that every thing I do is for myself and my children. I would not give the enjoyment I have had since I have been in Africa for all I have seen in America. My son, George Washington, is spelling in three syllables."[33]

But this group of chosen people was cruelly unfortunate, even beyond the usual hazards of the acclimating fever. Reuben Hatter left Liberia. After returning to the United States for a visit, he shipped out as a seaman on the packet *Richmond* from Liberia and did not return. Reuben Hatter had not been nurtured to be an emigrant—he had been simply purchased before departure—and he did not share the sense of national destiny fostered in the enslaved families of the Blackburns and Washingtons. Eliza Hatter struggled on as a teacher for several years before dying of a lung ailment. Shortly after writing his letter, Andrew Green's wife and three of his four children died, including Lott Cary Green. Green had his mother-in-law, Lydia Carroll, to aid in caring for the remaining child and to combine resources with him, but even remarriage to an American woman did not stop the downward trend in his fortunes, and within a decade he had been forced to sell all the property he was allotted, as well as that of his new wife.[34]

Mary Lee Custis, the wife of Washington Custis, served as a conduit for the Blackburn women's letters to the Reverend Gurley of the ACS. The Custis and Lee families that lived at Arlington House maintained close connection with their scattered cousins, especially those engaged in African colonization. Washington Custis, proprietor of Arlington House, had been raised at Mount Vernon as the grandson of Martha Washington and the adopted son of George Washington. He was an avid hunter and a socializer but not a scholar. He served the ACS with some zest as a writer and speaker, happy to work African colonization into the grand patriotic narrative that starred his adoptive father. Although he showed his reverence for George Washington by collecting as much memorabilia as his household and budget could bear, he never took Washington's advice on issues of education, discipline, order, and duty. Custis wished to be surrounded by the artifacts of Washington but not be permeated by his virtues.[35] His one lifetime passion was maintaining the memory of Washington.

Washington Custis was another of Virginia's gentleman amateurs in literature. His interest in Virginia history went beyond accumulating artifacts to retelling one of the central legends of Virginia history. His 1830 play, *Pocahontas, or the Settlers of Virginia*, retold the legend that the baptism and marriage of the Indian princess had validated the Virginians' claim to the New World in a manner that northern legends of Plymouth Rock could never match. Growing sectional divisions gave importance to the efforts to place Pocahontas ahead of the Pilgrims in a national patriotic narrative.[36] For Custis, this racial mixture was acceptable, even admirable, perhaps because the Indian posed no threat to Virginia. There was, however, "no footing [here] for the colored man. . . . He can but shine by borrowed light." Whether mixed or not, "They have no right to a homestead in the white man's country. Let this fair land, which the white man won by his chivalry . . . be kept sacred for his descendants."[37]

Quaker Samuel Janney was a member of the ACS in Alexandria and had an encounter with Custis that contributed to Janney's change of mind about African colonization. Seeking signatures for a petition to Congress to end slavery in the District of Columbia, Janney approached his fellow colonizationist at his Arlington estate. Despite the fact that the petition had the signature of "about a thousand respectable citizens," Custis declined to sign. Janney commented: "Although he made high professions of patriotism in his public orations, he made no effort nor submitted to any sacrifices to remove an evil which he seemed to deplore." Although Janney had believed that "removing the free people of color and liberated slaves to Africa would be the means of promoting emancipation in the Southern States," such caution from a highly placed member of the ACS made him think that "the tendency of the scheme . . . was to quiet the conscience of the people, lead to a sense of false security, and put off, to a distant day the work of emancipation."[38] Janney soon abandoned the ACS as an organization, although he maintained working contact with many Virginia members.

At Custis's Arlington House, there was the usual gender divide over African colonization, with Custis and his son-in-law, Robert E. Lee, happy to regard slavery and colonization as moral and political abstractions, while Mary Randolph Custis and her daughter, Mary Custis Lee, worked at raising money and preparing certain enslaved families for emigration. Washington Custis perceived the benefits of African colonization for white Virginians. It would restore "the good ship Virginia," the barque that "bore the Genius of Chivalry" back to its rightful place at the head of the ship of state instead of "following in the wake of those she formerly led."[39] For his part, Robert E. Lee did not share the enthusiasm of his wife and mother-in-law for African colonization, but he was not opposed to their experiments, and the slaves involved were not his to control. The U.S. Army officer shared the common view that slavery was "a greater evil to the white than to the black race" and that the blacks were "immeasurably better off" as slaves in America, undergoing a "painful discipline" in civilization.[40]

Mary Lee Randolph Custis and her daughter, Mary Custis Lee, were among the most devoted evangelical colonizationists and engaged steadily and constantly in letter writing and promotion for the cause. Decades of effort brought them a few emancipations and the departure of the William and Rosabella Burke family to Liberia. A few months after her mother's death, Mary Lee wrote, "In looking over my dear mother's papers, the great desire of her soul was that all our slaves should be enabled to emancipate to Africa—for years this has been the subject of her hopes and prayers. . . . William [Burke] and his family who I hope will go to Africa this fall will act as pioneers. . . . Eleanor and her family who are *now* all *free*—children and grandchildren—must always be protected and cared for. . . . I have always promised Eliza her freedom to emigrate to Africa in a few years." Seven years later she added this notation: "Eliza has her freedom and lives at Newport."[41]

William Burke, his wife, Rosabella, and their four children traveled to Liberia in late 1853 and experienced good health and considerable success by their own assessment and that of the Virginia women who had nurtured and prepared them. After two months in Monrovia, they went up St. Paul's River to the town of Clay-Ashland. Burke built a home, called Mount Rest, and set up as a shoemaker. Soon he enrolled in a seminary, where he hoped to learn to read the New Testament in Greek.[42] The Burkes were trained in the values that they were believed to need to found a Christian republic and reflect well on the prominent family that sponsored them. Their views usually reflected those of Mrs. Custis and Mrs. Lee.

"Dear Madam," Rosabella Burke wrote to Mrs. Lee. "According to my promise I take this opportunity to write you a few lines. During my stay of two months at Monrovia I was very much pleased, except that the people were too gay and fashionable for me. I being not able to rank with them."[43] These sentences may well have caused a brief satisfied smile to cross the face of Mrs. Lee. Rosabella Burke's response to the high society of Monrovia, Liberia, in 1854 mirrored precisely the polite disdain with which the socially secure but financially pressed women of Arlington House viewed all strivers and boasters. One of the few pleasures the Custis women permitted themselves was a subtle ridicule of those who sought the attention and approbation of the public. For Rosabella Burke, former domestic slave of the Custis family and tutored in their social and religious values, to say that she lacked rank served as both an expression of her piety and an acidic reflection on the pretensions of Monrovian society. It was a comment worthy of the plantation mistresses with whom she and her family had lived in close connection and who had sent her, along with her husband and their children, to Liberia.

The letters of Rosabella Burke must have been reassuring to her white sponsors. She sent advice to relatives and patriotic sentiments back from Africa. "Remember me to Aunt Eleanor; tell her that I love Africa, and would not exchange it for America."[44] But the Burkes' enthusiasm for Liberia was not contagious among their friends. "If it were not for yourself & Mrs. Lee," William Burke wrote to the Reverend Gurley, "I should hardly ever hear a word from Arlington the home of our youth as our Coloured friends do not write."[45]

Lack of interest in Liberia was scarcely the only sign of recalcitrance among the enslaved at Arlington House. The Arlington estate of the Custis-Lee family had domestic problems common to Virginia gentry households, but these were even more glaringly apparent at Arlington House, due to the family's privileged and public position near the center of society and history in the nation's capital. One domestic dilemma was the lack of order in the household. Year after year, Arlington House had more slaves than it needed to maintain the house and grounds, yet both house and grounds appeared neglected. The local market for hired labor in Washington and Alexandria was a source of income but offered dangers to the control of an enslaved workforce. Most of the people enslaved at Arlington House were aware that Custis's management style was to ignore problems, and they took advantage of that to structure their own time and encourage disorganization.[46] One young northern woman visiting Arlington House wrote: "I would not care to live at the South, however. The responsibility and bother of those servants would be enough to deter one. Just fancy waiting tea until 8 o'clock because they couldn't find anything to milk the cow in. Mrs. Lee was fairly provoked when they told her they had gone to the dairy maid and to this, that and the other and couldn't get a pan and exclaimed, 'Why didn't you come to me, the *maid of all?*'"[47]

The lack of order, even chaos, evident in this charade of the missing milk pail and its corresponding chain of calamities is very similar to the uproar, disorder, and "hurryscurryation" of Dinah's kitchen in Harriet Beecher Stowe's *Uncle Tom's Cabin*, where sixty-five sugar jars were crammed into every space and no clean tea towel was to be found. Stowe's slaveholder's kitchen was similar to the experiences of many southern women, and the kitchen was a site that novelists such as Tucker, Ruffin, Heath and Kennedy did not visit. Mrs. Lee's lack of order and method was perhaps greater than that of many mistresses, but Dinah's kitchen and Mrs. Lee's both pointed to the fact that domestic order could not be achieved without reforming the system of enslaved labor that was as wasteful and disorderly and full of recalcitrance as the southern kitchen.[48] This was something that the women of Arlington House and Mount Vernon understood.

The disorder at Arlington House also meant that runaways were hidden there by their fellow slaves. As early as 1813, a reward was offered for "a Negro Woman named Hannah . . . [who] it is now supposed . . . is harbored by Mr. Custis's negroes at Arlington, or is about the City or Navy Yard."[49] One Mississippi planter accused the Reverend Gurley, ACS secretary, of hiding a slave woman and three of her children after the planter had purchased them in Washington. Gurley, he continued, came to him and offered a nominal price for them so that they might stay in Washington near the husband and father. Fearing total loss, the planter sold, but "Mr. Gurley or his agent continued to steal the oldest boy and one of another family which I have never got—although they are in the District on Custis's plantation where the husband of the mother lives and who no doubt was Gurley's agent."[50]

Arlington House and Mount Vernon demonstrated African colonization's continued appeal in the Upper South, especially in urban areas. The two sites were located at the edge of cities with substantial free black populations and with many opportunities for slaves to take part, legally and illegally, in a cash economy and to escape to a free state. As Bushrod Washington complained, the best workers ran away to the North or to Canada. In 1855, Robert E. Lee paid E. W. Paine $19 for arresting and confining fugitive slaves from the Custis estate.[51] A few years later, Mrs. Lee wrote from Canada, "Tell nurse there are a great many runaways here, but I have not met with any acquaintances. The white people say that before long they will be obliged to make laws to send them all out of Canada. So I see no place left for them but Africa."[52] That she believed she needed to mount arguments against Canada to persuade her slaves to consider Africa reveals the extent to which Canada and the North were seen as alternatives to African colonization, even among slaves.

The second domestic problem, common to many southern households but more visible at Arlington House, was that of white males who maintained relationships with or took sexual advantage of black women under their control. Washington Custis was widely believed, in the neighborhood, in part through his pattern of emancipating young women with mulatto infants, to be the father of perhaps half a dozen children on his plantations.[53] It is doubtful that the Custis women ever acknowledged such possibilities. Even as descendants of Virginia patriots, and even as accomplished, aware, and deeply religious women, they had little power to alter the private conduct of their husbands, fathers, and sons. Rumors of Washington Custis's mulatto children reached a national public after his death in 1857 and were published by the antislavery *New York Tribune* in 1859. One anonymous letter writer claimed, "I live one mile from the plantation of George Washington P. Custis. . . . Custis has fifteen children by slave women. I see his grandchildren every day; they are of a dark yellow."[54] Custis's dilettantish character and lack of personal discipline — the despair of George Washington — and the nature and timing of his manumissions make it plausible. While few men active in Virginia colonization can be attached directly to evidence of sexual license, George Washington Parke Custis provides an example of something that southern women knew and deeply lamented, though seldom, if ever, discussed. The gentility that was so prominent a feature in the Arlington House women did not serve them well. As historian Richard Bushman has suggested, gentility "hid what it could not countenance and denied whatever caused discomfort."[55]

Washington Custis left a will specifying that his slaves were to be freed within five years, but his debts appear to have prevented the will's provisions from being carried out. With the tone of exasperated affection that gentry women often assumed in discussing their feckless fathers and husbands, Mrs. Lee observed, "My dear father in his usual entire ignorance of the state of affairs has left provisions in his will which it will be almost impossible to fulfill even in double five years and no provisions for manumitting them[,] so I do not know what can be done at the end of that time as it is obligatory to send them out of the state and for that purpose a large sum will be required." Mrs. Lee also feared insurrection among the slaves when they learned that they were not to be emancipated immediately. "Scarcely had my father been laid in his tomb," she wrote, "when two men were constantly lurking about here tampering with the servants and telling them they had a right to their freedom *immediately* and if they would unite and demand it, they would obtain it."[56]

The Arlington House slaves could not be freed until the debts of Washington Custis were paid. It was more than five years before Robert E. Lee was able to file the manumission papers. It was then early 1864, and the Civil War had forced the Lee family to leave Arlington three years before. The Lee family had not been able to supervise the plantations of Romancoke and White House, and many bondpersons had, by this time, emancipated themselves by leaving. All this was deeply interesting to the

Flanking the entrance to George Washington's tomb at Mount Vernon are two obe-
lisks marking the burial sites of Bushrod Washington and John Augustine Washington, late owners of Mount Vernon. Both men and their female relatives maintained
a connection with the American Colonization Society and with Liberia, based on
a Virginia patriotism that needed a plan for ending slavery and on their own need
for a more profitable farm labor system. (Mount Vernon Ladies' Association)

Burke family, now comfortable in Liberia. They had followed the fortunes of the Lee family and the American nation since their departure in
late 1853.

The death of George Washington Custis in 1857 caused William Burke
to reflect in a letter to Gurley: "Mr. Custis . . . lived 7 years beyond his allotted time and I have no doubt enjoyed as much of this Lief [life] as any
man ever did, so fare as health, food, and raiment is intended to make one
comfortable and happy. But my Idea is that it requires more than all these
to make a man truly happy in this Lief and if we would be happy in the
world to come we must have a foretast of it in this Lief." Burke obliquely
criticizes Custis's self-indulgent life here—his sympathies were always with
Mrs. Custis and Mrs. Lee. He also anticipated that slaves emancipated by
Custis's will would emigrate to Liberia and helpfully pointed out to Gurley
that "he [Custis] brought it [his will] home in a small box and gave [it] to

Daniel[,] charging him to be very careful to put it in the bank for every-thing as regard him or us depended on that."[57]

Burke worried that his relatives and friends at Arlington and on the other Custis plantations were not prepared for freedom and would be "to-tally unable to act for themselves."[58] He first offered to return to the United States to prepare the slaves for settlement in Liberia at their emancipation five years after Custis's death. At the close of the Civil War, Burke hoped that the freedmen might be encouraged to emigrate to Liberia.[59] He was to be disappointed. The freedmen and women from the Custis holdings were not interested. The Burkes had apparently found the utopia they desired and all that their life in Virginia had taught them to want, but their fellow ex-bondmen and relatives did not share their views.

Seven

Virginians in Liberia

I N THE PALM GROVE CEMETERY in Monrovia, Liberia, there were and perhaps still are gravestones erected by the children and grandchildren of early settlers. One marker is inscribed: "In Memory of Charles Cooper, born in Smithfield, Virginia, U.S.A. in March, 1799. Died in Monrovia on March 24, 1881. He was a kind father, a true friend and a veteran soldier of the cross. I have fought a good fight. I have finished my course. I have kept the faith." Near Cooper's grave are those of family members who accompanied him from Portsmouth, Virginia, on the *Elvira Owen* in May 1856 and other relatives who came earlier on the *Banshee* in April 1853. Cooper had been a comparatively old man of fifty-six when he left Portsmouth, a town where he had free relatives and had lived as a free man himself. Perhaps his departure was delayed by the necessity of purchasing his wife and four adult children who were enslaved. Three years earlier, an older son's freedom had been purchased to enable him to leave Virginia with his wife and two children. There are other Coopers from Virginia in Palm Grove Cemetery—seamen, grocers, and servants. The most recent recorded is Hilary Cooper, who was born in 1941 and who died in an automobile accident in 1964.[1]

Cooper's grave inscription proclaimed to the world what his family saw as important about his life. He had fought the good fight, stayed the course, and kept the faith. This was the self-assessment of many emigrants to Liberia who survived the fevers and prospered to some extent. And it was a part of the patriotic narrative evolving in Liberia. But it was not the assessment of others whose families were decimated by illness, accident, or lack of proper supplies or of those who emigrated without commitment, who were given only a choice between Liberia and slavery. Among Virginians, urban free blacks with skills and literacy did relatively well in Liberia, while emancipated slaves and rural free blacks lacking those advantages tended to do less well. Still, the stories of all emigrant families from any part of the United States had similarities, whether they were advantaged or not. Members of any extended family, however constituted, were likely to experience death, calamity, and occasional small triumphs.

The earliest years of the ACS settlements were reminiscent of other colonial ventures: the initial sites proved unhealthy or unsafe; indigenous peoples resisted the incursion; many people died; and the leadership faced rebellion from the settlers. For the first dozen years, from the arrival of the *Elizabeth* at Sierra Leone in early March 1820 to the docking of the *James Perkins* at Monrovia in January 1832, each shipload of people carried the power to change the fate of the little colony. A crucial reinforcement of people and supplies meant survival; but illness or lack of supplies among new emigrants drained resources and discouraged future emigration. After 1832, ships continued to arrive regularly, but their arrival no longer meant the difference between failure and survival of the colony. By the time Liberia became a republic in 1847, the names of these early ships would be invoked as a patriotic trope, celebrating the early settlers.

Emigrants to Liberia before the Civil War were overwhelmingly from the Upper South, with Virginia providing the most—one-third of all emigrants between 1820 and 1860. At the time of the Liberian census of 1843, Virginia, Maryland, and North Carolina emigrants made up almost three-quarters of the population, and these states maintained their dominance, although at slightly lower levels, throughout the Civil War era. In the first dozen years of settlement, the emigrants from Virginia were primarily free blacks, and most of those who emigrated from Virginia, at any point in the forty-year period, came from towns and cities or from moderate-sized agricultural holdings. Although Virginia contributed the highest number of emigrants to Liberia, emigration from the state was always sporadic, with numbers ranging from 12 in 1826 and 19 in 1843 to a high of 521 in 1832 and early 1833, after Nat Turner's insurrection.

After the fear-induced exodus of 1832, free black Virginia emigration nearly ceased, and the number of emancipated slaves directed to Liberia remained low throughout the 1830s and much of the 1840s. In the late 1840s, free black numbers rose and stayed modestly high through 1857. In part, black Virginians shared with all African Americans a renewed interest in leaving the United States when national legislation, such as the Fugitive Slave Act of 1850, further restricted African American rights. But the Virginia emigration after 1847 was also part of regional colonization efforts in the state and, to a lesser extent, the creation of the Liberian

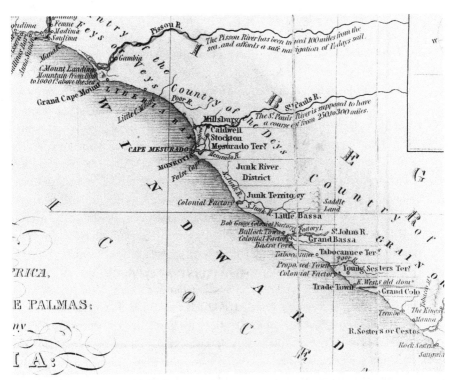

Early maps of a region undergoing colonial settlement were often as much a device for persuading investors and emigrants of the commercial possibilities as they were an accurate description of a geographic site. This 1828 map of Liberia by Jehudi Ashmon places the small coastal settlements and factories within the territory held by indigenous ethnic groups such as the Dey, Vai, and Bassa, who maintained their own commercial and political networks between the coast and the interior. (Virginia Historical Society)

Republic in 1847, with Virginians as the most prominent leaders. Virginia emigration fell again after 1857 and essentially ceased after one post–Civil War exodus. Late in 1865, 172 Virginia blacks left the Lynchburg region for Careysburg, Liberia, in a voyage planned and executed by the black Virginians who constituted the Lynchburg Emigration Society. The voyage was coordinated by William Douglass, a Liberian from Albemarle County, acting as agent for the ACS, which paid the expenses of the group. But the era of Chesapeake migration ended with the Civil War. Only a few persons left Virginia over the next twenty-seven years. Maryland, the other Chesapeake state that had sent out a large portion of Liberia's free blacks, also ceased to contribute emigrants.[2]

At the beginning, in 1820, the *Elizabeth*, carrying the first emigrants recruited by the ACS from diverse parts of the United States, landed at Sierra Leone, and the settlers moved to Sherbro Island, where they were attended to by John Kizell, an African who had escaped slavery in South Carolina by leaving with the British Army for Nova Scotia during the American Revolution. In time, he returned to Africa and became a trading partner of Paul Cuffe, whose death interrupted plans for an African American commercial colony in Africa. Among the settler party of eighty-six were nine Virginians, among them the young Nathaniel Brander from Petersburg. The island proved very unhealthy, and the three white agents soon died of West African malaria. Most settlers moved to Fourah Bay, in Freetown, Sierra Leone, where they encamped, awaiting the purchase and distribution of land by the ACS. Here they were modestly reinforced by the arrival of the *Nautilus*, with thirty-three persons, twenty-six of them from Virginia, including Lott Cary, Colin Teage, and other Richmond Baptists. A newly arrived ACS agent and an armed American naval officer used threats and gifts to persuade the Golah leader, King Peter, to cede a narrow strip of land on a high coastal promontory, which was called Cape Mesurado.[3]

Although the Vai and the Golah peoples had authority over this region, it had long been inhabited by the Dey, who resented the ACS incursion on their land, especially without compensation to them. The area that was to become Liberia shared with Sierra Leone, Guinea, and the Ivory Coast a history of fluid populations and shifting power for centuries before African American settlement. Wars and disturbances in the interior empires sent populations to the west, and the increase in European trade on the Atlantic coast made that region more subject to competition for control of the trade routes from the interior. Trade rivalries intensified with the growth of the slave trade in the eighteenth century. Some sixteen groups came to the area known as the Grain Coast, for its pepper grains. The Krus, Bassas, Deys, Mambas, and Grebos arrived at the coast in about the sixteenth century and developed trade with the Portuguese and later with the Dutch, French, and English. The Vai, known for their system of writing and their complex social and political organization, arrived in the sixteenth and seventeenth centuries. Loose confederations formed and reformed. Because the Golah maintained both an interior and a coastal presence, they were the principal trade rivals of the Mandingo, especially in the slave trade. The latter had the most highly developed trade networks, with their center at the town of Bopolu, fifty miles north of Cape Mesurado, where they shared power with a confederation of ethnic groups. Into this web of trade arrangements and governance came the African Americans, unaware and perhaps unconcerned that their presence was disruptive.[4]

Early in the spring of 1822, the settlers took possession of Cape Mesurado and founded the town that was later to be named Monrovia, in honor of President James Monroe. In accordance with the 1819 Slave Trade Act, a primary goal of the ACS was to prepare housing for Africans recovered from the slave trade. Lott Cary chafed at the agent's authority, in letters to the Baptist Board of Missions, and reminded the board that it had not been his idea to unite Baptist missions with the ACS. He complained that the ACS had "abandoned them as colonists" and "received us as laborers and mechanics" for housing construction. They were "confined to the field by law and by necessity,"[5] but it was indeed by necessity that the colonists struggled to nurse the sick, raise shelter, obtain food, and protect themselves from the unhappy Dey peoples surrounding them. In August, a white missionary arrived with a group of rescued Africans. Jehudi Ashmun, not yet an agent, undertook to prepare fortifications for an attack by the Dey that came on December 1 and was repulsed by the settlers, though outnumbered, giving them a sense of providential intervention and divine purpose. In this crisis, settler leadership and Ashmun worked together well.[6]

A few months later, the *Oswego* brought sixty free blacks from Pennsylvania, Maryland, and Virginia to Liberia. From Petersburg came Colston Waring, a Baptist minister. Waring's task was to report to the Gillfield Baptist Church, where he was a trustee and frequent exhorter, whether Liberia was a suitable destination for the free blacks of Petersburg. By August, Waring had decided in favor of Liberia, and, late that year, he returned to Virginia to report his findings to the free blacks of Petersburg and Richmond. Waring led one hundred people from that region, many skilled and literate, to Liberia early in 1824 on the *Cyrus*. Most were from Petersburg, but fourteen were members of the free black Clark family from Southampton County. All suffered from the fever, but most survived, aided only by Agnes Barbour, a fifty-three-year-old Petersburg midwife, and the self-taught Lott Cary. Most of the Gillfield Church members followed trustees Colston Waring and Joseph Shiphard into Cary's Providence Baptist Church.

Ashmun's cordial relations with the settlers, especially with Cary and Waring, deteriorated when his method of allocating town lots and rationing food angered settlers. He encountered a resistance that apparently surprised him. Led by Cary, settlers seized control of the stores of food early in 1824 and rejected Ashmun's rationing plan, insisting that settlers should be making their own decisions in this and other matters. The revolt forced Ashmun to leave the colony for the Cape Verde Islands in April

1824, and ACS secretary Gurley traveled to Africa to mediate a settlement that included Ashmun's return. Although the ACS managers in Washington wanted Cary arrested, Ashmun and Gurley realized that this might cause even greater insurrection and persuaded the white ACS board that a more participatory set of laws was needed. A body of law adopted in 1825 put the settlement under common law, with authority divided between the ACS and the settlers.[7]

Ashmun again worked amicably with the settler leadership, forming a partnership with Colston Waring. Ashmun's housekeeper, Martha Thompson, from Richmond, served as an informal hostess in the governor's house. When poor health forced Ashmun to return to the United States, Cary became the acting agent for the ACS, a position he held until his accidental death in 1828.[8] Under the leadership of Ashmun and Cary, the colony expanded its borders through treaties in the 1820s. Ashmun commissioned Waring, the colony's vice agent, who was seen as a skilled negotiator, and Jacob Warner, an emigrant from Maryland, to acquire a tract of land south of Monrovia in October 1825. In December 1827, the colony acquired the northern part of Bushrod Island at the mouth of the Mesurado River, and, the next April, Cary signed an agreement with African chiefs that ceded a large tract of land on the St. Paul's River to the colony.[9]

The *Indian Chief* that arrived in February 1826 carried the first emancipated family from Virginia. The family's former owner, an outspoken Virginia Presbyterian minister, had been forced from his pulpit because of his denunciation of slavery. Frances Paxton and her ten children and two grandchildren were emancipated by John D. Paxton, a clergyman at Hampden-Sydney College in Prince Edward County. The aged Frances Paxton had not wanted to leave Virginia, but her family would not go without her. The group waited four months in Norfolk for the *Indian Chief*, probably staying with friends of the ACS or with people known to the Reverend Paxton. Perhaps they attended church and sought temporary work in town. It was to be their last time together. Despite the good intentions of Paxton, emigration meant death from the fever for eight of her children and grandchildren, but the elderly Frances Paxton survived for several years.[10]

Late the next year, another group of emancipated Virginians embarked for Liberia, when the *Doris* from Baltimore stopped in Norfolk to pick up three families that had been emancipated by David Bullock of Louisa County from among his bondmen. The Bullock group carried with them the hope of the Richmond auxiliary officers that this example would first move Colonel Bullock to further emancipations and then move more slaveholders to emancipate for African colonization. But this emigrant group frustrated ACS expectations once they arrived in the farming community of Caldwell. Although Colonel Bullock and Benjamin Brand thought that the emigrants were adequately supplied, the Bullocks, from Liberia, assessed the situation differently and wrote that "a man has to work very hard here to make a living and then he can just live: and as for becoming Rich it is out of the question unless he come out well provided."

The Bullocks reported: "We have all been sick. . . . Our situation is deplorable. . . . Our provision is not more than half enough to support us. We have found nothing here as it was told us in America." They described their weekly rations as one pint of rice, one pint of meal, a half pint of palm oil, a half pound of meat, one hogshead of tobacco, two pipes, and two ounces of soap. The ex-bondmen were told by ACS agents to use the tobacco and pipes to buy cassava and plantain from the natives. Lack of adequate provisions was made worse for them by a lack of tools and money and by the fact that their clothes had rotted on the voyage. They asked for "a cross-cut saw, three axes, three spades, some tobacco powder, an old lock and keys, augers and anything else you can think of."[11] The experience of the emancipated Paxtons and the Bullocks provided a sharp contrast with the narrative of progress that Virginia auxiliaries and free black emigrants were developing even in the first decade of settlement.

By the time that the Bullocks arrived in Caldwell and assessed their situation, some 200 farms of five to ten acres each, most of them located near Monrovia, were established. The majority of the rest were located at Caldwell, a farming community on the St. Paul's River, in an area of fertile lowland where agriculture appeared most promising. Experiments and adaptations led to sugarcane and coffee as the most viable cash crops, but few in the Liberian experiment anticipated the extent to which American lives and agriculture would have to be adjusted to the terrain and climate of West Africa. The weather was divided into a dry season, with hot, sandy winds, and a rainy season, in which water fell in torrents. Despite the apparent lushness, arable soil was scarce, and American draft animals were vulnerable to the insect-borne diseases.[12]

Much of the labor supply in the colony came from either recaptive or indigenous Africans. The Slave Trade Act of 1819 had provided funding for the ACS's West African colony based on the colony's ability to absorb and care for Africans taken from slave ships. Africans recaptured by American vessels, frequently called Congoes, were brought to land at Monrovia and put in the care of an agent. But recaptives were few in the early years. The group of 152 Africans, rescued from the slave trade in 1819 and then

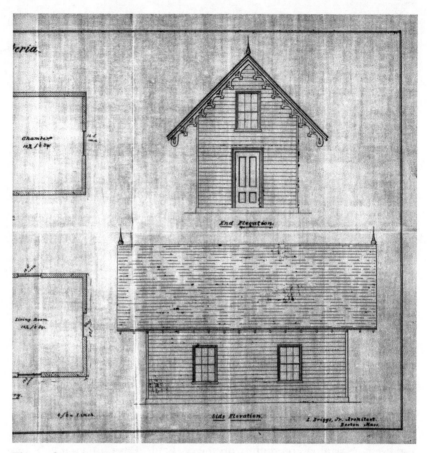

These 1850 plans by a Boston architect for model cottages to be built in Liberia show a modest but adequate frame structure that has made no concessions to the West African climate or terrain. Whenever possible, emigrants to Liberia maintained the American standards and preferences they had brought to Africa. (Library of Congress)

held in Georgia, had provoked the Slave Trade Act, but they were not sent to Liberia until 1827, much reduced in numbers. Most of them were sent to create a settlement called New Georgia, near Monrovia, which became a source of agricultural staples for the larger town.[13] The system of receiving recaptive Africans did not place a severe strain on Liberia until the 1840s and after, when large numbers of rescued Africans reached the colony. Ultimately, the recaptive Africans worked to the advantage of Liberians, because they populated many of the outlying settlements and extended Liberian influence.

Liberians were frequently criticized for their use of recaptured and local Africans as domestic and agricultural labor, but the policy combined aspects of indenture, apprenticeship, exchange, and African systems of slavery that allowed for much variation in practice. The actual status of such persons appears to have ranged from near-enslavement to adoption. The African tradition of apprenticing children in the homes of others made it easier for settlers to hire or adopt African children. Adult Africans were also hired, and they worked for less than Americans. An early account, observed just five years after the founding of Monrovia, noted, first, "a number of the natives attached to families, who act as servants and perform all the drudgery," and, a paragraph later, that "in almost every family of our colonists are one, two or more native children who have been sent to [the] cape by their parents to 'learn the fashion of the white man.'"[14] Lott Cary urged the ACS to pay tuition for the schooling of recaptive children who were now "running at large."

The problem of incorporating recaptives and developing alliances with local peoples was a core concern of settlers, who feared that their mission to convert and civilize Africa would be overwhelmed by a rapid infusion of Africans into their midst. The written evidence suggests that Liberian settlers understood that they were a small fraction of the region's inhabitants and that their cultural survival depended not only upon maintaining their own standards with vigilance but also in inducing or enticing recaptive Africans and members of neighboring groups to adopt settler practices and beliefs. Abuse or neglect of recaptives or indigenous people certainly occurred, but it seems to have been understood that such practices would eventually undermine the republic they were attempting to found.[15]

Cary's death in November 1828 marked the end of the first era of Liberian history, an era that would later be presented as the era of intrepid pioneers and explorers. Many of the persons who would govern Liberia for the next four decades arrived just four months after the death of Cary and are counted among the founders. The *Harriet*, from Norfolk, docked in Monrovia on March 17, 1829, well provisioned with household furniture, tools, agricultural implements, and articles of trade. All but 22 of its 147 passengers were from Virginia, and 101 of them were free blacks, the majority from Richmond. Typically, farming was the occupation most frequently listed, but the emigrants included six boot- and shoemakers, three blacksmiths, two coopers, two seamen, a cabinetmaker, a tobacconist, a seamstress, and a schoolteacher. The *Harriet* passengers included extended free black families of education and substance, but some of the most prominent died of the fever, among them David Payne, a Methodist minister who headed a large group from Richmond.[16]

David Payne's death from the fever, as well as that of Joseph Turner, a Presbyterian minister who was also from Richmond, robbed the group of much of its senior leadership. Frederick Lewis, an early emigrant who was returning to Liberia with his wife, raged at the notion that the deaths were based on risky behavior by the emigrants, saying "I have to say it has turned out as I ferd it would in comeing in the dry season to this place, and my reason for saying so is this the people that came with me ware of the best habets found among our color in the State of virginia, and yet, . . . we lost my kinsman David Payn." When he concluded the letter, Lewis was still counting the dead: "The whoel is 21." The total, according to the ACS agent, would eventually be twenty-six, and it was likely greater. Frederick Lewis, kin to the Paynes, had lived in Washington, D.C., for fourteen years and his wife had lived in New York City before joining him in Washington. His belief that arrival in the dry season was more deadly than in the wet season went against experience, as the malaria-carrying mosquitoes were more active and numerous in the time of heavy rain. But his ability to share his earlier experience in Liberia with free blacks from New York City to Petersburg, Virginia, illustrates once again the permeability of informational borders between North and South, for at least those African Americans in Maryland and Virginia.[17]

Initially surviving the fever was Joseph Shiphard, the one schoolteacher among the *Harriet* emigrants. He had conducted schools for free blacks in both Richmond and Petersburg in the years before he left Virginia, advertising that he sought "callow chiefs and embryonic statesmen" to educate for Liberia.[18] Also among the living were James Sprigg Payne, son of the deceased David Payne, who became the fourth president of Liberia, and Beverly Yates, later a vice president of the republic. All six of the children of Amelia Roberts survived the fever, among them Joseph Jenkin Roberts, the future first president of the Liberian republic. Other emigrants on the *Harriet* included fourteen persons manumitted by Margaret Mercer of Cedar Park, Maryland, and a family of nine Hunts, liberated by the Reverend Thomas Hunt, a Presbyterian minister from Brunswick County, Virginia. The farmers among them were sent to Caldwell on the St. Paul's River, while those who identified themselves as mechanics and traders drew for Monrovia town lots.[19]

The *Harriet*, in 1829, marked a transition in Virginia emigration to Liberia, not simply because it was the last large and self-organized exodus of free blacks from the state until 1865, but also because by 1829 emigrants encountered a town that they recognized as American, with a legal system, a social hierarchy, patterns of trade, and boundaries, however tenuous, with their Dey neighbors. The fact that Liberia was not, in reality, American and was as subject to African realities as to American ones was made apparent by the two largest emigrations to Liberia from Virginia in the 1830s. One was prompted by a massacre in Virginia; and the other prompted a massacre in Liberia. Together these events were an enactment of the sense of constant peril that settlers in Liberia experienced from enemies both outside and inside their colony.

On January 4, 1832, the *James Perkins* arrived in Monrovia with 338 individuals, most from Southampton County and the rest from adjoining counties in North Carolina. All but 12 had been born free.[20] They were fleeing the United States in the aftermath of the Nat Turner insurrection that had massacred 55 whites in Southampton County before turning into a reverse bloodbath for African Americans in the region. The January arrival was the first of five ships that would bring a record 521 emigrants from Virginia to Liberia in fifteen months. The impact of this migration was to reinforce the Virginia dominance in Liberia in the colony's second decade. With the arrival of the *Jupiter* in March 1833 as the last of the five ships, emigration from Virginia slowed considerably.[21]

For the rest of the decade of the 1830s, just 412 persons left Virginia for Liberia, and nearly one-quarter of those were the bondmen of Dr. Aylett Hawes of Rappahannock County, who had freed them in his will.[22] They were to play a part in a massacre that was the result of Liberian territorial expansion into established trade systems, in this case, the slave trade system. The territorial expansion that met its grimmest response at Bassa Cove was part of the central problem of African American settlement in what the settlers called Liberia. Along the Atlantic coast, the settlers' campaigns against the slave trade and their attempts to control trade from the interior used land acquisition as a central strategy, provoking recurrent skirmishes with Bassa, Vai, Dey, and Glebo peoples. The upriver settlements, small and weak compared to their Mandingo, Gola, and Kpelle neighbors, adopted more African practices and negotiated more carefully but were frequently caught in disputes over trade or even domestic relations among these groups.[23]

The Young Men's Colonization Society of Pennsylvania, with help from the New York City Colonization Society, purchased land for an independent settlement at Grand Bassa at the mouth of the St. John's River. It was a utopian experiment independent of the ACS, formed on pacifist and temperance principles and designed to prove that settlers could live peacefully among the natives and could trade successfully without dealing in rum. Virginia emancipators Dr. Aylett Hawes of Culpeper County and

Dr. James Jones of Lynchburg heard the echoes of Enlightenment ideas that they had absorbed in Edinburgh while youths in medical school and both directed that the slaves freed in their wills be sent to this settlement.[24] Dr. Jones survived until 1848 and his wishes were partly thwarted, but Dr. Hawes died in 1833 and approximately sixty of his former bondmen traveled to Liberia late in 1834.

In early December 1834, the ship *Ninus* brought the Hawes contingent to Liberia. They put ashore near Edina, on land purchased from Bassa chief Bob Gray, and proceeded to the 700-acre tract called Port Cresson, purchased from another Bassa leader, King Joe Harris. Rumors reached Monrovia that slave traders active in Bassa country had persuaded Joe Harris to destroy the settlement, telling him they could do no business with him while the Americans were so close. Aid came in the form of a rescue detachment of thirty men led by William L. Weaver, formerly a barber in Richmond and now superintendent of nearby Edina, who drove Joe Harris's men away from the settlement. What transpired between the former Richmond barber and the ex-slaves from Rappahannock and Culpeper Counties is not conveyed. It is easy to imagine that the new emigrants welcomed the military presence, but it was not acceptable to the pacifist principles of the white administrator, and Weaver's militia returned to Edina.[25]

On the night of June 10, 1835, Bassas, led by King Joe Harris, attacked the settlement, set fire to the buildings, and massacred twenty-two members of the emigrant party. When news of the massacre reached Monrovia, Nathaniel Brander, the colony's acting agent and chief administrator, met with the council and declared war. Six months of war followed that forced King Joe Harris to promise to make restitution, to abandon the slave trade, and to submit territorial disputes to the "colonial authorities at Monrovia." Bassa Cove was rebuilt further up the St. John's River and continued for several years to be populated by Virginia emigrants, especially those who had some connections with northern colonizationists.[26]

Future settlements were less utopian and had more of the standard pragmatic elements for founding settlements. These included seeking or rewarding patrons through town-naming practices and emphasizing the Christian conversion aspect of settlement through black ministers as settler leaders. One example was the Reverend Amos Herring, a Presbyterian minister and ex-slave from Augusta County, who had first come to the colony in 1833 and then returned to the United States to study at Wesleyan Academy in Wilbraham, Massachusetts, for two years, before returning to Liberia. He led the seventy Virginians on the *Luna* that brought them to Bassa Cove in August 1836. This time the enemy was the fever, and twenty-three died within the first year. Earlier that year, the same ship landed at Bassa Cove with a group of eighty-two persons, most from Virginia. This group founded a settlement on the Junk River, called Marshall, for John Marshall, the recently deceased Supreme Court chief justice and president of the Virginia Colonization Society (VCS). Notable among them was Beverly R. Wilson, a black Methodist minister from Norfolk, who had come out on the *Jupiter* in 1833 and then returned, after a year, to get his wife and four children.[27]

Such connections between Virginia colonizationists and Pennsylvania, New York, and Massachusetts colonizationists are more apparent than their connections with the VCS in the 1830s and 1840s. The legislative act of 1833 that provided funding for emigrants to Liberia restricted that funding to free blacks and was almost never used. At the 1837 meeting of the VCS Board of Managers, William Maxwell suggested that Virginia sponsor its own colony in Liberia. Nothing came of this. In 1845, an anonymous Virginian issued an appeal in the *African Repository* for Virginians to collect $5,000 and purchase a tract in Liberia to be called Virginia. Less than two years later, such a site did appear as New Virginia, located about five miles northeast of Monrovia on the right bank of the St. Paul's River and mentioned casually in correspondence and publications. Although it was never large or prosperous, the settlement survived.[28] Support for the Virginia settlement from the VCS appears to have been somewhere between modest and nonexistent. Other state colonization societies set up state colonies out of a desire to control their own donations and their state's settlers. The most successful of these state efforts was the Maryland Colonization Society's in Liberia, founded in the Cape Palmas region in 1831. In 1838, the Mississippi State Colonization Society founded a settlement called Mississippi in Africa, at the mouth of the Sinoe River, but it lasted only a short time.[29]

Emigrant responses to Liberia ranged from satisfaction to despair, and often those emotions could be found in the same person at different times. Most frequently, newcomers wrote first of their delight in the landscape and their liberties. "I like the country very well indeed & have no reason to return to America, for we believe there is no Country on the Earth can Equal it in the world." Mars and Jesse Lucas, emancipated slaves from Loudoun County, were initially positive. Mars Lucas wrote: "I. am very much pleased with this Country. I Could not have belived, it if I has. not seen it, myself." But these letters were frequently followed by grim lists of those who had sickened and died and, especially among emancipated slaves, accounts of their difficulties in making an adequate living.[30]

Complaints about the dispersal of land and the first six months' food supplies were common, but the emancipated slaves who felt betrayed by ACS descriptions of Liberia wrote or dictated the most angry and anguished letters. Three months later, Mars Lucas wrote again: "I. may state to you. that I. am much deceiv'd, with, this Country[;] the reports, is all a lie, mearly to Encourage people. To come to this Country." In a final letter in this correspondence, Jesse Lucas responded bitterly to complaints from friends who, perhaps excusing themselves for not sending supplies, wrote that times were hard. Jesse Lucas wrote: "You wrote to me that times were hard in America—I have not eaten once of flour for four years—The meat when I receive any is monkey or something like a rat." In a cry from the heart, Jesse Lucas wrote: "We never knew what slavery was until we came to this country and that is the cry with every living man in the colony."[31]

Such despair was not universal, but tragedies did seem to multiply for those who "have not the necessaries, far less the comforts of life."[32] The unfortunate Andrew Green from Jefferson County, who had named his babies for George Washington and Lott Cary, lost his wife giving birth to twins and lost two children to fever. Green's quarter-acre lot in town was sold by court order for debts that he had to the firm of Dailey and Russwurm, and Julianna Green, the widow he married after his wife's death, was forced to sell the lot she had inherited in Monrovia to Colin Teage, the Baptist minister from Richmond.[33] Perhaps what was universal in this experience was the opportunity for those with resources to profit from others' distresses.

Some of those who found Liberia's shortages, squabbles, wars, and deaths too much to bear were able to leave the colony. The Atlantic traffic went both ways, and it was not uncommon for dissatisfied emigrants to return to the United States or travel on to Sierra Leone. As early as 1825, two women from Southampton County relocated a year after arrival. Nancy Clark moved to Sierra Leone with her husband, and Matilda Clark and her husband returned to the United States, with the latter's departure officially attributed to her "caprice." A few years later, Southampton County shoemaker Lemuel Clark also returned to the United States.[34] This was a pattern that would be repeated with almost every shipload of emigrants. In each year, there were some who relocated within Africa or returned to the United States to complain bitterly of Liberia or its inhabitants.

In his first letter back to Virginia, Sampson Ceasar wrote: "The natives are numerous in this place and they do most of the work for the people in this place [Monrovia]. They will Steal every Chance they have. They are most all Croomen." Gilbert Hunt complained that the Kru men who rowed out to the ships in canoes had cheated him of his tobacco, his chief trading commodity. In fact, the Kru were experienced mariners and traders whose knowledge of geography and trade values gave them an edge over the American emigrants in any transaction.[35]

Gilbert Hunt's return to Richmond from Liberia caused Richmond colonizationists much distress. Hunt was well known in Richmond as the hero of an 1811 theater fire in which he caught women lowered from the burning building. After purchasing his own freedom many years later, Hunt traveled to Liberia on the *Harriet* in 1829, but he returned the next year. He recounted only the episode in which he was relieved of his tobacco by the sharp practices of the Kru boatmen, but he appears to have been generally disappointed by Liberia. He was not averse to saying so back in Richmond, causing the secretary of the Richmond-Manchester Auxiliary to refer to him as "a complete croaker" who was hurting the cause.[36]

Those who were content seemed to find their satisfaction in economic opportunity and civil liberties and were more likely to have brought resources with them. Joseph Shiphard, schoolmaster from Petersburg, was among the convinced colonizers. He wrote, "The most sanguine of my expectations for happiness in this Colony, have been surpassed in point of acquiring wealth, ease, respectability and the pleasures attendant on civil and religious liberty." Abraham Blackford from Fredericksburg, who had changed his name from Abram once in Liberia, wrote more bluntly: "It is much better than to be in the State[s] for them to call you Boy. There are a few white people out hear, though they are very polite. . . . The white man never calls me by my name unless they call me Mr. Blackford." In the Liberian republic, white persons could not become citizens, and Henry Roberts wrote, with evident satisfaction: "There is now in our port an American Steamer for California—with about 227 immigrants white of course. They are all about our City—many of them highly delighted and feign would remain, but as to that, no go you know."[37]

Separation from all that they had known was wrenching, even for those who prospered in their fields. Sampson Ceasar left the small Lewis County town of Buckhannon for Liberia late in 1833. Writing to white Henry Westfall, he exclaimed: "O Henry when I look back and reflect on the many hours I spent with you and your family I am led to wish that I could see you all. . . . Let me know all about the people how many have died and who they are and how many have married and who they are and who was elected to the next Legislature." Ceasar addressed a teasing comment to a young white girl. "Tell Lydia that there was A vessel from Jermany landed here About ten days Ago and I never saw better looking men in my life than some of them wer if She wants a Jerman and will write to me I wil try to send her one for I think they will suit her."[38]

The initial shock of seeing Africans, and experiencing so little identification with them, sometimes gave way to an appreciation, particularly among those Virginia missionaries who lived in missions or settlements in the interior. Ceasar, who ran a Methodist mission school at New Georgia, later admitted: "When I first saw the natives all naked, I thought that I never could get used to it," but "if I could talk with you face to face and tell you about the natives you would not believe me to See their cloth that they make and other articles. To be Short, their natural talents are great Indeed. Some of them can read and write." John Day and John Cheeseman, Baptist missionaries among the Bassa, acquired a cultural understanding that they tried to convey to their Baptist supporters. Day founded a school for the Bassa in Bexley and operated a press that published at least two primers in the Bassa language. Cheeseman learned to speak Bassa. Still, the view of Peyton Skipwith remained a common one: "It is something strange to think that these people of Africa are called our ancestors. In my present thinking, if we have any ancestors they could not be like these hostile tribes."[39]

In other letters, questions about the fate of children left behind in Virginia had a painful urgency. William Douglass, an industrious and prosperous sugar refiner who must have been one of the few Liberians able to send money back to the United States, tried to support his children in Virginia. After receiving no news during the Civil War, Douglass heard upsetting secondhand information that drove him to inquire once more about them. "I have been very anxious. I has written you four letters during the war and could hear nothing. . . . Also inform me something about my children. I could hear nothing from them nether during the war though I has often written them, but I chance to hear mention of them in a letter to George Walker from Mrs. Reeves that two was dead and one she never mention her name at all[,] Julia, which made me very unhappy. In 1861, when Dr. Hall [Addison Hall] was over here last I gave him $30 in gold . . . requesting you to . . . give it to my children but the war broke out . . . and I have heard nothing about it since."[40] Perhaps Douglass learned something of his children from the 1865 Lynchburg emigrants to Liberia for whom he acted as agent, but it is as likely that he was never able to locate them.

The delicate question of the holding power of slave marriage, when its participants were involuntarily separated, appeared in Liberia to depend on the couple's future prospects as well as depth of affection. Adaline Southall wrote: "Give my love to my husband Henry Southall & tell him

I am not married yet & miss him very much & like him to come out."[41] A gruffer note to a spouse came from another person in the same Albemarle County group: "I add these few lines to my wife I am well and may this find her in good health. I received your former letters but I had no time to write, my house is almost finished. I have 20 coffee trees I think they shall bear next year, my love to every persons on the plantation, I shall try to be over sometime the last part of the following year, in the returns of the ship. I should like to hear from you."[42]

Scholars have frequently commented on the entreaties for money and materials that took up a good part of the letters from Liberia. Some have interpreted these requests as evidence of ACS betrayal, as expressed by the Lucas brothers. The ACS's promotional efforts can frequently be attributed more to self-delusion than to calculated bad faith, but the tragedies suffered by emigrants were just as real, either way. The society's ability to maintain emigrants for six months was always marginal, and emigrants frequently suffered from shortages of every kind, unless they were privately supplied. ACS records and letters indicate that most Virginia emancipators had ongoing concern for the welfare of the families they emancipated. Liberia differed from other colonial ventures in lacking government sponsorship, and emigrants turned to those persons associated with the colonization movement or known to them personally. Free blacks sought basic supplies from African missionary societies, their families, their home churches, and their trading partners. Emancipated slaves turned to their former masters and to ACS agents or members.

Few settler requests were frivolous. They reflected the most basic needs of a transplanted culture: "Send me some garden seeds . . . a keg of butter . . . a barrel of sugar . . . some white shirting . . . a bed tick and a counterpane."[43] "Please send me one Doctor Book, Please Send me four Baptist hymn Books."[44] "Send law books."[45] "I am very glad of the saw you sent me. . . . I received all you sent me but the cloth."[46] Adaline Southall was building her own house when she wrote with requests, and her list reflected the construction supplies she needed and basic supplies for living that were either not available or overpriced in Liberia. "I wish you would send me a Keg of flooring nails & broad Axe & some Door hinges & anything you have money to get them with. Please to send some bed ticking & some blue Cottons and Cloths for Horras [Adaline Southall's son Horace] & a hat 2 pieces muslin, 1 is unbleached one is bleached, 1 Box Soap as it is Scarce here. I would like to have some handkerchiefs, some Cotton & some linen & a pair of shoes for Horras. Please send some Leaf tobacco & a Piece of Calico. Please send me a Door Lock and Padlock."[47]

Even well-considered supply efforts often fell short. Boxes frequently did not survive the voyage because the contents became waterlogged and then molded or rotted. Or they were stolen. Richmond Auxiliary secretary Benjamin Brand lamented to Lott Cary: "Poor Page Carter is dead but he did the colony an essential disservice by breaking open the bag of clothes and books and using them."[48] Sometimes boxes and trunks simply never appeared. "My wife Maria and all of the children, they did not get any of the clothes that was intended for them the box was robbed or something else; as there was no bill of lading for them, we have not seen any of them."[49] Desserline Harris worried: "Uncle John wishes you to remember *his crate.* . . . I hope you will relieve his anxiety by forwarding them in the packet."[50]

Letters suggest that African fruits and vegetables became part of the diet quickly and that substitutes for wheat flour were rapidly if reluctantly utilized, out of necessity. Tibey Scott was one of many to list local products: "We have great many and different kind of vegetables grows here . . . sweet potato and plantain banans and sometimes rice and corn these are our breadstuff and we have beans and peas cabbage greens . . . okra we can raise cowpeas . . . fruits of all kinds grows here too . . . fine apples gorgeous cherries and oranges lemons meat is hard to get here." Despite claims by upriver farmers that settlers rejected local foodstuffs and preferred imported American food, few could afford to buy such luxuries and most adapted to available produce. A major problem was the lack of meat, especially pork, the loss of which meant the loss of a staple seasoning and rendered fat for many purposes.[51]

When letters from Liberia or a returned and disillusioned emigrant described the colony as a site of illness and death, military skirmishes, and material scarcity, the ACS and its Virginia agents attempted to counter these accounts in the only way that would be effective among Virginia blacks. They encouraged successful colonists to visit the United States and, if from Virginia, tour their home regions to refute the statements of the naysayers. William Draper, of Fredericksburg, freed by his mother's purchase of him in 1812, emigrated to Liberia with his wife in 1824 and returned for a visit in 1829 to persuade others to emigrate.[52] The state of Virginia had an uneasy and inconsistent response to such persons. In 1841, in Bedford County, a Liberian named Harris, probably Sion Harris, had a "most happy effect"; in Abingdon and in southwest Virginia he aroused such "intense desire among slaves" that masters became uneasy, but Harris was not impeded in his travels. At the same time, in the Tidewater area, the presence of a Liberian named Brown was declared unlawful and he was forced to leave the state.[53]

The best of the trusted informers were family members writing or returning from Liberia. In at least one case, a prominent Liberian returned, but, despite his personal success, his family's fate in Liberia sobered his Virginia friends. James B. Barbour emigrated to Liberia from Petersburg on the *Cyrus* with his mother, Agnes Barbour, and nine siblings, all free-born. A kinsman, tobacconist John J. Barbour, had preceded them on the *Nautilus*, with Lott Cary. Agnes Barbour was a midwife, and two brothers, William and John W., were stonemasons. James and Robert were young men who had worked in tobacco factories in Petersburg and perhaps done some trading in tobacco. A grandmother and two young sisters had died within months, succumbing to the fever. The others appeared to be doing well. Agnes Barbour was given a prime building site in Monrovia. The younger Barbours were put in school, and the young men joined militia units, in which James Barbour became a major. He was later a vice agent of the ACS in Liberia.

But, within a few years, successive accidents and illnesses decimated the family. William Barbour died of drowning in 1828, and the matriarch Agnes Barbour died of what the census described as "a decline" in the same year. Robert died of a "deranged brain" two years later, and kinsman John J. Barbour died of a decline the next year. Burwell Barbour would soon be convicted of second-degree murder and sent to prison for two years. When James Barbour returned in 1832, Benjamin Brand complained to Gurley, "His conversation in regard to the colony was not very satisfactory."[54] Even if Barbour intended to promote Liberia upon his return to Virginia as a militia major, answers to inquiries about his family from friends and acquaintances had to acknowledge many deaths, including that of his well-known midwife mother.

Because Desserline Harris of Alexandria went to Liberia by himself, he acquired no family history of deaths. When one bellwether expedition from Rockbridge County, led by emigrant Samuel Harris, likely a kinsman of Desserline Harris, ended badly with significant deaths, it appeared that free blacks from the Shenandoah Valley would not volunteer again to go to Liberia. But letters from Desserline Harris, now the acting secretary of state in the Liberian republic, encouraged his uncle, John V. Henry of Lexington, to accompany Diego Evans, leader of a subsequent group from that region. John V. Henry sold his house and possessions and brought his family to Liberia with Evans in 1849. Upon their arrival, Henry, his son

Patrick Henry, and his nephew Desserline T. Harris started a mercantile firm, perhaps hoping to capitalize on their connections to the port of Alexandria. Harris announced that "John V. Henry and Company . . . will import and sell—I will say, most everything."[55]

The history of the Henry family was murky in a manner similar to that of other relatively prosperous Virginia free blacks with white male patronage. Patrick, Williamson, Dunkin, and John V. Henry had begun as slaves in Westmoreland County, owned by Martin Tapscott. Their mother, Lavinia, was registered as freed by Tapscott. At Tapscott's death, Williamson Henry was freed. Tapscott intended to free Patrick, but he died suddenly and Patrick purchased his freedom. How the other two brothers came to be free is not known. All four brothers moved to Rockbridge County in the Shenandoah Valley. Two of the brothers, Williamson and Dunkin (now Duncan), had only modest amounts of property, but the other two, Patrick and John V., were particularly favored by obtaining sinecures. Thomas Jefferson hired Patrick Henry to be caretaker of Natural Bridge, a scenic rock natural wonder that Jefferson then owned. Patrick farmed nearby and gave tours of Natural Bridge. John V. Henry lived in Lexington, where he was employed to work on the buildings and grounds of Washington College. He was literate and a property owner, and, like Patrick, he purchased his enslaved wife.[56]

How the Henry and Harris families are related is not known, but they were able to maintain their connection through migrations in Virginia—from the Tidewater to the Shenandoah Valley for the Henrys and Samuel Harris, and to Alexandria, still a part of the District of Columbia, for the other Harrises. The Harris family members, father John Harris and children Desserline and Bathsheba, were property owners and soap makers in Alexandria. After the city of Alexandria left the District of Columbia and reverted to the state of Virginia in 1846, John Harris and daughter Bathsheba moved to Washington, and Desserline Harris emigrated to Liberia in 1848. Although he encouraged his father and sister to follow and they made tentative inquiries, there is no record of their leaving the United States.[57]

The family connections among Virginia free and emancipated blacks emigrating to Liberia are frequent and layered. Southampton County supplied three sets of cousins, even before the Nat Turner insurrection caused a much greater surge of emigrants, including their relatives, to Liberia. Southampton County residents on the *Hunter* in 1825 included Alan and Elsie Davis and their children, Washington, Amanda, and Martha. Five years later, the *Valador* carried cousins of the Davises, John and Catherine

Gardner, along with their sons, Anthony, Jesse, and Alfred. Both families were cousins of fellow Southampton County emigrants Charles and Eliza Davis, who also brought two sons to Liberia. Charles Davis, a seaman, was captured by a Spanish slaver, and his wife survived only four years in Liberia, but their sons, William and Patrick, prospered as traders and businessmen in the town of Marshall.[58]

These interconnected free black Southampton County families became part of the settler elite, second only to the free black emigrants from the Virginia port cities. Washington Davis, fifteen at the time of his departure from Virginia, became one of the most influential of the settler Liberians. He returned to the United States for medical education and then practiced as a physician at Edina. While in the United States, he was frequently a spokesman for and interpreter of Liberia at fund-raising meetings for the ACS. His cousin, Anthony Gardner, eleven when he left Southampton County in early 1831, was schooled in Liberia, studied law there under Lewis Sheridan, a prominent and outspoken emigrant from North Carolina, and rose through clerkships and public office to be a delegate to Liberia's national convention to frame Liberia's Declaration of Independence. He served for sixteen years in Liberia's legislature and was president of the republic from 1879 to 1883.[59]

But not all emigrants were filled with civilizing impulses and Christian zeal. Some were prepared to take on whatever role or guise appeared to benefit them at the moment and to change form or shape opportunistically over time. Accompanying the Reverend Colston Waring to Liberia on his first trip in 1823 were Augustus Curtis, a twenty-one-year-old Petersburg blacksmith, later described as a Cherokee Indian, and his nineteen-year-old wife, Minerva.[60] The Curtises were literate and more than a little intrepid to venture to Liberia at this early stage, when Petersburg free blacks were still withholding judgment until Waring's return. They traveled with a group of free blacks from Philadelphia, Georgetown, D.C., and Baltimore. Despite his connections, his skills and literacy, and his early arrival, Augustus Curtis was described by 1831 as "well known to be a notorious character." In that year, he was brought into court on the charge of misappropriating money entrusted to him for the benefit of a young girl, Malvina Fleet, for whom he had been appointed guardian. When he was found out, her guardianship was changed to Colston Waring.[61] In 1834, Augustus Curtis moved to Grand Cape Mount, and Minerva Curtis moved to British Accra, a coastal trade port considerably south of Monrovia.[62]

The Curtis family had more than its share of troubles in Liberia. The year after Augustus Curtis left Monrovia for Grand Cape Mount, Edward and Mary Curtis, also from Petersburg, arrived in Liberia. Edward was two years older than Augustus and likely his brother. Within five months, he had been convicted of burglary and robbery and sentenced to two years imprisonment. Released early, he was rearrested on similar charges a few months later and was sentenced to four years in prison. Edward Curtis's quick rearrest suggests that it was a long-term pattern for him. That spring, Mary Curtis was convicted of receiving stolen goods.[63] The charges of burglary were more serious than the charges of larceny, which were not infrequent among the settlers in an economy of scarcity.

Larceny, the wrongful taking of another's property, could be a pair of shoes sitting outside a door, a kettle, or a knotted handkerchief filled with coins. Or it might be valuable lumber. These were the pilferings of ordinary threadbare persons from each other. The Virginians caught at larceny were usually accompanied by other Virginians in these activities. Burwell Brown, who arrived in Liberia from Southampton County on the *James Perkins*, was sentenced to twenty-five lashes and a six-month imprisonment for being an accessory to the grand larceny of J. Rix (or Ricks) and Albert Banks, who was also from Southampton County; Rix and Banks received sentences of thirty-nine lashes and two years imprisonment in 1835 for their thieving. Three years later, Ann Brown, wife of Burwell Brown, was convicted of petty larceny, along with five native men, and sentenced to five months in jail.[64]

However Augustus Curtis arrived at his reputation as a "notorious character," it was not from petty thievery. Ambitious and opportunistic, he was not burdened by a sense of Christian duty or the superiority of Western civilization, and this worked to his advantage once he left the American settlement. After his move to Grand Cape Mount in 1834, he settled among the Vai people and married the daughter of a chief, Fan Toro, who was also the sister-in-law of an important war leader, George Cain. Curtis was hired by the well-known slave trader Theodore Canot to oversee a blacksmith shop, sawpit, and ship dock when Canot attempted to start a legitimate business at that site.[65]

The complex intrigues at Grand Cape Mount in the 1840s remain unclear. When George Cain went to war with Fan Toro over the issue of the extent to which the latter had relinquished sovereignty to the British, Augustus Curtis became chief advisor to Cain, and Canot aligned with Fan Toro. Canot courted British protection, but it was the Liberians who offered him citizenship in order to bolster their claim to the region. Both the British and the Liberians suspected Canot of returning to the slave trade and watched his actions closely. Meanwhile, the destructive battles between Vai factions caused the Methodist Episcopal Church to send Anthony Williams to negotiate with Canot and Fan Toro to assure the safety of a missionary in the region. Williams, the former Norfolk shoemaker, may have conferred with Curtis, the former Petersburg blacksmith, now the chief advisor to a Vai war leader, as to the possibilities for peace. Curtis disrupted any such resolution when he reported to a British Navy officer that Canot trafficked slaves outside the Vai people's local system of slavery. He added as proof that hundreds of manacles were being made at the blacksmith shop. When an inspection of the shop appeared to corroborate this claim, Canot and his ship were seized, and the ship was taken to New York, where it was ultimately released. Canot never returned to his settlement, which was burned by Fan Toro, and always claimed that he had not reentered the slave trade. Prince George Cain became leader of the Vai upon the death of Fan Toro. The Liberians made treaties with the Vai and became the dominant power at Grand Cape Mount. Curtis lived out his life among the Vai and may have aided them in creating a written alphabet for their language. He was reportedly killed in the 1850s.[66]

Few Virginians came to identify with West African peoples as completely as did Augustus Curtis. But in the decades between 1832 and 1865, Virginia emigrants turned inward and became Liberians, whether this was their desire or not. While clinging to the American cultural forms that they remembered or were told of, they inevitably adapted their agricultural practices, their dietary habits, and their modes of interaction with local peoples to the daily realities of West Africa. Visitors might comment on the extent to which Liberians were a mixture of African and early-nineteenth-century American practices, but it was difficult for Liberians to see the extent to which their culture was frozen in American time and the extent to which it was merged with West Africa.

Eight

Liberians in Africa and America

A VISITOR TO MONROVIA IN 1860 professed surprise at the "degree of refinement and taste" that he found among its residents and concluded that "an aristocracy of means and education is already set up." "THE VIR-GINIANS," he added, "are said to be the leaders of the aristocracy." But the traveler did not really approve of the display of quality clothing: "The people generally dress above their means, extravagantly so, and the quantity of kid gloves and umbrellas displayed on all occasions does not promise well for a nation whose hope rests on hard and well developed muscles."[1] This observation by a white American was similar to those that might be found in antebellum American newspapers, where, as part of a general effort to maintain racial hierarchy, African American Sunday dress was often ridiculed as inappropriate for those of humble station. But from the perspective of the Monrovians, certainly including "THE VIRGINIANS," it was as important to distinguish themselves from the indigenous Africans when new arrivals formed first impressions as it had been to display their Sunday best in America. For Monrovians, elaborate dress was an outward manifestation of civilized standards.

Those on shipboard approaching Monrovia were usually favorably impressed by the lush beauty of the Cape Mesurado promontory. Because that coast's heavy surf and sandbars made it nearly impossible for ships to get near the dock, vessels weighed anchor some distance out and passengers watched as lightly clad Kru boatmen rowed dexterously toward the ship to take them and their goods over the surf. Occasionally someone gazing out asked, "Are those the Liberians?" Just before shore, if the sea was turbulent, the boatmen sometimes left their canoes and carried the new settlers to dry land. This was the first contact with Liberia that many emigrants and visitors had. Perhaps to counter this initial impression, Monrovians became known for their hospitality, and they sometimes ventured out in boats to greet the ships, well-dressed and bearing flowers and food.[2]

Although such displays may have encouraged class distinctions as well as a distancing from indigenous peoples, African Americans in Liberia felt themselves to be watched closely from the United States for signs of reversion to African norms. They believed their formal manners and formal clothing to be central to their survival as a distinct group in Africa and to their status as citizens, first in a colony and then in a republic. James Minor advised a potential emigrant from his native Virginia: "In your selection of ladies wear, do get some lady to assist you to make choices, for the ladies here are very flashy and wear no mean dresses." Other Liberians complained that such former Virginians were "most too high-headed, and . . . all the time claiming that they are the quality of Liberia." Baptist minister John Day agreed. Although he was a native Virginian and an educated man, he was not one of the urban free blacks who made up the James and Appomattox Rivers ascendancy in Monrovia. Instead, Day established a mission up the St. Paul's River among the Bassa people. Skeptical of Virginian pretensions, Day once praised a fellow minister by saying: "He is not like our Virginia folks, who will venture into every discipline and show at first sight, the depth and brea[d]th of their little intellect."[3]

Distinctions of class, color, and education that were a legacy of the American experience were exacerbated in Liberia by the fact that the earliest Virginia settlers were predominantly freeborn mulattoes of some education and financial resources who tended to cluster in Monrovia and engage in trade. Even among emancipated slaves from Virginia, class distinctions might prevail. Some accepted the widespread Virginian sense of superiority and felt themselves to be more culturally and socially elevated than emancipated slaves from the Lower South. For their part, the elite among the emigrants could pass swift judgment on the less polished. "Do not think much of the Kentucky delegates, (or *explorers* as they call themselves,) who came out in the 'N. Rich.' They appear to be rather self-consequential, blustering and ignorant—perhaps 'field hands,' as [Liberian] President Roberts told me he took them to be."[4]

The social divisions apparent in these assessments demonstrate the extent to which the Liberian experience was shaped by the internalized American cultural and political beliefs carried by African Americans to Liberia. The American patriotic narrative and the American evangelical urge to conversion were basic reference materials that could be drawn upon to explain and justify Liberia. The ACS construction of Africa's past emphasized vanished early civilizations and suggested that the cultural achievements of returning African Americans could restore Africa to its former glories. Free black and some previously enslaved emigrants experienced a form of sea change in their self-perceptions between Virginia and Liberia. In Liberia, culture, not race, was central to their self-image and their project of aiding blacks in America. Settlers saw the uplifting of Africans in Africa as the uplifting of Africans in diaspora as well. These were the concepts that framed their patriotic narrative, and two enduring iconic figures came to exemplify that narrative. The first was Lott Cary, from Richmond, the independent-minded missionary who successfully resisted the autocratic tendencies of the ACS and led military expeditions against indigenous African groups in the colony's first decade. The second enduring iconic figure was Joseph Roberts, from Petersburg, who served as an exemplar of entrepreneurial and diplomatic ability, dominating the history of Liberia from the 1830s until 1870.

Liberia was expected to become self-sufficient in agriculture, but it was trade that offered the quicker prospect for providing a sufficiency.[5] The American Colonization Society (ACS), although it had a dozen or so years of some funding due to an advantageous interpretation of the Slave Trade Act of 1819, was left with only donations in the early 1830s, and this meant that Liberia lacked the sustained and predictable support so necessary to fostering any colonial enterprise. Emigrants had only their own resources, and those resources were primarily their connections in Liberia and the United States. Education, skills, and a supply of dollars were all helpful, but the rapid rise of a merchant elite in Monrovia was due to family and community relationships formed in the United States or in the first decade of settlement. Settler society was rooted first in these family connections and region of origin and then in business arrangements and church membership. Family relations encompassed extended bloodlines but were also established around earlier plantation, farm, or town ties. Such ties were consciously affirmed when people organized themselves into a church or into a temperance or mutual aid society, which served as important displays of settlers' commitment to the values they brought with them.[6]

By 1826, Liberia was trading with increasing numbers of foreign vessels, as well as with its African neighbors. In that year, the number of vessels engaged in the colony's coastal trade increased from four to fifteen, and the colonists were beginning to build their own trade vessels. Trade and transportation were enhanced when the Colonial Council, the lawmaking body, chartered the colony's first public utility company. The Mesurado Channeling Company, a joint stock company organized by Lott Cary and Colston Waring, constructed a channel up the Mesurado River that allowed oceangoing vessels to reach the Monrovia wharves, rather than being forced to offload cargoes at sea and bring them across the bar by longboats.[7]

Mercantile firms were organized by even such stalwart Baptist ministers as Lott Cary and Colston Waring, who formed trading companies and traded in ardent spirits. Waring also founded a partnership with Francis Taylor to import firearms, ale, and rum from Liverpool. The trading firm of Roberts, Colson, and Company consisted of the young Joseph Roberts, whose parents had owned and operated boats on the James and Appomattox Rivers, and his partner, William N. Colson, a black barber in Petersburg. Their lucrative trade in camwood, palm oil, and ivory for clothing and fancy goods was disrupted by Colson's death but continued to be profitable under Roberts. John Russwurm, an editor from the northern antislavery camp, set up the successful trading firm of Dailey and Russwurm upon emigrating to Liberia. Desserline Harris, son of an Alexandria soap maker, formed a trading firm with his uncle and cousin, John V. Henry and Patrick Henry from Lynchburg.[8]

The Monrovian merchant elite consolidated its wealth and leadership through careful marriage, with an affinity for people of similar regional, religious, and commercial backgrounds. The lives of Harriet Graves Waring and her daughter, Jane Rose Waring Roberts, offer an example of Liberian family formation and consolidation that began in Norfolk in the 1790s and peaked at the court of Queen Victoria in the 1890s. Harriet Graves was born free in Norfolk, a busy port city, in 1796, into "tolerable circumstances" and in a post-Revolutionary moment when prosperous and educated free black families were hoping to gain from the spread of liberty. In October 1813, at seventeen, she married a young and promising Norfolk free black, Colston Waring. They were, she remembered, "both very young, but bid fair to do well in life."

After a few years in Norfolk, Waring felt called to preach, and he moved his young family to Petersburg. Harriet lacked his assurance about this calling, but she and their children accompanied him. Waring became a trustee of Gillfield Baptist Church in Petersburg, and his work among the people of color there caused a revival of religion and a substantial number of converts. Soon he was approached by Petersburg friends to "go out and make an examination of the state of the Colony [Liberia], its prospects &c, as many were anxiously desiring to know the truth respecting it—and their adopting it as the home of themselves and their children depended on the report he might bring back."

After Waring traveled to Liberia and back in 1823, "people were daily flocking to our house" to hear his "highly favourable" report. Nearly one hundred free blacks from Petersburg arranged to go to Liberia with Waring and his family on the *Cyrus* in 1824. Again, Harriet Waring accompanied her husband on a religious pilgrimage, this time with the six children that had been born to them in the dozen years since their marriage. Once in Monrovia, the two youngest boys soon died of malarial fever. Four years later, another two children died of varied causes. In a decade in Liberia, Harriet and Colston Waring had four more children, and their oldest child, Susanna, married John N. Lewis, whose family had accompanied the Waring family from Petersburg in 1824.

Colston Waring had gone to Liberia as a missionary for the African Baptist Missionary Society of Petersburg, but its inability to sustain him financially meant that he had to become a commission merchant to support his family, although "he was not born a merchant, of which he was fully aware." After the death of Lott Cary in 1828 and after the colonial agent, Jehudi Ashmun, left the country, Waring was chosen as vice agent, in charge until the arrival of Ashmun's replacement. Waring also replaced Cary as pastor of Providence Baptist Church. This busy life ended in August 1834, when Waring died. Harriet was left "a widow with four small children." Fortunately, she noted, "my son-in-law, John N. Lewis, carries on the business in part that Mr. Waring conducted."[9]

Five years later, Harriet Waring married Nathaniel Brander, the Petersburg native who had sailed to Sierra Leone on the first ship in 1820. The ceremony was performed by a Norfolk native, Abraham Cheeseman, who must have known the Graves and Waring families in Norfolk. Nathaniel Brander had done well in Liberia, serving as vice agent—and then acting agent the next year. By 1843, he was a Supreme Court judge, she was a milliner, and they had had one child, Albert Brander, Harriet's eleventh child. Milliner was a higher status occupation among laboring women in America, and Mrs. Justice Brander could remain genteel while making and selling bonnets.

By this time, Harriet Waring Brander's other Virginia-born daughter, Jane Rose, had married Joseph Jenkins Roberts, once of Norfolk and Petersburg, who would become president of Liberia and the republic's most important statesman and ambassador. Conversely and typically for extended families, Charles Brander, apparently a brother of Nathaniel, who had been a ditcher (a ditch digger) in Petersburg, was now a stonemason in Liberia, and his wife was a whitewasher. Their son, James, had been convicted of grand larceny in 1841 and had served seven months in prison.[10] In such small communities as Liberia offered, family connections that included both high achievers and lawbreakers were bound to be common and commonly known.

The existence of the small colony and its modest port town, while of central importance to the ACS and the settlers, also could not be ignored in the nineteenth-century debate over African American identity. The fact that both African American colonizationists and their opponents used concepts of racial origins that blended science, history, and scripture as arguments for equality meant that, although most northern blacks remained deeply opposed to colonization, it was possible to employ those same arguments in favor of emigration. The most prominent black intellectual to do so was John Brown Russwurm, a native of Jamaica and a graduate of Bowdoin College in Maine, who became a journalist and cofounder in 1827 of *Freedom's Journal*, a New York weekly that was the first black newspaper in the United States. Unsympathetic to the ACS and Liberia at the outset, Russwurm gradually changed his view over a two-year period and emigrated to Liberia in 1829, amid severe criticism from angry northern free blacks who saw his emigration as an act of apostasy.[11]

Before he left the United States in 1829, Russwurm published an argument for black equality that drew creatively on the standard sources. "The Mutability of Human Affairs," published in *Freedom's Journal*, stressed that just as the black Egyptian and Ethiopian empires had fallen, so would the current European and American empires, and Africa might rise again. Russwurm changed the newer argument—that blacks were the descendants of Noah's cursed son, Ham—by making blacks descendants of Ham's nation-building sons. Russwurm, like other African American writers, found it very difficult to step outside the parameters of race to refute racism. Free blacks held to racial arguments drawn from history and scripture as proslavery arguments of black inferiority were popularized in the 1830s. Russwurm's arguments eventually convinced him that emigration outside the United States was the answer, while other black writers, especially David Walker, found reinforcement for their own views that white oppression must be confronted and overcome in the United States.[12]

In Liberia, Russwurm's superior education quickly found an outlet as the first superintendent of schools and then as editor of the *Liberia Herald*. Russwurm's experience in the politics of Liberia demonstrates the constant pressure by settlers for more autonomy and the factional political strategies that were worthy of urban Jacksonians in the same 1830s decade. As editor of the *Herald*, and probably inevitably, Russwurm became involved with these colonial factions. The newspaper came into existence when Charles Force, a white printer, came to Liberia on the *Vine* in 1826 with a printing press purchased with Boston donations. He managed to put out the first issue of the *Liberia Herald* before succumbing to disease at about the time that Jehudi Ashmun left the colony ill and returned to the United States to die.[13]

After Ashmun's death, the Board of Managers of the ACS sent out a series of agents to Liberia in the 1830s, none of whom lasted long enough to make any serious difference in the colony. As each left the colony, they ceded power to a leading settler as vice agent, at first appointed and later elected. Vice agents who held power in the 1820s and 1830s were Virginians Lott Cary, Colston M. Waring, James C. Barbour, Anthony D. Williams, Nathaniel Brander, and George McGill from Maryland. In this and other ways, the incremental power of the settlers grew, and emerging political factions clustered around the men who acted as agents and vice agents. Russwurm aligned himself with the ACS agents against their frequent rivals for power among the Monrovia merchants.[14]

The alliance between Russwurm and the ACS agents foundered in 1835 when, in a crisis over control of the judicial system, Russwurm sided with the colonists against the agent, the Reverend Joseph Pinney, who dismissed Russwurm as colonial secretary as well as editor of the *Liberia Herald*.[15] Hilary Teage was appointed editor in Russwurm's place, although Teage was aligned with the core opposition, the Virginia-born Monrovia merchants. Hilary Teage had lived in Sierra Leone with his parents, Colin and Frances Teage, for at least five years after their arrival in West Africa with fellow Richmond Baptist Lott Cary in 1821. On their return to the ACS settlement, Colin Teage served as a Baptist minister and merchant. Hilary Teage inherited his father's trading business and ministerial mantle in 1839 when his father died on board ship, returning from a trip to Virginia. The younger Teage also served as a consignment agent for British firms and traders as well as the editor of the *Liberia Herald*.[16]

Russwurm appealed his firing to the Board of Managers of the ACS, and the Reverend Pinney resigned as colonial agent. The next agent sent out was empowered to return Russwurm to the editorship, but he did not. Russwurm then ran against Petersburg native James C. Barbour for vice agent and won with a plurality, but the new ACS agent, Dr. Ezekiel Skinner, set the election aside and gave recaptured Africans the franchise before a second election. This time Barbour won, and the angry Russwurm then moved to the new colony of Maryland in Africa, a settlement at Cape Palmas about fifty miles south of Monrovia, where in 1836 he became governor, a position he held until his death in June 1851.[17]

Among the Monrovia merchant faction, no firm was more successful than Roberts, Colson, and Company, and their business practices sometimes drew envy and criticism. John B. Russwurm wrote to Rev. R. R. Gurley: "There has been considerable stir against the circulation of certain paper notes issued by Roberts & Co. and also a copper coin of the ostensible value of one cent issued by the same firm. The community are determined not to receive them." An ACS doctor railed against the same circulation of store notes as money, saying that the currency was backed by a firm of "the greatest swindlers and imposters that ever disgraced any country."[18] If the young Roberts was thought to be a bit grasping, it did not impede his financial and political progress in the colony.

Monrovia grew on Cape Mesurado because of its trade and government functions, but new arrivals were urged to journey on to the settlements of Caldwell and Millsburg on the St. Paul's River, where farmers were needed to develop the hoped-for agricultural economy. In time, many small villages, each with its own history and supporters, appeared on the coast and along the major rivers. Monrovia bore some resemblance to southern towns in the United States, but its rain-rutted dirt roads, luxuriant weedy growth, mildew and mold of the rainy season, and hard dry winds of the dry season seemed an exaggeration of any American climate. Still, the more optimistic saw the wide streets and attempts at dignified stone and brick buildings as more worthy of comment than the weather. Lack of money meant that urban planning went little further than unpaved broad avenues. In later decades, the agricultural region along the St. Paul's River became prosperous, and successful farmers built large houses along the river. In the 1850s, the new settlement of Robertsport, north of Monrovia at Grand Cape Mount, offered rows of evenly spaced white houses. These and other settlements remained small and, in the later nineteenth-century, became shabby from lack of upkeep.[19]

Although public buildings and all public works such as wharves and roads were seriously deficient in Monrovia, Liberia's governing class had elaborate homes, equipped with parlors that offered sofas, sideboards, and paintings. A young white woman, one of a party visiting President Roberts, described his parlor as containing folding doors, walls hung with oil portraits, a tapestry carpet, embroidered curtains, and numerous books and ornaments. At least one Liberian from Virginia was not impressed with the learning implied by the Victorian comforts obtained by President Roberts and his brothers, one an American-educated doctor and the other a leading minister. In a comment typical of the carping rivalries between leaders, John Day said of the cleric, "The great Dr. Roberts is a very fine man. He has a library of about 25 books. All of Gill's works. The rest trash. . . . Fortunate for Mr. Roberts he can't read them. If either of the big volumes has ever been opened I did not see the sign." But the display and style of the Roberts household, as conducted by Jane Rose Roberts, who was variously described as "a beautiful and interesting woman" and "a thorough lady," among other compliments, served the function of convincing visitors that the settlers had not lost any part of their civilized backgrounds.[20]

While settlers, agents, and the ACS Board of Managers contested for civil powers, the legal status of the Liberian colony remained uncertain and the U.S. Congress showed no interest in claiming Liberia as a colony. This lack of imperial oversight meant that all lines of responsibility were unclear. Could individual American states, such as Maryland, create colonies that did not acknowledge either American law or ACS contractual principles? When settler ventures collided with European trade patterns, what nations should be engaged in negotiations? How much self-government would settlers have? The first settler rebellion in Liberia, after only two years of settlement, brought colonists some political representation, and conditions in the colony frequently forced the ACS to make more appointments from the black leadership. In a first attempt at colonial consolidation, Hilary Teage, as secretary of commerce, in 1838, prepared the "Monrovia draft" of a constitution that limited citizenship to men of color and gave settlers final authority over policy. The ACS Board of Managers soon wrote their own draft constitution that differed chiefly in keeping the colonial governor as chief justice and final authority.[21]

The ACS Commonwealth Constitution of 1839 that merged the two documents united the settlements into a commonwealth administered by one government that shared authority between an appointed governor and an elected council. The proposal did not include the Mississippi and Maryland settlements. The Colonial Council agreed to all except the provision that gave the governor irrevocable veto power, and the ACS ceded the point. It would go into effect when a majority of settlers voted for it. Mississippi in Africa soon asked that Liberia take over its settlement at Sinoe, between Bassa Cove and Cape Palmas, and there was a formal union in 1841, but Maryland remained independent until 1857.[22]

The new Commonwealth of Liberia kept the current white ACS agent, Thomas Buchanan, as its governor until his death in 1841. After his death, Joseph Roberts, with whom he had worked closely as second in command, was appointed the first black governor of the colony. In the first years of the commonwealth, Buchanan and Roberts had seen attacking the slave trade as a central part of the Liberian mission in Africa. When slavers at

Joseph Jenkins Roberts left Petersburg for Liberia with his family in 1829. In the course of a long career, he held office in colonial Liberia, became a wealthy trader, was twice president of Liberia, and visited the United States with some frequency to promote Liberian emigration. On official visits to England, he negotiated for English recognition and support, and he sought always to extend Liberia's dominion on the land and off the coast. (Library of Congress)

Little Bassa refused to leave, Buchanan sent the militia on a successful expedition to destroy the barracoon, burn the villages involved, and pour out the slavers' rum. This operation, done as a Liberian commonwealth, attracted more international attention than had the many raids and forays by settlers against slave traders in the preceding decades.[23]

The most cynical opponent of African colonization could not deny that the colony of Liberia had been planted where it would inevitably have to confront the slave trade. This was the basis on which the Slave Trade Act of 1819 had granted money to the ACS — to make its colony a site for receiving and maintaining Africans rescued from the slave trade. Although the society had a larger view of its mission in Africa, it was necessarily diligent in its pursuit of slavers and in its attention to recaptive Africans. In the early decades, however, the Liberian colony was not asked to absorb many recaptives, in part because the American navy had a very modest fleet on the western coast of Africa and slavers frequently flew the American flag to avoid search by the British. As long as the American nation was divided, North and South, over slavery, national policy aimed at enforcing the ban on slave importations would be modified, if not dismantled, by southern congressional reluctance to support such enforcement.[24]

In the mid-1840s, an American naval officer described the manner in which slave ships slipped into and out of the coast: "The greatest hurry and anxiety prevails to clear the coast after a cargo is taken on board. A good look out is kept in the river for man of war boats and daily reports sent up from the coast in the vicinity of the river mouth where trusty per-

The daughter of Colston Waring of Petersburg, Jane Rose Roberts appeared ideally suited for her role as the wife of the first Liberian president. Frequently praised for her cultivated charm, she presided over social gatherings and traveled with Roberts on his many trips to the United States and England. In 1892, she traveled with Martha Ricks to be presented to Queen Victoria, the culmination of Ricks's desire but also the result of England's long involvement with the Liberian republic. (Library of Congress)

sons, in the employ of Baracoon owners are always stationed in readiness to pilot vessels up the river and warn the parties from any danger of cruisers. They either then watch [for] some favorable moment when no vessels are cruising off, or make sail on the darkest and stormiest nights to clear the coast."[25]

The colonial agents and the settlers made real efforts to eliminate the slave trade, both because they truly opposed it and also because the slave trading chiefs were the ones most likely to seek their destruction. Away from the coast, Liberia's interior settlements were threatened by chiefs who resented the interruption of their lucrative trade in slaves or by the warriors attached to trade caravans.[26] Liberian settlers complained of "the establishment of slave factories within the limits of the colony" and that "our trade is interrupted on the beach to please our foes, the slavers." For decades, the slave trade was carried on in sight of Liberia's coastal settlements. There were slave factories or barracoons in every direction, especially to the north of Monrovia at Gallinas and Cape Mount. Clashes with the slave trade took place in settler raids, slaver attacks on settlements, or in sea chases. The United States flag was flown by slave ships of many countries because its display meant that only a United States cruiser could board and search. But some slave ships and traders were indeed American. They left the United States with proper paper and cargo and then took on slaves in Africa. At this point, the Spanish or Portuguese "passengers" became the crew and took charge of the vessel.[27]

The sensationalized but revealing autobiography of one famous slaver tells much about the slave trade off the Liberian coast and the efforts of the skimpy American fleet and the British fleet, the latter handicapped by its inability to board vessels with American flags, to interrupt slavers. Theodore Canot had lost one cargo of wretched Africans too many, because he was pursued and could find no port to put in for supplies, and he gave up the slave trade. Always having been careful to maintain good relations with the Liberians, he began farming operations at Cape Mount, under the Liberian government. But he did not prosper, and within a few years he began to allow slavers to use his land as a beachhead, and soon he was selling them supplies and then slaves. Then came a British raid on Canot's property and his arrest by the Americans. He was transported to New York, and he lost or abandoned all his possessions, his family, and his business partners. Fleeing creditors and various indictments, he was eking out a bare existence near the Baltimore docks in 1854.

There he encountered James Hall, an agent of the Maryland Colonization Society, whom he had met when Hall was engaged in setting up Maryland in Liberia at Cape Palmas. Ever courteous, Canot had provided small favors to the colonists. Now Hall could aid him and the cause of African colonization at the same time. Hall encouraged Canot to tell his story to Brantz Mayer, a prominent journalist and founder of the Maryland Historical Society. One goal was to promote Liberia and describe that nation's opposition to the slave trade. The other goal was to make money, and the memoir employed many of the sensationalist strategies of the day in order to attract a popular audience. In his long and rambling narrative, crammed with exotic horrors, the brutality of the illegal slave trade is made apparent.

Canot describes an Africa long open to adventurers and entrepreneurs from many parts of the globe and containing its own multitude of differences. Large and imposing castles, such as Goree, slave pens or barracoons at New Sestros or Gallinas, and simple ropes and chains near the beach held Africans captive until they were sold. Bribes, flattery, and much negotiation were involved in trading gold, cloth, swords, gunpowder, rum, and other products for the ivory and slaves of the interior. Cuba and the Key West area were the destinations for most slave vessels in this era when the trade was illegal. Although Canot did describe the efforts of the Liberians to close down slave factories and chase away slave ships, he could not resist bragging of outwitting the Liberians and describing the times his vessels tricked or escaped them.

The slave factories were run by such men as Mongo John Ormond, mulatto sons of European traders and African women, who had often been educated in Europe. When Mongo John committed suicide in 1828, Canot, who had served in several navies and been on the fringes of the slave trade as a bookkeeper, took over part of his trade, setting up his factory at New Sestros. It was almost required that Canot write about his long visit to Mongo John Ormond's seraglio and the special attention he received from "Esther, the quarteronne." He described murders, an auto-de-fé, and the particularly lurid cannibalistic practices of an African chief named Jenken.[28] Canot did not mention Rosaline Cyrus, the Liberian woman whom he had taken as his mistress and deserted when he left New Sestros. Cyrus, a young woman from Georgia, had one child when she arrived in Liberia in 1835. By 1838, according to colonial governor Buchanan, Canot had "formed an intimacy" with her and "took her away with him as a mistress." Later, two of her sisters, a brother, and a maid had been transported to Canot in New Sestros by a British sea captain to "share in the munificence of his paramour." Rosaline Canot, as she identified herself, had at least one child with Canot, and, when his munificence ended, she bought a small house in Monrovia where she lived until her death.[29]

Groups such as the Bassa, Kru, and Glebo, long dominant in the role of trade middlemen, were particularly displeased with the settlers' disruption of their trade and efforts to usurp it. The settlers sought to establish their own trade connections between the interior and the coast, and they were not willing to pay fees and tolls to any group. In 1828, Reuben Dongey, a part–American Indian tanner from Richmond, and three others traveled far inland to Bopolu, the center of the Condo confederacy that included the Mandingo traders. There the powerful leader Sao Bosu joined with the settlers in the hope of dominating trade from Bopolu to the coast. This was galling to many African tradesmen operating in the interior out of Sierra Leone, and to British merchant vessels that were asked to pay for docking and trading that they had formerly done without duties.

To add to their injuries, Governor Buchanan, in the early 1840s, sought to extend Liberian sovereignty from Cape Mount to Cape Palmas. To further limit the coastal slave trade, Buchanan permitted only two ports of entry—Monrovia and Bassa Cove. Two men were appointed as directors of Public Works and Commercial Operations to oversee trade—at Monrovia, Joseph Roberts, and at Bassa Cove, Louis Sheridan from North Carolina.[30] This restriction to two ports annoyed British traders, who also objected to paying customs duties, instead of bribes, called "dash." Despite trader pleas, Britain at first refused to interfere. But trade rivalries ultimately brought conflict and confrontation between Britain and Liberia. Later, Liberians realized that although England and France had given diplomatic recognition to Liberia long before the United States did, European diplomacy had an interest in maintaining Liberia as a minor trade partner, one neither attached to the United States nor powerful in its own right.

As Liberian merchants expanded down the coast and competed with British traders, the British inquired of the United States as to the status of Liberia. The American government disclaimed all responsibility for the colony, and it became clear that British and other foreign merchants were not willing to pay duties and docking fees to a benevolent society. There was some nervous bickering between the ACS and the Liberian Council over who had first suggested sovereignty and who should, therefore, take responsibility, but it was clear to both parties that lack of sovereignty hurt Liberia commercially and diplomatically, as well as politically.[31] The Liberian Council determined to issue a declaration of independence and called a constitutional convention. Hilary Teage wrote the Declaration of Independence, purposely modeling it on the American version.[32]

Hilary Teage played an active political role in the decade that led up to Liberia becoming a republic. Never happy with the ACS and its inability to provide financial or military support for Liberia, Teage, as early as 1841, explored the possibility of uniting Liberia with Sierra Leone under the British government. His letter to William Fergusson, lieutenant governor of Sierra Leone, was an accurate assessment of Liberia's position and an indication of what Teague's state of mind would be when he wrote the Liberian Declaration of Independence: "You are probably aware of the nature of our relations with the people of the United States. With them as a nation we have nothing to do. From the first the Government disowned us, and up to this hour disclaims all political connexion. With a few American citizens confederated under the title of the American Colonization Society, we hold a temporary and conditional relation. . . . Our relations are contingent and will be de facto dissolved by the Society's failing to perform its stipulations." He asked if the British would support such a dissolution. Fergusson responded politely but without encouragement, suggesting to his superior in London that such a merger would bring unwelcome "Republican ideas" to Sierra Leone.[33]

Delegates to a constitutional convention called in 1847 were predominantly early settlers, and they brought to their deliberations the same awareness of American political ideals that Hilary Teage had reflected in the Declaration of Independence. One vexing question at the constitutional convention was the issue that had caused the delegates to leave the United States in the first place: Who is a citizen? Unlike the United States in the 1840s and 1850s, where the answer was increasingly based on race, Liberian qualifications for citizenship were based on meeting measurable settler cultural standards. In the colonial era, Liberian citizenship was a privilege, earned by "responsible" conduct, as verified by three disinterested citizens. A responsible citizen was a homeowner who, over at least three years, had consistently attended church services, dressed in Western clothes, and cultivated two acres. The Constitution of 1847 restricted citizenship to black male Liberians who owned real estate. Indigenous people were not considered to be citizens, in part because many groups were seen as "nations" in their own right, separate entities living within and without the physical bounds of the republic and able to negotiate treaties. In theory, however, individual Gola or Vai, for example, who converted to Christianity and adopted a Westernized life could become citizens.[34]

In search of such competent citizen-emigrants, the barque *Nehemiah Rich* left Monrovia for the United States in the next year, carrying Harriet Waring's son-in-law, President Joseph Roberts, her daughter, Jane Rose Roberts, and her granddaughter. They were accompanied by Harriet's other daughter, Susanna Lewis. Also in the party were other Virginians and Zion and Martha Harris, a prosperous couple originally from Tennessee. The purpose of their trip was to conduct business, visit major cities, promote Liberia, and counteract negative statements made by other returnees.[35] This was not the first trip to the United States for Roberts. He had returned in 1833 and in 1841 on Liberian business, visiting major cities. But on this trip, as the elected African American president of Liberia, he was accompanied by more than a dozen other Liberian citizens.[36]

Roberts, along with James Sprigg Payne, Beverly Wilson, and Anthony Russell, spoke to full houses in New York City churches, where the Liberians argued that the "founding of the [Liberian] republic had done more for the regeneration and manumission [of African Americans] than any other agency adopted." After listening to Roberts speak in Rev. Jacobus's church in Brooklyn, the white reporter for the *New York Recorder* wrote: "We saw the African race under a new aspect. . . . The tone of conscious inferiority and servility, so universally and so naturally characteristic of the race here, had given place to a manly bearing which at once commanded respect."[37] Probably that reporter had never heard black abolitionists, such as Frederick Douglass, speak. For black male abolitionists, too, a commanding presence was as important as any words they might speak to an audience. In projecting an aura of "manliness," the Liberians were aided by the fact that their saga of exploration, settlement, and republican institutions was in harmony with the doctrine of manifest destiny so popular in the United States during the 1840s.

The bearing that made such a deep impression on those they visited may have contributed to the Liberians' ability to travel between northern and southern cities with more freedom than American free blacks. Their Liberian nationality sometimes meant they were less subject to the restrictions on free blacks entering Virginia. Or their being accompanied by whites may have made other whites hesitant to accost them. Either way, Liberians disrupted American categories, and they felt validated in their choice to leave the United States and take up citizenship in their own African republic. From the United States, in this 1848 trip, the Liberians traveled on to England, where Roberts negotiated a treaty with the British and may have placed his daughter in school. Again in 1852 and 1856, Roberts visited England and the United States on official business that included rallying support for Liberia.[38]

Roberts and other founders of Liberia were effective ambassadors for the country, and indeed they needed all the skills they could muster because of the pervasive hostility toward the ACS found among the great majority of northern free blacks. Among their detractors, few were more hostile than Martin Delany, born in Charles Town, Jefferson County, Virginia. He had left that area for Pennsylvania as a boy of ten, just as Jefferson County was organizing three or more colonization auxiliaries. Whether Delany remembered some of the respectable colonizationist gentlemen of

Jefferson County as slaveholders whose support for colonization was based on fear of runaways and free blacks is speculation. But Delany was outspoken in his contempt for the ACS and Liberia, describing Liberia as "that miserable hovel of emancipated and superannuated slaves, and deceived colored freemen, controlled by the intrigues of a conclave of upstart colored hirelings of the slave power of the United States."[39]

Delany, who had edited a newspaper in Pittsburgh and trained as a physician before working with Frederick Douglass on the *North Star* newspaper, was a prominent black nationalist leader who sought emigration sites in the years between the passage of the Fugitive Slave Act in 1850 and the Emancipation Proclamation in 1862. But even when considering African colonization, Delany scorned association with the ACS and continued to heap insults on Liberia and its leadership, especially President Roberts.[40] Delany's critique of Liberia in 1854 included claims that the whole nation was daily flooded by the ocean, that the Liberians practiced the slavery that most of them had known in the South, and that the missionaries were rum-dealing hypocrites who regularly betrayed the indigenous people.[41] Within five years, Delany and Robert Campbell, tenuously representing black emigration organizations, traveled to West Africa to explore the possibility of a colony on the Niger River, pointedly ignoring Liberia as a site.[42]

Their itinerary took them first to Cape Mount, then to Monrovia for almost a month, and then to Cape Palmas for an equal amount of time. Although they were well aware of his attacks, Delany was received cordially by the Liberians and was asked to lecture to them on conditions and prospects for blacks in the United States. His experiences in Liberia caused him to modify considerably his earlier assessment. Although he continued to want a separate colony, he abandoned his view that the Liberians were mere tools of the white ACS. Now he saw them as equally capable of regenerating Africa. He wrote a survey of Liberia's climate, soil, products, and settler accomplishments, which might have been done by the most ardent colonizationist.[43]

Some free black leaders looked at Liberia with more interest in the 1850s, but it was a disappointment to Liberians that the republic was not diplomatically recognized by the United States until fifteen more years had passed, although they understood that this was connected to ever-growing sectional tensions and suspicions. In Government House, Monrovia, in 1855, Roberts was bitter but not entirely surprised that men of color in Liberia had demonstrated every quality that Americans valued, and yet they were not recognized as men or Liberia as a nation. He wrote: "With regard to the acknowledgment of the independence of Liberia by the

United State Government, it may be 'some of these days': but I have ceased to cherish the hope that it will be accomplished in my day. Why should European nations be more magnanimous than enlightened America? Oh, you plead the peculiar institution! — Well be it so. Heaven is just."[44]

Liberians hoped, at least, that their independence would encourage emigration. Their African history seemed to them to be a triumphal story — from oppression and enslavement to the establishment of a republic in one generation — while their fellow Africans in America seemed to have progressed little, if at all. One earnest Liberian queried, "All along the free colored people in the U. States, have refused to come and live in Liberia, because it was under the control of your Society. Can you tell me if their views are now changed? I learn from some of our gentlemen who lately visited the U. States, that the condition of the colored people in the free states, is very little removed from that of the people in the Southern states. How . . . can [they] remain in so degraded a state?"[45] Liberians had a perennial hope that more educated free blacks would emigrate, and they repeatedly asked the ACS to try harder to find qualified emigrants. One recent and successful emigrant wrote: "I hope the Society will particularly regard the sending to Liberia *now* a due proportion of immigrants of *the proper class*. We are politically and socially in a transition state, hence a disproportion of *improper immigrants* would greatly retard, instead of enhance, our national interests."[46]

Liberians faced true dilemmas in the decades after their independence. They lacked the capital and labor to become competitive in commerce or, in the 1880s, to dissuade the English and French from carving at their boundaries as Europe colonized Africa. But the greatest dilemma was the status of ethnic groups in Liberia, who generally showed little interest in Christianity and Western civilization. Should the Liberian government impose conversion and Western standards? They were hardly capable of doing so. Liberians knew it was in their best interest to expand their citizenry but were unwilling to consciously lower their standards. The Liberian national narrative was one in which Christianized African Americans returned to Africa with all the benefits of civilization. The ships from America that landed on the West African coast in the 1820s were a patriotic catechism for Liberians. The *Elizabeth*, the *Nautilus*, the *Oswego*, the *Cyrus*, the *Vine*, the *Indian Chief*, the *Doris*, the *Harriet*, the *James Perkins* — these and others told the story of the construction of the republic. The heroic acts enshrined in narrative consisted almost equally of resistance to the indigenous Africans and resistance to the Board of Managers of the ACS.

"Thatched huts have given place to commodious brick or stone buildings, both in Monrovia and on the banks of the St. Paul. The tenants live happy under their own vine and fig tree, or, literally true, under banana and plantain, and wondering why our friends in the United States think us foolish for fleeing from contempt in America to respectability in Africa. . . . Let those who think best stay in America and talk and we, who are otherwise minded, stay out here and act and at the end of the nineteenth century, it will be seen who have operated to the greater advantage in putting down prejudice."[47] This triumphal tale was framed around events in the United States, and it was by events in the United States that Liberians continued to measure themselves. James Sprigg Payne, the Richmond-born Methodist minister who became the fourth president of Liberia, declaimed, "O Africa, rise, shine, for the glory of the Lord is upon thee. Africa is dark. . . . But I can see a better day, when there will be telegraphs and railroads from tribe to tribe, and nation to nation; when fetish religion will be changed for Christianity; and a [telegraph] station will be planted on Lover's Rock where Liberia's sons and daughters will get messages from proud America."[48]

But proud America sent few messages in any form, and Martha Erskine Harris Ricks was among those who hoped for a closer alliance with Great Britain when she made a visual contribution to the construction of Liberian history. Married first to Zion Harris, she and her husband traveled from Clay-Ashland in Liberia to the United States with the Roberts entourage in 1848 and may have been part of the continuation of the journey to England where the Liberians were well received. After Zion Harris's death, she married Henry Ricks. An industrious farm woman who raised turkeys, ducks, and sheep, she won a prize for her stockings, made of Liberian cotton silk, at an 1858 agricultural fair.[49] Deeply invested in Liberia and her family's prosperity there, she was an English partisan who was particularly admiring of Queen Victoria. For some twenty-five years, she worked on an intricate cotton silk quilt depicting a Liberian coffee tree in bloom that she hoped to present to the queen.[50] The quilt design had over 300 pointed green leaves with bright red coffee berries, all hand appliquéd onto a white background with a center tree trunk.

In 1892, Martha Erskine Ricks accompanied Jane Rose Roberts, the elderly widow of Joseph Roberts and the daughter of Colston Waring, to England and, through the aid of Liberian ambassador Edward Blyden, gained an audience with Queen Victoria, presenting her with the quilt at Windsor Castle. It appeared to be an acknowledgment of Liberia's status as a nation among nations. And it was surely a personal triumph for the two elderly black women, born in Virginia and Tennessee, who had advanced so conspicuously in Liberia. But it was among the last public acts of the founding generations. The arc of progress peaked in the 1890s, and the twentieth century produced little but tired rhetoric to inspire pride. It was the writings and careers of such men as Ambassador Blyden that would move assessment of Africa and its diaspora away from American and European standards of measurement.[51]

Almost fifty years earlier, when Joseph Roberts became Liberia's first president, he spoke in his inaugural address of the first African American colonists in Liberia as "a mere handful of isolated Christian pilgrims, in pursuit of civil and religious liberty, surrounded by savage and warlike tribes bent on their ruin and total annihilation." Liberia's existence was threatened both internally and externally, and it was in the interests of leaders in the colony and republic to emphasize these threats in order to maintain unity among fractious settlers of varied backgrounds. This echo of the American origins myth might have been a transitional national identity under some historic circumstances, but, cut off from the main currents of African American postemancipation thought and without the resources for independent economic development, Liberians, after the first two generations of American settlement, made only modest adjustments to their national myth and continued to interpret their history though the prism of antebellum America.[52]

Nine

Civil War to White City

I N PARIS, IN THE LATE 1850S, two men who knew a great
deal about Liberia may have passed each other in the en-
virons of the Luxembourg Gardens, near their residences.
Theophile Conneau, restored to his birth name and protected by his brother, who was court physician to Napoleon III,
had recently retired from a modest and brief position as collec-
tor of the port of Noumea in New Caledonia. With him was his
young American wife, the former Elisa McKinley of Philadelphia.
A small, smartly dressed man, he charmed the friends of his older
brother, Dr. Henri Conneau, with his discreetly censored stories
of the slave trade and the African interior—stories with which
he had extracted drinks from Brantz Mayer in Baltimore several
years earlier.

Conneau's charm was not as dissipated as his body, and he had
managed to court an American girl of good family with his hints
of an exotic world not imagined in Philadelphia. By the time that
the book he dictated to Mayer, *Memoirs of a Slave Trader*, appeared
in print, Conneau had once again moved on, taking his new wife
with him. He died in Paris of a heart attack in 1860 while scheming to be appointed the civil governor of New Caledonia. His
young wife, who perhaps thought twice about returning to Philadelphia on the eve of the Civil War as the widow of a notorious
slave trader, attached herself to the Empress Eugenie and outlived
her husband by seventy-two years.[1]

There was another man in Paris in those days, aging and slight
of build, whose life had also long centered on the African slave
trade and Liberia. Charles Fenton Mercer, the congressional
founder of the American Colonization Society and the man who
had worked obsessively to tie American suppression of the slave
trade to the finances of the Liberian colony, could be said to have
been the source of many of Conneau's slaving losses. Mercer had

fared no better among American politicians than Conneau had among the West African slavers. It had been twenty years since Mercer had resigned from his seat in a sectionally divided Congress to work first in a bank in Tallahassee and then in real estate in Texas, to travel in Europe, and now to linger on in Paris, the city that had so excited him as a youth.

Mercer knew he should return to the United States. But there were excellent reasons not to do so, the most excellent of which was the fact that, once in the United States, he would never leave it again. The sore in his mouth that would not heal would have to be doctored. He would have to go back to Virginia where his heroes were dead and his friends were attacked by North and South. His old colleague, Meade, had been labeled "satanic" by William Lloyd Garrison and criticized by the *Petersburg Democrat* as encouraging insurrection among slaves.[2] Mercer wrote a long letter to his niece about the history of the Mercer family in Virginia but stayed on in Paris, visiting the leading reformers of the day. In time he was forced to leave the contemplative peace of Paris for the agitations of Virginia, where his mouth cancer took his life in 1858.

Mercer, the evangelical Christian and advocate of American internal improvements, still envisioned an Africa that would save America from slavery for the sake of white Americans. This Africa, elevated above savagery and heathenism, was dotted with little republics, mission stations, farms, and small factories, all directed by the most advanced free blacks and ex-slaves from the United States. Why could not his fellow citizens accept the genius in this vision, the natural fit with the most advanced ideas of progress? His friends in Paris never ceased to marvel at this example of enlightened and benevolent philosophy.

The Liberian leadership held this view. They expected hundreds of thousands of emigrants from the United States when the course of the American Civil War made diplomatic recognition of Liberia and the Emancipation Proclamation expedient. There were other hopeful portents, viewed from Liberia. In order to make emancipation acceptable, President Lincoln offered financial compensation to slaveholders not in rebellion and suggested that the American government might sponsor emigration for those freedmen willing to go to Africa, Central America, or the Caribbean. But delegations of African Americans told Lincoln that they were not interested in Liberia, and he was forced to abandon that plan. The other destinations failed to gain support or present a plan for settlement that could be enacted. It was up to the ACS or the freedmen themselves to sponsor postwar emigration.[3]

A few months after the end of the Civil War, 172 members of the Lynchburg Emigration Society, a black organization, with a Liberian from Albemarle County acting as their agent, left Lynchburg for Careysburg in Liberia on the *H. P. Russell*. Their well-organized exodus suggests that planning had begun before or during the Civil War and that they had conferred with Virginia emigrants in Liberia. The claims made in 1860 by free black Washington Copeland that he was responsible for the many Lynchburg emigrants in the antebellum era suggest that African Americans had played such roles in Virginia before the Civil War and continued to do so.[4] This was to be the last group from Virginia. Post-Reconstruction migration and inquiries came primarily from South Carolina, Arkansas, and Texas, places where freedmen were experiencing deepening poverty and a violent backlash to Reconstruction.[5] Emigration to Liberia was no longer of interest to black Virginians, possibly because they could emigrate north or west more easily than could freedmen from the Lower South. But perhaps more likely was the nature of post-Reconstruction politics in Virginia, in which the black vote was an important factor in politics, especially in the third-party racial alliance that gained control of the state in the 1880s. African Americans were not truly excluded from political participation until the adoption of the 1902 Virginia constitution.[6]

But as an example of a black republic, Liberia after the Civil War was again a malleable symbol for Virginians, and strange reversals of opinion took place in the postwar political climate. The Petersburg press, which had frequently pronounced Liberia a failure in the 1850s, now took a certain pride in that country once the Civil War ended. It noticed when Joseph Jenkins Roberts visited Petersburg again in February 1869 and delivered an address at the Union Street Methodist Church, following his address in Washington to the fifty-second annual meeting of the American Colonization Society.[7] In an attack on African American suffrage in Reconstruction Virginia, the *Petersburg Index and Appeal* took satisfaction in pointing out that in Liberia only "qualified suffrage exists, whereas in America the most ignorant negroes [are] holding political positions."[8]

In another reversal, in the autumn of 1865 a woman who identified herself as "Richmonia Richards" gave an address to a large audience at the Abyssinian Baptist Church in New York City. She praised the accomplishments of African American emigrants in Liberia, the climate of West Africa, and the cultures of certain indigenous groups, such as the Mandingoes. The woman was, in fact, Mary Jane Richards, the young Richmond woman whom Elizabeth Van Lew had sent to Liberia and then brought back when

Richards was unhappy. It was fortunate for the Union cause in the Civil War that Richards returned from Liberia, because she served an important function, evidence suggests, as a spy for the Union and as part of the Richmond-based spy system operating from Van Lew's household.[9] In her October 1865 address, Richards disguised some aspects of her recent activities, perhaps because full disclosure would have endangered persons still living in Virginia.

The experience of the Civil War and emancipation had modified Richards's earlier unhappy view of Liberia. Richards now made a case for full citizenship and equality for African Americans by offering both Liberians and ethnic Africans as models of black capability. She pointed out that Mandingoes "never drink, lie, nor steal and have a religion based upon these principles." Described as "sarcastic" and "humourous" by a reporter for the *Anglo-African*, she cautioned her audience that New York City blacks paid too much attention to clothing styles, "the only condition of admission to social circles here," and urged young people to "turn your attention to the education and adornment of your mind."[10]

At the moment in 1865 when Richards urged emulation of both Liberians and Africans, the future of the African republic appeared modestly hopeful. It was not yet apparent how few African Americans would end up leaving the United States for Liberia in the postwar period. During the Civil War, the United States bought coffee and sugar from Liberia, encouraging farmers to think they had found their cash crop and to hope that palm oil, camwood, and various spices might also increase in market value. Liberian goals in the late 1860s were to increase trade internationally and into the interior, as well as extending political control and more settlements into those regions.

But in the decades after the Civil War, the United States soon turned to Cuban sugar and Brazilian coffee. In this case, as in that of other products, Liberia lacked economies of scale both in production and in shipping. Liberia's staple crop production and extractive industries could not compete in the world trade without capital or industrialized trading partners. A few years after the Civil War, Liberia began to have trade conflicts with Britain that presaged European colonization of Africa in the 1880s and further determined Liberia's destiny as a minor player in an international commercial world. Liberian seizure of a British ship in 1869 over trading rights led to a British-imposed indemnity on Liberia. A British loan to pay off the indemnity was acquired at such usurious rates that it brought down the government of President Edward Roye in 1871, and the nation never recovered from that indebtedness. The aged John N. Lewis, as secretary of state, was sentenced to death for "treason" for his part in the loan ne-gotiations and was saved only by a pardon from his brother-in-law, Joseph Roberts, when Roberts again became president.[11]

The disastrous British loan and the management of the loan money was only part of Roye's undoing. Roye represented the Whig Party, a col-lection of upriver farmers, recent emigrants, and recaptured Africans or-ganized in Clay-Ashland in 1860. They were generally in opposition to the Republican Party, made up of merchants and early settlers and established in the 1840s, which had dominated Liberian politics and included most prominent Virginians. Part of the Whig campaign against the Republican merchant elite, many of whom were mulatto, was an attack on them as "mongrels" who were genetically unstable and unable to govern or even survive in Liberia. This particular form of eugenics had some appeal to darker-skinned voters, especially those who resented the virtual monopoly of commerce and government that the Republicans had exercised. Roye believed he could not make the sweeping changes necessary to integrate education and politics in one two-year term and tried to extend his presi-dency to four years. It was when Roye attempted to prohibit the scheduled presidential elections that he was deposed by force in Monrovia.[12]

When Joseph Roberts was again elected president, after the failed Roye presidency, he traveled to England in an effort to renegotiate the terms of the loan, as well as to settle a boundary dispute. Roberts's final trip to England was essentially a failure. He was unable to reach an agreement on the boundary question, and he could not get significantly better terms for the loan. Roberts turned his office over to James Sprigg Payne in January 1876, and he died on February 24 of that year. Republican Party rule did not long survive Roberts. Struggles for power in the tumultuous 1870s led to the long victory of the True Whig Party, made up of West Indians, St. Paul's River settlers, and others who resented the Monrovian dominance. The True Whig Party had control of the presidency from 1884 until the Liberian coup of 1980.[13]

Within the United States, a few African American leaders in the 1890s turned to emigration as the answer to the desperate economic and civil plight of many freedmen. Bishop Henry M. Turner of the African Method-ist Episcopal Church, a primary advocate of African emigration, returned from trips to Liberia in 1892 and 1893 convinced that African Americans needed to leave the United States. In the early 1890s, African American newspapers devoted much space to the debate over emigration, and in the midst of this debate, the Liberian republic set up its exhibit at the World's Columbian Exposition in Chicago in 1893.[14]

The exposition was designed to commemorate the 400th anniversary of Columbus's arrival in the New World and to celebrate American nationalism, imperial reach, and consumer goods production. The fair was divided into a Midway Plaisance, of exoticized attractions and popular amusements, and the great Court of Honor, known nationally as the White City, so named for the construction material used to quickly erect and take down replicas of American historic icons in the Court. The Midway was the exposition's most remarkable feature, combining the then-current ideas of evolutionary principles with entertainment on a broad mile-long walkway that led to the White City. Along the route had been built representations of medieval villages, mosques, pagodas, and German and Irish villages; the dwellings of South Sea Islanders, the Javanese, the Egyptians, the Bedouins, and the Indians; and the rude huts of those considered truly primitive.

In each representation were "natives" of those regions, and the dwellings were positioned according to their assigned level of civilization, with the Teutonic and Celtic races nearest the White City, followed by Mohammedans and Asians, and finally by the Africans and the North American Indians.[15] This ethnographic hierarchy reinforced the Great Court or White City as the utopian pinnacle of civilization by projecting ignorance and barbarity on darker-skinned peoples. The double message of the fair's supposed scientific categorization was that darker people must be tutored in order to progress to American standards, but also that their degraded position just might be as innate and permanent as their shade of color.[16]

Not incidentally, the lack of material and moral advancement of the dark-skinned primitives, as the exposition presented it, was an excellent argument for continued racial control and segregation in the United States. African Americans had no part in planning the design or themes of the American exhibits, and their contributions had to be approved by an all-white committee. These "Negro departments" within the fair exalted blacks only as industrial workers in the New South. Many African Americans understood that the fair's cultural representations of Africans and African Americans would give support to those who wanted to limit black ambitions, and they rejected the implications of the exposition. Leaders such as Frederick Douglass and Ida B. Wells collaborated on a pamphlet entitled *The Reason Why the Colored American Is Not in the World's Columbian Exposition.*[17]

There were clear echoes in the exposition of the early-nineteenth-century ACS message that the American republic was a white republic. A separate-but-equal republic was a doctrine that the Supreme Court would soon make into national law as separate-but-equal facilities in one republic. But from the Liberians' perspective, though disappointed in the lack of emigrants after the Civil War and under increasing pressure from European imperialism, they had succeeded in proving their abilities. At century's end, they were still insisting that American identity was based on culture, not race, and this was the theme of their exhibit. The Liberians were able to structure their exhibit without exposition supervision, and they managed to be in harmony with the general theme of Western civilization as the highest achievement of man even as they insisted that this civilization was not linked to race.

The Liberian exhibit displayed trade goods and agricultural products of the indigenous peoples, along with subsequent attempts at cash crops. Ivory, coffee, camwood, and animal skins were displayed along with Liberian rubber, palm oil and kernels, and cocoa. Relics of the slave trade reminded visitors of Liberia's role in combating it. Palm leaf and bamboo huts were placed next to American-style settler homes to illustrate Liberia's progress. Westernized Vai at the exhibition were of less interest than the exotic living tableaux of natives placed in their re-created site. Inevitably, there were photographic images of stiffly posed "native" families and bare-breasted maidens, who usually stare straight at the camera even as they are posed provocatively by photographers in studio portraits. Such photographs show the extent to which simply placing the "country people," as the Liberians called them, on the Midway made them exotic. Their treatment illustrates the extent to which neither Liberians nor African Americans could control the public presentation of their lives and histories. Still, Liberia was honored with its own day at the fair, July 26, 1893, the forty-seventh anniversary of its independence, and newspapers praised the intelligent and cultivated young Liberian who was the spokesman for the exhibit.[18]

The Liberian exhibit, which sought to blend seamlessly into a narrative of progress, was subtly made exotic and distant by the themes of the exposition, but more direct misrepresentation happened to Martha Ricks's quilt. Brought to the exposition and displayed by the British, its later fate is unknown. A quilt that looks very similar, reportedly commissioned of Martha Ricks by Bishop Turner, was displayed at the 1896 Atlanta Exposition and later recorded in a photograph that shows it among items labeled "Uncivilized Africans Exhibits: Hands Off." That Martha Ricks, the very model of an industrious Victorian woman as well as an artist, could have her quilt clustered with the work of unknown primitive artists in Africa illustrates how difficult it was for Liberians to overcome the cultural assumptions of Americans, as well as the racial stereotypes.[19]

Martha Ricks is said to have made, at the request of African Methodist Episcopal bishop Henry Turner, a second copy of the coffee tree quilt that she presented to Queen Victoria. The first was exhibited by the British at the 1893 World's Columbian Exposition. This image was taken at the 1896 Atlanta Exposition, where it was placed among the "uncivilized Africans" exhibits. (Reproduced from Kyra Hicks, *Black Threads* [Jefferson, N.C.: McFarland, 2003])

The exposition, with its hierarchy of Midway ethnological villages and its representations from Liberia, provided a context for the Congress on Africa that met for a week during the fair and brought together black and white intellectuals, including Liberians, to discuss Africa's past and future. An important aspect of the seven days of meetings was the debate over African American emigration to Liberia, even as the outlines of America's twentieth-century racial policies became apparent. But slavery was ended, and the African colonization effort that had seemed important enough to warrant vituperative attacks in the antebellum era was now only an interesting footnote in history and a distraction to racial progress in the United States for most African Americans and their supporters.[20]

For their part, Liberians did not easily modify the standards of the early-nineteenth-century world they had created. There is no doubt that they were proud of their accomplishments, but the Columbian Exposition demonstrated the internal contradictions in the African republic. Most of the indigenous inhabitants of Liberia were still outside the constitutional covenant, based on cultural grounds that acted almost as strongly as racial proscriptions to keep them economically, politically, and socially marginal. The settler belief continued to be that Africans must be brought up to settler standards in order to be citizens and that citizenship was based on achieved status, not ethnicity. Modest adjustments in that policy brought some token improvements in the status of the indigenous inhabitants and conferred limited voting rights in the legislature. But these modifications were never sufficient to shift power from the settler Liberians.[21] The marginalization of the majority indigenous groups encouraged Liberian citizens to continue to exaggerate their attachments to the United States in clothing, rhetoric, public ceremonies, and religious services. By the turn of the twentieth century, the isolated republic was still maintaining the values and attitudes of a bygone America, and it appeared a trifle curious and quaint to visitors.[22]

Edward Blyden, a Liberian intellectual of West Indian origins, assessed the failed mission of Liberia as based on the fact that the republic did not develop an independent set of beliefs and aspirations suitable to Africa and continued to believe that everything American was superior, even as the negative results of such thinking became apparent. This explained the second failure: that the African republic did not incorporate Africans into Liberian society and political systems.[23] Blyden was perhaps too severe on the early settlers, for his own political reasons. In reality, the settlers had picked and chosen those parts of the American experience that worked for them and had never been passive recipients of ACS direction. Critical of the ACS and the American government in both official and private letters, they had consistently petitioned or confronted the ACS Board of Managers and its agents for more autonomy from the earliest years of settlement. Their definition of "citizen" was one based on achievement, as they understood achievement. However hierarchical, it was nominally available to native Africans as well as to settlers. The theory was exemplary, but the results remained minimal even over generations, because the act of incor-

The Vai people were centered near Cape Mount, in what became northwestern Liberia and southwestern Sierra Leone. Primarily Muslim and long part of the coastal trade culture, the Vai developed their own alphabet and writing system in the 1820s. These studio portraits of a Vai prince and princess, although taken from a Western perspective and part of the 1893 Columbian Exposition, suggest the differences between ethnic groups in Liberia and grant dignity to the subjects. (Library of Congress)

porating ethnic groups into the Liberian republic involved a loss of status and control for the settler Liberians that they viewed as devastating to the entire enterprise.

In 1919, almost one hundred years after the *Elizabeth* had carried thirty-eight emigrants from New York to Sierra Leone, the African American poet and scholar Benjamin Brawley was hired by the New York Colonization Society to teach at Liberia College and submit a report on Liberia. Brawley became ill and returned to the United States early, but he offered a written assessment of the republic. In it, the contrast that he felt between his own reality and that of the Liberians is apparent. In the aftermath of World War I, 1919 was the worst year for lynchings in the United States, but Brawley was part of a vibrant intellectual movement of African Americans that was on the cusp of a rich cultural and intellectual advance, and he felt himself to be far removed from the Liberians.

The Liberians are, he said, "a combination of conservatism, aloofness, and self-satisfaction. They have departed little from the ideals that actuated the settlers a hundred years ago. These ideals included much church-going and a Puritanical observance of the Sabbath; but they knew nothing of the broad social and economic outlook that the western world has cultivated within the last half-century. Shut up within their little world, with little opportunity for culture, with only occasionally issued newspapers or other means of contact with the great world without, the people have made comparatively little progress in the modern sense."[24]

But Liberia was intended to be "a nation in the bud—a coloured America on the shores of Africa."[25] That was what the settlers—none more hopeful and ambitious than the Virginians—had done. They had created an early-nineteenth-century American republic and become early national Americans through a frontier experience, resistance to colonial authority, and the rituals of nation-making. Yet they had failed in the impossible task of their larger aims—they had been unable to westernize an African population that greatly outnumbered them and that was unwilling to become part of the new nation. After a century in which most ordinary settlers and their leaders had responded as inventively as possible to an almost unending series of difficulties, they had not Christianized even their portion of Africa, prospered as a nation among nations, or made themselves respected and welcomed in the United States.

Note: References to Virginia emigrants to Liberia—their ages, occupations, skills, level of literacy, family members, place of origin, ships on which they traveled, and time of arrival in Liberia—are taken from a database titled Virginia Emigrants to Liberia (VEL), compiled by Marie Tyler-McGraw and Deborah Lee. The project was funded by a grant from the Virginia Foundation for the Humanities with the support of the Afro-American Historical Society of Fauquier County. The database was compiled primarily from the ACS journal, the *African Repository and Colonial Journal*, 1825–92; emigrant rolls in the Records of the American Colonization Society (RACS), Library of Congress, Washington, D.C.; and U.S. Senate, *Roll of Emigrants That Have Been Sent to the Colony of Liberia*, 28th Cong., 2nd sess., 1844, S.Rep. 150, 152–414. I also used emigrant lists compiled by Tom W. Shick, "Emigrants to Liberia, 1820–1843: An Alphabetical Listing" (Liberian Studies Working Paper Number 2, Department of Anthropology, University of Delaware, Newark, for Liberian Studies Association, 1971); and Robert T. Brown, *Immigrants to Liberia, 1843–1865: An Alphabetical Listing* (Philadelphia: Institute for Liberian Studies, 1980). This database will be at the center of a website provided by the Virginia Center for Digital History and funded by a further grant from the Virginia Foundation for the Humanities.

Abbreviations

ACS	American Colonization Society
AR	*African Repository and Colonial Journal*
JNH	*Journal of Negro History*
JSH	*Journal of Southern History*
LC	Library of Congress, Washington, D.C.
LSJ	*Liberian Studies Journal*
LVA	Library of Virginia, Richmond
RACS	Records of the American Colonization Society, Manuscript Division, Library of Congress, Washington, D.C.
RMCS	Records of the Maryland Colonization Society, Maryland Historical Society, Baltimore
SHC	Svend Holsoe Collection, Archive of Traditional Music, Indiana University, Bloomington
UVA	University of Virginia, Charlottesville
VCS	Virginia Colonization Society
VEL	Virginia Emigrants to Liberia database
VHS	Virginia Historical Society, Richmond
VMHB	*Virginia Magazine of History and Biography*

Introduction

1. Recent studies that explore this aspect of African colonization include Eric Burin, *Slavery and the Peculiar Solution* (Gainesville: University Press of Florida, 2005). Burin investigated the long national history of the ACS and concludes that it tended to undermine slavery. Other studies have focused on emigration from Maryland, Mississippi, Arkansas, and North Carolina, using those regions to ask larger questions about the intentions and realities of African colonization. See Robert Hall, *On Afric's Shore: A History of Maryland in Liberia, 1834–1857* (Baltimore: Maryland Historical Society, 2003); Alan Huffman, *Mississippi in Africa* (New York: Gotham Books, 2004); Kenneth C. Barnes, *Journey of Hope: The Back-to-Africa Movement in Arkansas in the Late 1800s* (Chapel Hill: University of North Carolina Press, 2004); and Claude A. Clegg, *The Price of Liberty: African Americans and the Making of Liberia* (Chapel Hill: University of North Carolina Press, 2004).

2. "Memorial of the ACS to the Senate and House of Representatives," reel 304, RACS. The final draft is printed in *National Intelligencer*, January 18, 1817; and in *Annals of Congress*, 14th Cong., 2nd sess., January 14, 1817, 481–83.

3. For early emancipation plans among black and white Americans, see Mary S. Locke, *The Neglected Period of American Antislavery, 1619–1808*, 1901 (reprint, Gloucester, Mass.: Peter Smith, 1965); Floyd Miller, *The Search for a Black Nationality: Black Emigration and Colonization, 1787–1863* (Urbana: University of Illinois Press, 1975); and Gary B. Nash, *Race and Revolution* (Madison, Wis.: Madison House, 1990).

4. For the history of American construction of race, cornerstone texts remain Winthrop Jordan, *White over Black: American Attitudes toward the Negro, 1550–1812*, 1968 (New York: W. W. Norton, 1977); David Brion Davis, *The Problem of Slavery in the Age of Revolution*, 1966 (rev. ed., Cambridge: Oxford University Press, 1988); David Brion Davis, *Slavery and Human Progress* (Cambridge: Oxford University Press, 1984); Edmund Morgan, *American Slavery, American Freedom: The Ordeal of Colonial Virginia* (New York: W. W. Norton, 1975); and George Fredrickson, *The Black Image in the White Mind: The Debate on Afro-American Character and Destiny, 1817–1914* (New York: Harper and Row, 1972). Very useful is Robert Forbes, "Slavery and the Evangelical Enlightenment," in *Religion and the Antebellum Debate over Slavery*, ed. John R. McKivigan and Mitchell Snay (Athens: University of Georgia Press, 1998). See also Bruce Dain, *A Hideous Monster of the Mind: American Race Theory in the Early Republic* (Cambridge, Mass.: Harvard University Press, 2002); and David Brion Davis, "The Culmination of Racial Polarities and Prejudice," *Journal of the Early Republic* 19, no. 4 (Winter 1999): 757–75.

5. Philip Staudenraus, *The African Colonization Movement, 1816–1861* (New York: Columbia University Press, 1961), 29–30, 50–56, 63–66. See also Douglas Egerton, *Charles Fenton Mercer and the Trial of National Conservatism* (Jackson: University Press of Mississippi, 1989). Although some of those appointed as vice presidents, such as Andrew Jackson, never joined or participated, the society claimed many Upper South politicians, such as Henry Clay, as well as influential clergymen and the men of business who ran the society.

6. Eric Burin's chapter on the Pennsylvania Colonization Society, in *Slavery and the Peculiar Solution*, 79–99, suggests what this northward tilt meant for the national society.

7. Examples include Jordan, *White over Black*, 551–68; William Freehling, *The Reintegration of American History: Slavery and the Civil War* (New York: Oxford University Press, 1994), 148; and William G. Shade, *Democratizing the Old Dominion: Virginia and the Second Party System, 1824–1861* (Charlottesville: University Press of Virginia, 1996), 191, 194.

8. "Tabulation of Emigrants to the End of the Year 1866, *AR* 43 (1867): 109–17; Tom W. Schick, "Emigrants to Liberia, an Alphabetical Listing," Liberian Studies Working Paper Number 2, Department of Anthropology, University of Delaware, Newark, for Liberian Studies Association, 1971; Robert T. Brown, "Immigrants to Liberia, 1843 to 1865: An Alphabetical Listing," Philadelphia: Institute for Liberian Studies, 1980.

9. Their arguments survive in the unpublished correspondence of such emigrants as Lott Cary, Joseph Jenkins Roberts, and John Day. Their private letters are frequently critical of the ACS and of American politics and society. An example is in John Saillant, ed., "'Circular Addressed to the Colored Brethren and Friends in America': An Unpublished Letter by Lott Cary, Sent from Liberia to Virginia, 1827," *VMHB* 104, no. 4 (Autumn 1996): 481–504.

10. Instructive on the creation of nationhood, moral authority, and patriotism among antebellum free blacks are Patrick Rael, *Black Identity and Black Protest in the Antebellum North* (Chapel Hill: University of North Carolina Press, 2002); and Dickson D. Bruce Jr., *The Origins of African American Literature* (Charlottesville: University Press of Virginia, 2001). For an influential and very negative black response to colonization after its first dozen years, see David Walker, *Appeal to the Colored Citizens of the United States*, ed. Peter P. Hinks (University Park: Pennsylvania State University Press, 2000); and Peter P. Hinks, *To Awaken My Afflicted Brethren: David Walker and the Problem of Antebellum Slave Resistance* (University Park: Pennsylvania State University Press, 1997).

Chapter One

1. *Commonwealth v. Sam Byrd*, testimony of Ben Woolfolk; *Commonwealth v. Solomon*, testimony of Prosser's Ben and Toby; Communication of Solomon, under sentence of death; Testimony of Patty, re trial of Daniel, box 8, "Gabriel's Insurrection," Virginia Executive Papers (September–December 1800), LVA; Douglas R. Egerton, *Gabriel's Rebellion: The Virginia Slave Conspiracies of 1800 and 1802* (Chapel Hill: University of North Carolina Press, 1993), 55–56.

2. *Commonwealth v. Gabriel*, testimony of Gilbert; "Information from Mr. Foster," September 23, 1800; *Commonwealth v. Isham*, testimony of Isham; for Gabriel's capture, see Thomas Hinton, Norfolk to Gov. James Monroe, Richmond, September 24, 1800, box 8, "Gabriel's Insurrection," Virginia Executive Papers, LVA.

3. *Commonwealth v. Gabriel*, evidence of Prosser's Ben; *Commonwealth v. Solomon*, evidence of Prosser's Ben; *Commonwealth v. Charles*, testimony of Patrick; *Common-*

wealth v. George, testimony of Ben Woolfolk; box 8, "Gabriel's Insurrection," Virginia Executive Papers (October–December 1800), LVA; Egerton, *Gabriel's Rebellion*, 104–8, 182–85.

4. That Gabriel and his followers saw themselves in the tradition of recent revolutionary movements is central to two studies of Gabriel and his milieu. Egerton, *Gabriel's Rebellion*, saw the conspiracy closely connected to the national politics of the era and Gabriel as a self-identified republican artisan. James Sidbury, *Ploughshares into Swords: Race, Rebellion and Identity in Gabriel's Virginia, 1730–1810* (New York: Cambridge University Press, 1997), placed Gabriel's Rebellion in an Afro-Virginian world in which enslaved and free blacks had multiple connections and identities, some grounded in evangelical Christianity and all more apparent in urban areas.

5. In *Jefferson's Empire: The Language of American Nationhood* (Charlottesville: University of Virginia Press, 2000), 147–88, and in other writings, Peter Onuf argues that, in Thomas Jefferson's thought, the evolution of an American political nation was dependent upon grouping African Americans as a separate nation.

6. *Records of the State Enumerations, 1782–1785* (Baltimore: Genealogical Publishing Company, 1966); Historical Census Browser, University of Virginia Geospatial and Statistical Data Center: <http://fisher.lib.virginia.edu/census> (accessed October 30, 2004).

7. Marie Tyler-McGraw and Gregg D. Kimball, *In Bondage and Freedom: Antebellum Black Life in Richmond, Virginia* (Chapel Hill: University of North Carolina Press for the Valentine Museum, 1988), 20, 64–66.

8. John H. Russell, *The Free Negro in Virginia* (Baltimore: Johns Hopkins University Press, 1913), 63–64; Winthrop Jordan, *White over Black: American Attitudes toward the Negro, 1550–1812* (Chapel Hill: University of North Carolina Press, 1968), 561–63; Philip Slaughter, *The Virginian History of African Colonization* (Richmond: MacFarlane and Ferguson, 1855), 1–7; Archibald Alexander, *History of Colonization on the Western Coast of Africa* (Philadelphia: W. S. Martien, 1846), 63–75. The Jefferson-Monroe-Page correspondence is reprinted in Slaughter and in Alexander.

9. Alden T. Vaughan, "The Origins Debate: Slavery and Racism in Seventeenth Century Virginia," *VMHB* 97, no. 3 (July 1989): 311–54; Warren Billings, "The Law of Servants and Slaves in Seventeenth-Century Virginia," *VMHB* 99, no. 1 (January 1991): 61–62.

10. Edmund Morgan, *American Slavery, American Freedom: The Ordeal of Colonial Virginia* (New York: Norton, 1975), 295–330; John H. Russell, *The Free Negro in Virginia, 1619–1865*, 1913 (reprint, New York: Negro Universities Press, 1969), 10–12, 19–21, 33–37, 39, 51, 56.

11. June Purcell Guild, *Black Laws of Virginia* (Richmond: Whittet and Shepperson, 1936), 53; Russell, *Free Negro*, 51–53.

12. James C. Ballagh, *A History of Slavery in Virginia* (Baltimore: Johns Hopkins Press, 1902), 23; Russell, *Free Negro*, 59; John Chester Miller, *The Wolf by the Ears: Thomas Jefferson and Slavery* (New York: Free Press, 1977), 12–18.

13. Thomas Jefferson, *Notes on the State of Virginia*, ed. William Peden (Chapel Hill: University of North Carolina Press, 1955), 134–43. Jordan, *White over Black*,

546–47, notes this usage; and Peter Onuf, in *Jefferson's Empire*, has developed it. Miller, *Wolf by the Ears*, 38–45.

14. Richard Dunn, "Society in the Chesapeake, 1776–1820," in *Slavery and Freedom in the Age of the American Revolution*, ed. Ira Berlin and Ronald Hoffman (Urbana: University of Illinois Press, 1986), 49–82.

15. Russell, *Free Negro*, 61–64; Theodore S. Babcock, "Manumission in Virginia, 1782–1806" (M.A. thesis, University of Virginia, 1974), 21–22, 65.

16. Sylvia Frey, *Water from the Rock: Black Resistance in a Revolutionary Age* (Princeton, N.J.: Princeton University Press, 1991), 4, 45; Lorena Walsh, "Slave Life, Slave Society and Tobacco Production in the Tidewater Chesapeake, 1620–1820," in *Cultivation and Culture: Labor and the Shaping of Slave Life in the Americas*, ed. Ira Berlin and Philip Morgan (Charlottesville: University Press of Virginia, 1993), 187.

17. Sylvia Frey, "Between Slavery and Freedom: Virginia Blacks in the American Revolution," *JSH* 49, no. 3 (August 1983): 376, 378, 380; Woody Holton, *Forced Founders: Indians, Debtors, Slaves, and the Making of the American Revolution in Virginia* (Chapel Hill: University of North Carolina Press for the Omohundro Institute for American History and Culture, 1999), 213; Richard West, *Back to Africa: A History of Sierra Leone and Liberia* (New York: Harper and Row, 1970), 40–51.

18. Frey, *Water from the Rock*, 194–201; Sheldon H. Harris, *Paul Cuffe, Black America, and the African Return* (New York: Simon and Schuster, 1972), 233–36, 255.

19. William Maxwell, *Memoir of the Reverend John H. Rice, D.D., First Professor of Christian Theology in Union Theological Seminary, Virginia* (Philadelphia: J. Whethan; Richmond: R. I. Smith, 1835), 32–34, in Special Collections, LVA; Sylvia Frey and Betty Wood, *Come Shouting to Zion: African American Protestantism in the American South and British Caribbean to 1830* (Chapel Hill: University of North Carolina Press, 1998), 97–102. Frey and Wood make the important point that such literacy and discipline were used by white preachers to point out the benefits of slave religion for slave masters.

20. Luther Porter Jackson, "Religious Development of the Negro in Virginia from 1760 to 1860," *JNH* 16 (April 1931): 170–75; Edward Smith, *Climbing Jacob's Ladder: The Rise of Black Churches in Eastern American Cities, 1740–1877* (Washington, D.C.: Smithsonian Institution Press for Anacostia Museum, 1988), 84; Mechal Sobel, *Trabelin' On: The Slave Journey to an Afro-Baptist Faith* (Westport, Conn.: Greenwood Press, 1979), 300; "Brief History of Gillfield Baptist Church," in "Records of Gillfield Baptist Church, 1827–1939," Acquisition No. 10041, box 2, Alderman Library, UVA.

21. St. George Tucker, "A Dissertation on Slavery: With a Proposal for Its Gradual Abolition in the State of Virginia," 1796 (reprinted in electronic format as *The Founders' Constitution*, v. 1, chap. 15, doc. 56, by the University of Chicago Press, 2000 <http://presspubs.uchicago.edu/founders/documents/v1ch15s56.html> (accessed July 30, 2006).

22. See the overview by Richard Newman in *The Transformation of American Abolitionism* (Chapel Hill: University of North Carolina Press, 2002), 1–38, and esp. 110–11, 117; see St. George Tucker, "A Dissertation on Slavery." Gary Nash, *Race and Revolution* (Madison, Wis.: Madison House Publishers, 1990), reviewed the

evidence for Revolutionary Era awareness of the incompatibility of slavery with natural rights, especially among the Chesapeake leadership; see pp. 42–50 for his assessment of northern failure to respond to southern abolition schemes. See also William L. Freehling, *The Road to Disunion: Secessionists at Bay, 1776–1854* (New York: Oxford University Press, 1990), 119–43; and Philip Schwarz, *Twice Condemned: Slaves and the Criminal Laws of Virginia, 1705–1865* (Baton Rouge: Louisiana State University Press, 1988), 242–61.

23. James O. Horton and Lois Horton, *In Hope of Liberty: Culture, Community, and Protest among Northern Free Blacks, 1700–1860* (New York: Oxford University Press, 1997), 71–75; David Brion Davis, *The Problem of Slavery in the Age of Revolution* (Ithaca, N.Y.: Cornell University Press, 1975), 119–31.

24. Jordan, *White over Black*, 551–63; Ferdinando Fairfax, "Plan for Liberating the Negroes within the United States," *American Museum* 8 (1790), in Nash, *Race and Revolution*, 146–50.

25. See the indirect communication between Tucker, Jeremy Belknap, and Prince Hall, in Jordan, *White over Black*, 555–56; Philip Hamilton, *The Making and Unmaking of a Revolutionary Family: The Tuckers of Virginia, 1752–1830* (Charlottesville: University of Virginia Press, 2003), 80–83; [George Tucker], *A Letter to a Member of the General Assembly . . . with a Proposal for Colonization* (Baltimore, 1801), in Nash, *Race and Revolution*, 159–65.

26. Deborah Lee, "'Life Is a Solemn Trust': Ann R. Page and the Antislavery Movement in the Upper South" (Ph.D. diss., George Mason University, 2003), makes the important point that many Anglican communicants maintained a personal discipline during the period when that church lost its political status and was generally weakened. It was these persons who encouraged aspects of evangelicalism in the Episcopal Church.

27. Rhys Isaac made this point strongly in *The Transformation of Virginia, 1740–1790* (Chapel Hill: University of North Carolina Press, 1983). See Christine Leigh Heyrman, *Southern Cross: The Beginnings of the Bible Belt* (Chapel Hill: University of North Carolina Press, 1997), esp. 9–27, for a more cautious estimate of the spread of dissenting religion in the South.

28. Douglas Ambrose, "Of Stations and Relations: Proslavery Christianity in Early National Virginia," in *Religion and the Antebelllum Debate over Slavery*, ed. John R. McKivigan and Mitchell Snay (Athens: University of Georgia Press, 1998); Sobel, *Trabelin' On*, 79–90, 300; Russell, *Free Negro*, 56–57; Donald Mathews, *Religion in the Old South* (Chicago: University of Chicago Press, 1978), 68–80; Isaac, *Transformation*, 146–72, 308–10; Jackson, "Religious Development," 170–75.

29. Mary S. Locke, *Antislavery in America, 1619–1808*, 1901 (reprint, Gloucester, Mass.: Peter Smith, 1965), 109–10; Ira Berlin, *Slaves without Masters: The Free Negro in the Antebellum South* (New York: Pantheon, 1974), 84–85.

30. Egerton, *Gabriel's Rebellion*, 147–62; Stanislaus Hamilton, *The Writings of James Monroe*, 7 vols., 1900 (reprint, New York: AMS Press, 1969), 3:275–79, 307, 328–29, 341, 344, 348.

31. Floyd Miller, *The Search for a Black Nationality: Black Emigration and Colonization, 1787–1863* (Urbana: University of Illinois Press, 1975), 44–51; Philip

Staudenraus, *The African Colonization Movement, 1816–1865* (New York: Columbia University Press, 1961), 15–30.

32. Douglas Egerton, *Charles Fenton Mercer and the Trial of National Conservatism* (Jackson: University Press of Mississippi, 1989), 105–12; Archibald Alexander, *History of Colonization on the Western Coast of Africa* (Philadelphia: W. S. Martien, 1846), 75–77.

Chapter Two

1. Samuel Mordecai, *Richmond in By-Gone Days*, 2nd ed. (Richmond: MacFarlane and Ferguson, 1860), 191–94.

2. Many scholars have discussed the manner in which Enlightenment theory could embrace both human rights and a race-based eugenics. For examples, see David Brion Davis, *Slavery and Human Progress* (New York: Oxford University Press, 1984), 109–11, 115, 224–26; and Dickson D. Bruce Jr., *The Origins of African American Literature* (Charlottesville: University Press of Virginia, 2001), 135–74, esp. 135–37 and 150–53. For the limits of corporate evangelicalism, see Christine Leigh Heyrman, *Southern Cross: The Beginnings of the Bible Belt* (Chapel Hill: University of North Carolina Press, 1997), 67–70, 76; and Donald Mathews, *Religion in the Old South* (Chicago: University of Chicago Press, 1977), 185.

3. Floyd Miller, *The Search for a Black Nationality: Black Emigration and Colonization, 1787–1863* (Urbana: University of Illinois Press, 1974), 44–46; Lamont Thomas, *Rise to Be a People: A Biography of Paul Cuffe* (Urbana: University of Illinois Press, 1986), 93–100.

4. Duncan Rice, *The Rise and Fall of Black Slavery* (New York: Harper and Row, 1975), 242.

5. Lamont Thomas, *Rise to Be a People*, 107–19, esp. 111; Miller, *Search for a Black Nationality*, 4–13, 25–44.

6. Dickson D. Bruce Jr., "National Identity and African American Colonization, 1773–1817," *Historian* 58 (Autumn 1995): esp. 15, 21, 27–28; and Peter Onuf, *Jefferson's Empire: The Language of American Nationhood* (Charlottesville: University Press of Virginia, 2000). Useful are Bruce Dain, *A Hideous Monster of the Mind: American Race Theory in the Early Republic* (Cambridge, Mass.: Harvard University Press, 2002); and Patrick Rael, *Black Identity and Black Protest in the Antebellum North* (Chapel Hill: University of North Carolina Press, 2002).

7. William Jay, *Inquiry into the Character and Tendency of the American Colonization Society and American Anti-Slavery Societies*, 1838 (reprint, Miami: Mnemosyne Publishing Company, 1969), 1–3.

8. Charles Mackay, *Extraordinary Popular Delusions and the Madness of Crowds*, 1841 (reprint, New York: Harmony Books/Crown Publishers, 1980).

9. Charles Fenton Mercer, "Autobiographical Sketch," March 14, 1849, Mercer-Hunter Papers, LVA, 14–22; *Annals of Congress*, 15th Cong., 2nd sess., 442; C. F. Mercer to John Hartwell Cocke, April 2, 1819, Cocke Letters, Alderman Library, UVA. The best account of the complex maneuvering by which Mercer and the society obtained their ends is to be found in Douglas Egerton, *Charles Fenton Mercer and the Trial of National Conservatism* (Jackson: University Press of Mississippi, 1989).

10. A sampling of donations in the Manuscript Account Books, RACS, from 1817 to 1831 showed more donations from Virginia than from any other state. The later history of the society suggests that donations dropped after 1831, but bequests from Virginians grew. Pennsylvania and New York became the predominant sources of funds.

11. J. Mitchie to R. R. Gurley, Washington, D.C., 1827, RACS.

12. Bushrod Washington lacks a scholarly biography. For Mercer, see Egerton, *Charles Fenton Mercer*. For Meade, see first Deborah Lee, "'Life Is a Solemn Trust': Ann R. Page and the Antislavery Movement in the Upper South" (Ph.D. diss., George Mason University, 2002). See also Philip Slaughter, *Memoir of the Life of the Rt. Rev. William Meade, D.D.* (Cambridge, Mass.: New England Historic Genealogical Society, 1885); and John Johns, *A Memoir of the Right Reverend William Meade, D.D.* (Baltimore: Innes, 1867).

13. Drew R. McCoy, *The Last of the Fathers: James Madison and the Republican Legacy* (Cambridge: Cambridge University Press, 1989), 282–86, 301; Alison G. Freehling, *Drift toward Dissolution: The Virginia Slavery Debate of 1831–32* (Baton Rouge: Louisiana State University Press, 1982), 123, 180–85.

14. Harriett Martineau, *Retrospect of Western Travel*, 1:189–98, in McCoy, *Last of the Fathers*, 5–6; Madison to Dew, February 23, 1832, in ibid., 303–4.

15. Horace Binney, *Bushrod Washington* (Philadelphia: C. Sherman, 1858), 9; Dumas Malone, ed., *Dictionary of American Biography*, 26 vols. (New York: Charles Scribner's, 1936), 19:508–9; Charles Fenton Mercer to James Mercer Garnett, December 8, 1854, Garnett Family Papers, LVA.

16. Typed notes from Bushrod Washington File Notebook, Mount Vernon Library and Archive, Mount Vernon, Va.; W. Hamilton Bryson, "Bushrod Washington," in *American National Biography* 22, ed. John A. Garraty and Mark C. Carnes (New York: Oxford University Press, 1999), 756–57.

17. Deborah Lee, "'Solemn Trust,'" 82–91, 111–12; Slaughter, *Memoir of Meade*, 1–20.

18. His cofounders included Francis Scott Key, a close friend and coreligionist, as well as Gerrit Smith and Arthur Tappan, who would later become active abolitionists; Philip Staudenraus, *The African Colonization Movement, 1816–1865* (New York: Columbia University Press, 1961), 189–92; Lee, "Solemn Trust," 147.

19. ACS, *Address of the Board of Managers of the American Colonization Society to the Public* (Washington, D.C.: Davis and Force, 1819), 1–4. Ship's records published in the *AR* (1828) suggest their return, in much diminished numbers, nine years later.

20. Lee, "Solemn Trust," 137–38.

21. Meade quoted in ibid., 142–43; Philip Schwarz, *Migrants against Slavery: Virginians and the Nation* (Charlottesville: University Press of Virginia, 2000), 122–48, esp. 129–40, for Gist slaves. Schwarz notes that legal entanglements hampered the freedmen as much as hostility did. John H. Russell, *The Free Negro in Virginia* (Baltimore: Johns Hopkins University Press, 1913), 70–72; Bishop Meade to R. R. Gurley, December 6, 1831, in Patricia Hickin, "Antislavery in Virginia" (Ph.D. diss., University of Virginia, 1968), 272–74; Mathews, *Religion in the Old South*, 116–18.

22. Staudenraus, *African Colonization Movement*, 70–74, 189–90.

23. Mercer, "Sketch," 1–3; Charles Fenton Mercer to Maria Garnett, December 8, 1854, and June 6, 1856, Garnett Family Papers, LVA.

24. First quotation, Charles Fenton Mercer, *A Discourse on Public Education Delivered . . . at Princeton* (published for American Whig and Cliosophical Societies, by D. A. Borrenstein, Princeton Press, 1826) (Rare Book Collection, LC, MIC 02191/reel 235), pp. xx, xxi, xxv, 76–77; second quotation, Charles Fenton Mercer to Maria Garnett, June 6, 1856, Garnett Family Papers, LVA.

25. The engraving is reproduced in Rhys Isaac, *The Transformation of Virginia* (Chapel Hill: University of North Carolina Press, published for the Institute of Early American History and Culture, 1983), 289–90; Isaac comments that "a claim to higher understanding" was the only real legitimation left to a republican gentry as a rationale for its traditional domination of "semiliterate husbandmen." But Mercer's career indicates that he wanted to democratize the struggle for learning and that some of those who scaled the mountain might be the husbandmen. Robert Forbes develops this theme well in "Slavery and the Evangelical Enlightenment," in *Religion and the Antebellum Debate over Slavery*, ed. John R. McKivigan and Mitchell Snay (Athens: University of Georgia Press, 1998).

26. In the House of Delegates, Mercer recommended and carried through an enlargement of the banking capital of Virginia and the creation of a Farmer's Bank. In 1812, he accompanied Chief Justice Marshall and others appointed by the legislature to examine the rivers in the western part of the state to see if they could be made to connect with the headwaters of the James River by canal. He also submitted a series of resolutions to the legislature to establish a general fund for the internal improvement of the state's roads and rivers. Mercer, "Autobiographical Sketch," 4–7, 10.

27. Mercer, *Exposition*, 115–20, 355. Mercer linked expanded suffrage with the need for education to prevent demagoguery: "This worst of all associations, ignorance and a general suffrage, throws everything into the hands of the dishonest, designing demagogues, who are enabled by a little flattery and, if necessary, a little bribery, to lead them to the support of all their measures, and convert them into the merest tools. I consider it the greatest defect of this confederation, both of the State and Federal governments, thus to neglect education and leave it to chance. The showing of the number that cannot read and write by the census in some of the States is frightful, amounting nearly to one-half the whole population. Ireland or Naples could not make much worse showing, with much more to excuse them than we have."

28. Douglas Egerton, "Charles Fenton Mercer and Public Education in Virginia," in *Rebels, Reformers, and Revolutionaries* (London: Routledge, 2002), 93–106.

29. Charles Fenton Mercer, "The Right of Instruction," folio for February 19, 1812, *Journal of the Virginia House of Delegates for 1811–1812*, 145–49; Mercer, "Autobiographical Sketch," 11–14; James Mercer Garnett, *Biographical Sketch of the Honorable Charles Fenton Mercer, 1778–1858* (Richmond: Whittet and Shepperson, 1911), 6.

30. Cabell, Richmond, to TJ, January 24, 1816, Thomas Jefferson Papers, se-

ries 3, roll 7, M122, International Center for Jefferson Studies, Charlottesville, Va.; Cabell to Thomas Jefferson, February 25, 1816, and Cabell to Thomas Jefferson, February 2, 1816, August 4, 1816, and January 12, 1817, in Cabell Papers, Special Collections, UVA (emphasis in original). Douglas Egerton has argued that Mercer's goal in promoting public education was an acquiescent white labor force that would ultimately supplant slave labor. See Douglas Egerton, "Charles Fenton Mercer and Public Education in Virginia," in *Rebels, Reformers, and Revolutionaries: Collected Essays and Second Thoughts* (New York: Routledge, 2002), 93–225.

31. Cabell to Thomas Jefferson, February 25, 1816, August 4, 1816, and January 12, 1817, Cabell Papers, Special Collections, UVA; William A. Maddox, *The Free School Idea in Virginia before the Civil War* (New York: Columbia University Teacher's College, 1918), 55–59; Garnett, *Biographical Sketch*, 14–15; Mercer, "Autobiographical Sketch," 12.

32. John Holt Rice to William Maxwell, January 10, 1819, in William Maxwell, *Memoir of the Life of John Holt Rice, D.D.* (Philadelphia: J. Wetham, 1835), 154–55. See Cameron Addis, *Jefferson's Vision for Education, 1760–1845*, History of Schools and Schooling, vol. 29 (New York: Peter Lang, 2003), 36–53, 63, 72–87, for Jefferson's extreme hostility to both Mercer and Rice; Louis Weeks, "John Holt Rice and the American Colonization Society," *Journal of Presbyterian History* 46 (1968): 27.

33. Forbes, "Evangelical Enlightenment," 87–88, in McKivigan and Snay, *Religion*; Addis, *Jefferson's Vision*, 81–85.

34. Jefferson-Cabell letters, Jefferson Papers, Special Collections, UVA; Nathaniel Cabell, ed., *Early History of the University of Virginia; as Contained in the Letters of Thomas Jefferson and Joseph Cabell . . .* (Richmond: J. W. Randolph, 1856), Special Collections, UVA.

35. Paul Finkelman, "Jefferson and Slavery: 'Treason against the Hopes of the World,'" in *Jeffersonian Legacies*, ed. Peter Onuf (Charlottesville: University Press of Virginia, 1993), 181–221, is a strong indictment of Jefferson on slavery. Balance this with William L. Freehling, *The Road to Disunion: Secessionists at Bay* (New York: Oxford University Press, 1990), 122–31, 152–57. For the quotidian realities, see Lucia Stanton, "'Those Who Labor for My Happiness': Thomas Jefferson and His Slaves," in Onuf, *Jeffersonian Legacies*, 162–63.

36. *The Second Annual Report of the American Society for Colonizing the Free People of Colour in the United States* (Washington, D.C.: Davis and Force, 1819) reproduced a letter of Jefferson to John Lynch (1811) commenting on the proposal of Mrs. Ann Mifflin for an establishment for free blacks on the coast of Africa. He reviewed his efforts of 1800 and noted that it was now a matter for the national government to pursue.

37. James H. Broussard, *The Southern Federalists, 1800–1816* (Baton Rouge: Louisiana State University Press, 1978), 176–77.

38. Charles H. Ambler, *Sectionalism in Virginia from 1776 to 1861* (Chicago: University of Chicago Press, 1910), 100; Charles Poland, *From Frontier to Suburbia* (Marceline, Mo.: Walsworth, 1976), 98–101; Bertram Wyatt-Brown, *Southern Honor: Ethics and Behavior in the Old South* (New York: Oxford University Press, 1982). Wyatt-Brown's survey of dueling in the Old South includes the Pope-Noland duel,

won by Charles Fenton Mercer Noland, who had Mercer's name but apparently not his religious principles.

39. Staudenraus, *African Colonization Movement,* 174–78, 186; Charles Francis Adams, ed., *John Quincy Adams Memoirs Comprising Portions of His Diary from 1795 to 1848,* 12 vols. (Philadelphia: J. B. Lippincott, 1876), 10:360–61.

40. William G. Shade, *Democratizing the Old Dominion: Virginia and the Second Party System, 1824–1861* (Charlottesville: University Press of Virginia, 1996), esp. 30–34, 55–64; Daniel P. Jordan, *Political Leadership in Jefferson's Virginia* (Charlottesville: University Press of Virginia, 1983), xi, 54, 57–58, 68–69, 209; Donald Robinson, *Slavery in the Structure of the United States, 1765–1820* (New York: Harcourt, Brace, Jovanovich, 1971), 386, 398, 400–423; Freehling, *Road to Disunion,* 122–57.

41. Thomas Jefferson to Marquis de Lafayette, December 26, 1820, in Onuf, *Jefferson's Empire,* chap. 5, and esp. 186–87; Thomas Jefferson to Jared Sparks, February 4, 1824, in *The Writings of Thomas Jefferson,* ed. Andrew A. Lipscomb and Albert Ellery Bergh, 20 vols. (Washington, D.C.: Thomas Jefferson Memorial Association, 1903–1904), 16:8–14.

Chapter Three

1. Charles D. Poland, *From Frontier to Suburbia* (Marceline, Mo.: Walsworth, 1976), 142–43.

2. Sources for Virginia auxiliaries to the ACS include *AR;* Philip Slaughter, *The Virginian History of African Colonization* (Richmond: MacFarlane and Ferguson, 1855); the Benjamin Brand Papers at VHS; and domestic letters to the ACS held in RACS. Virginia counties, cities, and institutions that left at least a minimal record of the formation of an auxiliary society include Alexandria, Albemarle (and Female Auxiliary), Amherst, Arlington, Augusta (and Female Auxiliary), Bedford, Berkeley, Botetourt, Brunswick (and Female Auxiliary), Buckingham, Campbell, Caroline, Charles City, Charleston/Kanawha, Chesterfield, Petersburg (and Female Auxiliary), Clarksburg/Harrison, Culpeper, Dinwiddie, Elizabeth City, Essex (and Female Auxiliary), Fairfax, Fauquier, Fluvanna, Frederick, Fredericksburg (and Female Auxiliary), Greenbrier, Hampden Sydney College, Hampton, Romney/Hampshire, Hanover, Harpers Ferry/Jefferson, Deep Run/Henrico, Isle of Wight, Charles Town/Jefferson, King William, Lexington (and Female Auxiliary), Loudoun, Ladies Colonization Society of Louisa, Lynchburg, Mangohick Union Colonization Society/Prince William and King and Queen Counties, Morgantown/Monongalia, Middletown, Nansemond, Nelson, Richmond-Manchester (and Female Auxiliary), Roanoke, Rockbridge (and Female Auxiliary), Shepherdstown/Jefferson, Sussex, Warrenton Female Colonization Society, and Wheeling (and Female Colonization Society).

3. Allan Kulikoff, *Tobacco and Slaves: The Development of Southern Cultures in the Chesapeake, 1680–1800* (Chapel Hill: University of North Carolina Press, 1986), 157–58; William G. Shade, *Democratizing the Old Dominion: Virginia and the Second Party System, 1824–1861* (Charlottesville: University Press of Virginia, 1996), 3–6, 33–35, 43.

4. Philip Staudenraus, *The African Colonization Movement, 1816–1865* (New York:

Columbia University Press, 1961), 105–7; John Brockenbrough to William Meade, June 8, 1819, in John Johns, *A Memoir of the Life of the Right Reverend William Meade* (Baltimore: Inness and Company, 1867), 122.

5. Minutes of the Richmond-Manchester Auxiliary Society of the ACS [1823–28], Benjamin Brand Papers, VHS.

6. William Crane to Rev. Obadiah Brown, March 28, 1819, cited in J. B. Taylor, *Biography of Elder Lott Cary, Late Missionary to Africa* (Baltimore: Armstrong and Berry, 1837), 15–16; Blanche S. White, *First Baptist Church, Richmond, 1780–1955* (Richmond: Whittet and Shepperson, 1955), 30; H. A. Tupper, *The Foreign Mission of the Southern Baptist Convention* (Philadelphia: American Baptist Publication Society, 1880), 277.

7. John Rutherfoord autobiographical fragment, LVA; Agnes Bondurant, *Poe's Richmond* (Richmond: Garret and Massie, 1942), 98, 145, 100, 152; Staudenraus, *African Colonization Movement*, 109; Benjamin Brand Papers, Section 5, VHS; *Richmond City Directory* (Richmond: John Maddox, 1819).

8. The Richmond-Manchester records are extensive because it was the most active auxiliary and became the Virginia Colonization Society in 1828. The best sources for the activities of other auxiliaries are the minutes of their meetings printed in *AR*. Members' letters to the ACS, held in the RACS, are scattered but very revealing.

9. Benjamin Brand to Lott Cary, Richmond, April 2, 1824, Benjamin Brand Papers, Section 4, VHS.

10. Staudenraus, *African Colonization Movement*, 169–73.

11. *Controversy between Gaius Gracchus and Opimius . . . Originally in the Richmond Enquirer* (Georgetown, D.C.: James C. Dunn, 1827), 6, Special Collections, UVA; Staudenraus, *African Colonization Movement*, 170–74.

12. "Alpha," in *Richmond Whig*, February 17, 1824, manuscript copy in Benjamin Brand Papers, Section 6, VHS; Philo Gracchus and Opimius, in *Controversy between Gaius Gracchus and Opimius*; "Liber" in *Norfolk Herald*, in Tommy Bogger, *Free Blacks in Norfolk, Virginia, 1790–1860* (Charlottesville: University Press of Virginia, 1997), 35–36; VCS Minutes, 20, 22, 36, in Patricia Hickin, "Antislavery in Virginia" (Ph.D. diss., University of Virginia, 1968), 256.

13. Thomas Miller, "Out of Bondage: The History of the Alexandria Colonization Society," *Alexandria History* 7 (1987): 18–19, held at VHS; Atkinson to Gurley, July 4, 1827, in Early Lee Fox, *The American Colonization Society, 1817–1840* (Baltimore: Johns Hopkins University Press, 1919), 82; Benjamin Brand to Lott Cary, February 3, 1827, Benjamin Brand Papers, Section 4, VHS.

14. David Burr to R. R. Gurley, September 24, 1826; Benjamin Brand to R. R. Gurley, October 17, 1826; William Crane to R. R. Gurley, January 1, 1827, and January 22, 1827; John French to R. R. Gurley, December 9, 1826; William Atkinson to R. R. Gurley, January 8, 1827; John Cocke to R. R. Gurley, February 9, 1827; all reel 1, RACS.

15. Richmond-Manchester Auxiliary Minutes, January 19, 1825, Benjamin Brand Papers, Section 6, VHS; John Tyler to Littleton W. Tazewell, Washington, D.C., May 21, 1826, Tyler Papers, LC.

16. John Tyler to John White Nash, Washington, D.C., May 6, 1820, Nash Papers, VHS.

17. Benjamin Brand to Richard Smith, ACS treasurer, December 15, 1828, Benjamin Brand Papers, Section 4, VHS; Staudenraus, *African Colonization Movement*, 176–77.

18. "Minutes of the Virginian Branch of the American Colonization Society," 1823–1859," Benjamin Brand Papers, VHS.

19. W. McKenny to Elliott Cresson, January 30, 1834, in reel 12, RMCS.

20. James G. Birney to R. R. Gurley, September 24, 1833, reel 18, RACS.

21. Capitalization as in original. *AR* 4 (August 1828): 172–79.

22. "Minutes of the Virginian Branch," Benjamin Brand Papers, VHS.

23. Gov. John Floyd to Gov. James Hamilton, November 19, 1831, Floyd Papers, LC; Brand to Gurley, January 3, 1832, reel 73, RACS.

24. Staudenraus, *African Colonization Movement*, 181–83. See Alison G. Freehling, *Drift toward Dissolution: The Slavery Debates of 1831–32* (Baton Rouge: Louisiana State University Press, 1982), for the best tracking of Virginia's convoluted debate, esp. 170–95; and Hickin, "Antislavery in Virginia," 531.

25. William Atkinson to R. R. Gurley, June 30, 1832, reel 14, RACS.

26. Edward Colston to R. R. Gurley, July 9, 1833, reel 17, RACS.

27. William Brodnax to R. R. Gurley, February 14, 1832, in Hickin, "Antislavery in Virginia," 276; Staudenraus, *African Colonization Movement*, 183–84; Freehling, *Drift toward Dissolution*, 179–86, 217–21.

28. William Crane, *Antislavery in Virginia: Extracts from Thomas Jefferson, Gen. Washington, and Others Relative to the "Blighting Curse of Slavery," etc.* (Baltimore: J. F. Weishampel, 1865), 22; *Baltimore Sun* cited in *Daily Richmond Whig*, October 2, 1866; George F. Adams, *A Brief Sketch of the Life and Character of the Late William Crane of Baltimore* (Baltimore: J. F. Weishampel, 1868), 30.

29. Crane, *Antislavery in Virginia*, 19–20; Adams, *Brief Sketch*, 30; *Liberia Herald* (February 24, 1842), reel 29, RMCS.

30. Slaughter, *Virginian Colonization*, 89–92; Hickin, "Antislavery in Virginia," 284–89.

31. Poland, *From Frontier to Suburbia*, 6–8, 131; Fairfax Harrison, *Landmarks of Old Prince William: A Study of Origins in Northern Virginia*, 1913 (reprint, Berryville, Va.: Chesapeake Book Company, 1964), 148, 150, 153–55; James W. Head, *History and Comprehensive Description of Loudoun County, Virginia* (Washington, D.C.: Park View Press, 1908), 110–13.

32. Pauline Maier, *The Old Revolutionaries: Political Lives in the Age of Samuel Adams* (New York: Alfred Knopf, 1980), 165–200; Burton J. Hedrick, *The Lees of Virginia: Biography of a Family* (Boston: Little, Brown, 1935), 183, 404.

33. Richard Henry Lee to Bushrod Washington, October 3, 1827, Letters to Bushrod Washington, RM-789/MS 5193, Mount Vernon Archives, Mt. Vernon, Va.; U.S. National Archives, U.S. Census, 1820, Loudoun County, Va.; Allen Johnson and Dumas Malone, eds., *Dictionary of American Biography*, 20 vols. (New York: Charles Scribner's, 1933), 11:117–21; Loudoun County Deed Book 3T, 239 (March 1830).

34. Poland, *From Frontier to Suburbia*, 111; Hedrick, *Lees of Virginia*, 405; John Jay Janney, *John Jay Janney's Virginia*, ed. Werner Janney and Asa Moore Janney (McLean, Va.: EPM Press, 1978), 16; Loudoun County Deed Book 2W, 357.

35. U.S. Census, 1820, Loudoun County, Va.; Poland, *From Frontier to Suburbia*, 114–21; Eugene Scheel, *The Story of Purcellville* (Warrenton, Va.: Warrenton Printing and Publishing, 1977); Harrison, *Landmarks of Old Prince William*, 300.

36. U.S. Census, 1820, Loudoun County, Va.; Scheel, *Story of Purcellville*, 5–6; Loudoun County Record Book P/63, inventory of will of James Heaton; Jesse and Mars Lucas to Albert and Townsend Heaton, March 10, 1830, and Townsend Heaton to Mars and Jesse Lucas (copy), April 29, 1830, manuscript letters held by Loudoun Museum, Leesburg, Va.; Loudoun County Petitions, Archives Division, LVA; Poland, *From Frontier to Suburbia*, 134; runaway advertisements at <http://www.balchfriends.org/Slaves/index.html> (accessed July 11, 2005); *AR* 10 (October 1834): 252.

37. Steven Weeks, *Southern Quakers and Slavery* (Baltimore: Johns Hopkins Press, 1896), 211, 215, 217, 243; Bronwen C. Souders and John M. Souders, *A Rock in a Weary Land, A Shelter in a Time of Storm: African-American Experience in Waterford, Virginia* (Waterford, Va.: Waterford Foundation, 2003), 8–13. Jay Worrall Jr., *The Friendly Virginians: America's First Quakers* (Athens, Ga.: Iberian Publishing, 1994), lists 62 weekly meetings in this area of northern Virginia in 1800 with about 5,500 members. By the 1890 census, they numbered about 600 souls and had disappeared from nearby Culpeper, Stafford, and Orange Counties in Virginia, as well as Hampshire, Berkeley, and Jefferson Counties in West Virginia.

38. *Genius of Universal Emancipation*, July 4, 1825, and October 29, 1825, in Poland, *From Frontier to Suburbia*, 143. Thomas Earle, *The Life, Travel and Opinions of Benjamin Lundy*, 1871 (reprint, New York: Augustus M. Kelly, 1971), gives the date for the printing of the constitution of the Loudoun Manumission and Emigration Society as September 1825.

39. Loudoun Manumission and Emigration Society to R. R. Gurley, n.d., but placed in 1828 file, p. 2 missing, reel 3, RACS.

40. "Address to the Public from the Manumission and Emigration Society of Loudoun," *Genius of Liberty*, May 15, 1827, 2; Jean R. Soderlund, *Quakers and Slavery: A Divided Spirit* (Princeton, N.J.: Princeton University Press, 1985), 184–85; Thomas Drake, *Quakers and Slavery in America* (New Haven: Yale University Press, 1950), 114–15.

41. Earle, *Lundy*, 218; Hickin, "Antislavery in Virginia," 454–55; *Genius of Universal Emancipation*, April 26, 1828, in Poland, *From Frontier to Suburbia*, 145. Thanks to Deborah Lee for verification of the Winchester meeting.

42. Weeks, *Southern Quakers*, 291–93; Drake, *Quakers and Slavery*, 114–15; Worrall, *Friendly Virginians*, 335–42, 352–54.

43. Margaret Crenshaw, "John Bacon Crenshaw," *Quaker Biographies*, ser. 2, vol. 3 (Philadelphia: Friends Book Store, n.d.), 165–68, in Mary Fran Hughes, *The History of Richmond Friends Meeting, 1795–1962* (Richmond: self-published, 1979); John Thomas Richardson to Nathaniel Crenshaw, and quote in Nathaniel Crenshaw to Moses Sheppard, both letters printed in *Virginia Colonizationist* (May 1852),

copy held at LVA; *AR* 3 (July 1828): 154; *Genius of Universal Emancipation*, July 4, 1827, in Earle, *Lundy*, 213; Fox, *American Colonization Society*, 212.

44. Samuel Janney, *Memoirs*, 4th ed. (Philadelphia: Friends Book Association, 1889), 28, 93, 97–106.

45. *AR* 14 (1838): 120; Gurley to Fendall, January 17, 1837, reel 27, RACS.

46. Franklin Knight to Samuel Wilkinson, January 23, 1839, reel 31, RACS; Hickin, "Antislavery in Virginia," 200–206, quote on 291; Andrews to Gurley, March 11, 1837, n.p., in ibid., 296.

47. John H. B. Latrobe to Cortland Van Rensellaer, July 10, 1833, quoted in Richard Hall, *On Afric's Shore: A History of Maryland in Liberia, 1834–1857* (Baltimore: Maryland Historical Society, 2003), 26–27; Philip R. Fendall to Joseph Gales, Richmond, April 5, 1834, reel 20, RACS; Staudenraus, *African Colonization Movement*, 208–9, 223–26.

48. T. B. Balch to R. R. Gurley, August 1, 1838, reel 29, RACS; McLain to Wilkinson, July 11, 1839, reel 32, RACS; Benjamin Brand to R. R. Gurley, March 22, 1842, reel 39, RACS; Hickin, "Antislavery in Virginia," 297–306.

49. See William Link, *Roots of Secession: Slavery and Politics in Antebellum Virginia* (Chapel Hill: University of North Carolina Press, 2003), for the geographic and political divisions in Virginia, esp. 1–11, 283–84.

50. Franklin Knight to Gurley, June 8, July 14, 1843, September 5, September 15, September 29, 1843, December 18, 1843, in Hickin, "Antislavery in Virginia," 307.

51. Ibid., 307–8; William Henry Ruffner to McLain, July 10, 1847, September 7, 1847, reel 52, and October 30, 1847, reel 53, RACS.

52. William Henry Ruffner to William McLain, September 7, 21, 1847, reel 53, RACS; Rufus Bailey to William McLain, September 28, 1847, reel 53, RACS.

53. Rufus Bailey to William McLain, Staunton, August 6, 1850, reel 62, RACS; Hickin, "Antislavery in Virginia," 311; Ellen Eslinger, "The Brief Career of Rufus Bailey, American Colonization Society Agent in Virginia," *JSH* 71, no. 1 (February 2005): 59.

54. John H. Russell, *The Free Negro in Virginia, 1619–1865*, 1913 (reprint, New York: Negro Universities Press, 1969), 74, 157; Rufus Bailey to William McLain, December 12, 1848, reel 57, February 2, 1849, reel 58, March 26, 1850, reel 61, RACS; Nathaniel Crenshaw to McLain, January 9, 1849, reel 58, RACS; "Minutes of the Virginian Branch," newspaper clipping on final page, n.p., n.d., Benjamin Brand Papers, VHS.

55. *AR* 27 (August 1851): 234, 238; *AR* 26 (May 1850): 151; Slaughter to McLain, December 12, 1849, reel 60, RACS; Starr to McLain, January 23, 1854, reel 72, RACS; Starr to Gurley, September 15, 1854, reel 73, RACS.

56. *AR* 28 (May 1852): 100, 149; *AR* 31 (March 1855): 74.

57. "Resolution of Mr. Dorman," *AR* 27 (August 1851): 235.

58. *AR* 26 (May 1850): 214–15.

59. Russell, *Free Negro*, 130; *AR* 26 (August 1850): 246; "Appeal by the Virginia Colonization Society," *AR* 26 (May 1850): 151.

60. Philip Slaughter to McLain, December 12, 1849, reel 60, April 4, 1850, reel 62, RACS; William Starr to McLain, January 23, 1854, reel 72, RACS; Starr to Gur-

ley, September 15, 1857, reel 82, RACS; *Virginia Colonizationist* (1852), Archives Division, LVA; Hickin, "Antislavery in Virginia," 274–320; Staudenraus, *African Colonization Movement,* 234–39; *AR* 29 (July 1853): 198–99.

61. Washington and Lee Special Collections, Washington and Lee Trustees' Papers 028, Folders 99, 113, 118, 119, Washington and Lee University, Lexington, Va. Thanks to Leila Boyer for this data.

62. Hickin, "Antislavery in Virginia," 311–17; William H. Ruffner to "My Dear Sir," May 20, 1848, reel 56, RACS.

63. Extract from letter by Mary J. Henry, published in *Lexington* (Va.) *Gazette,* June 20, 1850. Thanks to Leila Boyer for citation.

64. Eslinger, "Brief Career," 60–65; Rufus Bailey to William McLain, August 6, 1850, reel 62, RACS.

65. *AR* 29 (1853): 161–63, 198–200.

66. Virginia Colonization Board Journal of Proceedings, 1853–58, Archives Division, LVA. The journal notes the final meeting, in August 1858, but gives no reason why the board disbanded.

67. Starr to McLain, January 24, 1861, reel 91, RACS.

Chapter Four

1. "Memorial of the Semi-Centennial Anniversary of the American Colonization Society," Washington, D.C. (January 15, 1867), reel 30, RMCS; Paul Cuffe to "Friend Roper," August 24, 1816, Barrett Collection, Special Collections, UVA.

2. William Crane to Obadiah Brown, March 28, 1819, in Miles Mark Fisher, "Lott Cary, the Colonizing Missionary," *JNH* 7, no. 4 (October 1922): 383; J. B. Taylor, *Biography of Elder Lott Cary, Late Missionary to Africa* (Baltimore: Armstrong and Berry, 1837), 15–16.

3. H. A. Tupper, "The Church in Its Relation to Missions," in *The First Century of the First Baptist Church in Richmond, Virginia, 1780–1880,* ed. H. A. Tupper (Richmond: Carlton McCarthy, 1880), 31; for Brander's role, see the account of the *Elizabeth* in Floyd Miller, *The Search for a Black Nationality: Black Emigration and Colonization, 1787–1863* (Urbana: University of Illinois Press, 1975), 57–68, esp. 61. References to ship departures to Liberia and emigrants are taken from the VEL, in the author's possession.

4. Miller, *Search for a Black Nationality,* 48–49; Richmond statement in *Boston Recorder,* February 17, 1817, 32, photocopy in AfroAmerican Communities Project, Smithsonian Institution, Washington, D.C. William Lloyd Garrison, *Thoughts on African Colonization,* 1832 (reprint, William Loren Katz, ed., New York: Arno Press, 1969); part 2, pp. 9–13, reprints the Philadelphia 1817 statement.

5. Luther Porter Jackson, *A Short History of Gillfield Baptist Church of Petersburg* (Petersburg: Virginia Print Company, 1937); *ACS Semi-Centennial Memorial,* 98–99, reel 30, RMCS; Blanche Sydnor White, *The First Baptist Church, Richmond, 1780–1955* (Richmond: Whittet and Shepperson, 1956), 30; R. R. Gurley, "Sketch of the Life of the Reverend Lott Cary," in *Life of Jehudi Ashmun, Late Colonial Agent in Liberia* (Washington, D.C.: J. C. Dunn, 1835), 147–60; Miller, *Search for a Black Nationality,* 68; James C. Crane to R. R. Gurley, September 21, 1826, reel 1, RACS.

6. David I. Burr to ACS, 7 May 1831, reel 11, RACS.

7. R. H. Toler to R. R. Gurley, August 22, 1833, reel 15, RACS. The results of that expedition, if it took place, are not known.

8. *Controversy between Caius Gracchus and Opimius . . . Originally Published in the Richmond Enquirer* (Georgetown, D.C.: James C. Dunn, 1827), 6.

9. Archibald Alexander, *A History of Colonization on the Western Coast of Africa* (Philadelphia: W. S. Martien, 1846), 243.

10. William Crane letter (February 22, 1855), printed in Tupper, "Missions," in Tupper, *First Century*, 221.

11. Alexander, *History of Colonization*, 244; William Crane to R. R. Gurley, March 30, 1829, reel 5, RACS.

12. Moncure D. Conway, *Testimonies concerning Slavery*, 2nd ed. (London: Chapman and Hall, 1865), 75. He comments that miscegenation is the new word for the "old horror" of amalgamation.

13. For the extent and particular culture of seventeenth- and eighteenth-century miscegenation in Virginia, see Joshua Rothman, *Notorious in the Neighborhood* (Chapel Hill: University of North Carolina Press, 2003); Rodney D. Barfield, "Thomas and John Day and the Journey to North Carolina," *North Carolina Historical Review* 78, no. 1 (January 2001): 1–31 (thanks to Claude Clegg for this article); and Paul Heinegg, *Free African Americans of North Carolina and Virginia*, 2nd ed. (Baltimore: Clearfield, 1994).

14. Ira Berlin, "From Creole to African: Atlantic Creoles and the Origins of African-American Society in Mainland North America," *William and Mary Quarterly* 53 (April 1996): 251–88. See also Tommy Lee Bogger, *Free Blacks in Norfolk, Virginia, 1790–1860: The Darker Side of Freedom*, Carter Woodson Institute Series in Black Studies (Charlottesville: University Press of Virginia, 1997); and Marie Tyler-McGraw and Gregg D. Kimball, *In Bondage and Freedom: Antebellum Black Life in Richmond, Virginia* (Chapel Hill: University of North Carolina Press for the Valentine Museum, 1988).

15. Quotation from Christopher McPherson, *A Short History of the Life of Christopher McPherson*, 2nd ed. (Lynchburg, Va., 1855), 17. Copy in VHS of original from the New-York Historical Society, New York City. James Sidbury, *Ploughshares into Swords: Race, Rebellion, and Identity in Gabriel's Virginia, 1730 to 1810* (Cambridge: Cambridge University Press, 1997), 214.

16. McPherson, *Short History*, 6–8, 13–14; Sidbury, *Ploughshares*, 214–15; *Richmond Enquirer*, March 1, 1811; *Virginia Argus*, March 10, 1811, March 18, 1811, LVA; Edmund Berkley Jr., "Prophet without Honor: Christopher McPherson, Free Person of Color," *VMHB* 77 (April 1969): 180–87.

17. John Day to Rev. J. B. Taylor, October 16, 1847. He added: "This matter has not come to the light. She was sent to the fork of the Yadkin to a quaker's house who came with R. Day from England, where she left my father and money for his education—returned to S.C. and married." John Day Missionary Correspondence, Southern Baptist Foreign Mission Board, Southern Baptist Historical Library and Archives, Nashville, Tenn. My thanks to Jane Leigh Carter for copies of the letters. John Day's mulatto grandfather, Thomas Stewart, owned a large Dinwiddie County

plantation. In his will, he left nineteen slaves to his family. "Unrecorded Wills of Dinwiddie County, Virginia," *Virginia Genealogist* 16 (October–December 1972): 255–57, in Barfield, "Thomas and John Day," 5.

18. James Wesley Smith, *Sojourners in Search of Freedom: The Settlement of Liberia by Black Americans* (Lanham, Md.: University Press of America, 1991), 45–46.

19. John N. Lewis to Samuel Wilkinson, Monrovia, April 12, 1840, letter enclosed to "Mr. Adam S. Naustedler, my Father who lives in Petersburg, Va.," reel 154, RACS. A year later, Lewis asked Wilkinson to "try to find his place of residence." John N. Lewis to Samuel Wilkinson, Monrovia, January 1, 1841, reel 173, RACS.

20. Among the tri-racial family names listed as emigrants to Liberia were Payne, Page, Sampson, Dongee, and Roberts. Virginia Easley DeMarce, "'Very Slitly Mixt': Tri-racial Isolate Families of the Upper South—A Genealogical Study," *NGS Quarterly* 80, no. 1 (March 1992): 5–36; "Looking at Legends—Lumbee and Melungeon: Applied Genealogy and the Origins of Tri-racial Isolate Settlements," *NGS Quarterly* 81, no. 1 (March 1993): 24–45; Helen Rountree, *Pocahontas's People* (Norman: University of Oklahoma Press, 1990), 160, 190–91, 203(nn. 107, 118). See Rountree for a cautious evaluation of the Virginia Indian/European/African relationship over four centuries.

21. Quoted in Debra L. Newman, "The Emergence of Liberian Women in the Nineteenth Century" (Ph.D. diss., Howard University, 1984), 137.

22. "At a Meeting of the Free People of Colour," Benjamin Brand Papers, Section 4, VHS.

23. "Table of Emigrants," *AR* 43 (1867): 109–17.

24. Lott Cary to Benjamin Brand, June 11, 1827, Benjamin Brand Papers, VHS; Entries for Sampson and Waring, newspaper index file, Petersburg Main Library, Petersburg, Va.

25. John Saillant, ed., "Circular Addressed to the Colored Brethren and Friends in America: An Unpublished Essay by Lott Cary, Sent from Liberia to Virginia, 1827," *VMHB* 104, no. 4 (Autumn 1996): 494–95. Cary's circular uses the same vigorous rhetoric and appeals to manhood, liberty, and theology as the contemporary David Walker's *Appeal*, published in 1829.

26. Three of the five committee members were Virginians—Colston Waring, James Barbour, and William Weaver. "Address of the Colonists to the Free People of Colour in the U.S.," Eleventh Annual Report of the ACS, *AR* (1828): 87–94; *American Baptist Magazine* 8: 50–53, reprinted in Mile Mark Fisher, "Documents," *JNH* 7, no. 4 (October 1922): 438–43.

27. Fifteen other passengers on the *Harriet* were the ex-slaves of Margaret Mercer, who was still of Maryland but was soon to move her school to Virginia. Eighteen had been emancipated by Rev. Thomas Hunt of Brunswick County. Another six slaves were manumitted by Edward Colston of Berkeley County, who was the nephew of Supreme Court Chief Justice Marshall (VEL); Patricia Hickin, "Antislavery in Virginia" (Ph.D. diss., University of Virginia, 1968), 278.

28. Beverly Page Yates, *AR* 49 (1873): 94–95 (emphasis in original); Dickson Bruce, "National Identity and Afroamerican Colonization, 1773–1817," *Historian*

58 (Autumn 1995): 15–28; Miller, *Search for a Black Nationality.* Both provide a framework for early African American colonization thought.

29. Thomas Parramore, *Southampton County, Virginia* (Charlottesville, Va.: University Press of Virginia, published for the Southampton County Historical Society, 1978), 71–72.

30. D. I. Burr, Richmond, to R. R. Gurley, D.C., May 7, 1831, reel 11, RACS.

31. Liberia is woven into the Nat Turner legend in black oral tradition. John Cromwell, a Southampton County African American writing in 1920, asserted that Nat Turner's father was "a native of Africa, escaped from slavery and finally emigrated to Liberia where, it is said, his grave is quite as well known as that of Franklin's, Jefferson's or Adam's is to the patriotic American." "The Aftermath of Nat Turner's Insurrection," *JNH* 5, no. 2 (April 1920): 208–34.

32. Ervin L. Jordan Jr., "'A Just and True Account': Two 1833 Parish Censuses of Albemarle County Free Blacks," *Magazine of Albemarle County History* 53 (1995), 114–37.

33. Mortality figures varied among emigrant expeditions, but all investigations concluded that the death rate within the first year was especially high. See Tom W. Shick, "Quantitative Analysis of Liberian Colonization from 1820 to 1893 with Special Reference to Mortality," *Journal of African History* 12 (1971): 145–59; Antonio McDaniel, *Swing Low, Sweet Chariot: The Mortality Cost of Colonizing Liberia in the Nineteenth Century* (Chicago: University of Chicago Press, 1995), 104; and Claude A. Clegg, *The Price of Liberty: African Americans and the Making of Liberia* (Chapel Hill: University of North Carolina Press, 2004), 159–60. Clegg used the 1843 Liberian census to calculate that 20 percent of emigrants had died of West African malaria in the first year. In all, 50 percent died in the first two decades.

34. James Wynn to "Dear Sir," September 6, 1850, reel 63, RACS.

35. Virginians who emancipated significant numbers for emigration in the 1830s and 1840s included Mrs. Ann R. Page of Clark County, General Samuel Blackburn of Bath County, Rev. James W. Stockdell of Madison County, General John Cocke, Mr. Lynch of Lynchburg, and William Hunton of Fauquier County.

36. William Grimes, *Life of William Grimes, the Runaway Slave, Brought Down to the Present Time, Written by Himself,* 1855 (reprinted in *Five Black Lives,* ed. Arna Bontemps [Middletown, Conn.: Wesleyan University Press, 1971]); William Blackford to R. R. Gurley, March 18, 1831, reel 10, RACS; Mary Berkeley Blackford and William Blackford to R. R. Gurley, June 16, 1831, reel 11, RACS; Hickin, "Antislavery in Virginia," 281; *AR* 9 (November 1833): 284; Blackford, *Mine Eyes,* 45.

37. William S. White, *The African Preacher: An Authentic Narrative,* 1849 (reprint, Freeport, N.Y.: Books for Libraries Press, 1972), 109–11, 122–25.

38. Eric Burin, "The Peculiar Solution: The ACS and Antislavery Sentiment in the South, 1820–1860" (Ph.D. diss., University of Illinois, 1999), 106–9; Randall Miller, ed., *"Dear Master": Letters of a Slave Family,* 1978 (2nd ed., Athens: University of Georgia Press, 1990), 7, 25–34; Diana Scott, "Louisa Maxwell Holmes Cocke, 1788–1843," *Bulletin of the Fluvanna County Historical Society* 53 (Spring 1992): 3–4, 10–14.

39. VEL.

40. James C. Minor to William Blackford, *AR* 9 (1833): 126.

41. Rev. J. B. Pinney to ACS, Monrovia, n.d., SHC.

42. Marie Tyler-McGraw, ed., "'The Prize I Mean Is the Prize of Liberty': A Loudoun County Family in Liberia," *VMHB* 97, no. 3 (July 1989): 355–74, quote on 366–67.

43. James O. Horton and Lois E. Horton, "Violence, Protest and Identity: Black Manhood in Antebellum America," in James Oliver Horton, *Free People of Color* (Washington, D.C.: Smithsonian Press, 1993), 80–97; James Oliver Horton, "Freedom's Yoke: Gender Conventions among Antebellum Free Blacks," *Feminist Studies* 12, no. 1 (Spring 1986): 51–76; R. J. Young in *Antebellum Black Activists: Race, Gender, Self* (New York: Garland, 1996), 57–67.

44. R. W. Bailey to William McLain, January 10, 1850, reel 61, RACS; Hickin, "Antislavery in Virginia," 311–17.

45. William Engle to Rev. McLain, January 15, 1850, reel 61, RACS.

46. John Kennedy to R. R. Gurley, April 11, 1831, reel 11, RACS; Bogger, *Free Blacks*, 44–45.

47. Works Progress Administration, *The Negro in Virginia*, 1940 (reprint, Winston-Salem, N.C.: John F. Blair, 1994), 119. The Herndon and Love families of Fauquier and Loudoun Counties manumitted sixty-three slaves and sent seventy-one persons to Liberia in 1856. The ACS mounted a national campaign to raise money for outfitting them. W. McLain to T. H. Rochester, Washington, D.C., August 4, 1854, reel 73, RACS; Thaddeus Herndon to W. McLain, Piedmont Station, Va., April 28, 1857, reel 82, RACS.

48. Benjamin Brand to R. R. Gurley, Richmond, November 3, 1827, reel 3, RACS; inventory and appraisal of estate of Willis Cowling, reel 66, 3–48, LVA.

49. William Starr to William McLain, Norfolk, 12 July 1850, reel 62, RACS; Bogger, *Free Blacks*, 44.

50. James C. Crane to R. R. Gurley, Richmond, January 4, 1827, reel 1, RACS.

51. J. D. Parker to [Gurley], Hampshire County, Va., November 10, 1834, reel 22A, RACS.

52. Benjamin Brand to R. R. Gurley, October 23, 1827, November 3, 1827, November 5, 1827, reel 3, RACS.

53. D. J. Burr to R. R. Gurley, November 10, 1827, and December 5, 1827, reel 3, RACS.

54. Miller, *"Dear Master,"* 93–94; Martin R. Delany and Robert Campbell, *Search for a Place: Black Separatism and Africa*, 1860 (reprint, Ann Arbor: University of Michigan Press, 1971); Wilson J. Moses, ed., *Liberian Dreams: Back-to-Africa Narratives from the 1850s* (University Park: Pennsylvania State University Press, 1997).

55. "Sentiments on Colonization in Liberia," *Colonization Herald* (n.p., n.d.), reprinted in *AR* 30 (May 1854): 144–46.

56. Washington Copeland to Rev. McLain, Circleville, Ohio, October 14, 1860, reel 90, RACS.

57. Forten initially supported African colonization, although most Philadelphia free blacks rejected it. Patrick Rael, *Black Identity and Black Protest in the Antebellum North* (Chapel Hill: University of North Carolina Press, 2002), 274–77, 209–10;

Henry Mayer, *All on Fire: William Lloyd Garrison and the Abolition of Slavery* (New York: St. Martin's Griffin, 1998), 173.

Chapter Five

1. Margaret Mercer to Major John Mercer (n.d., n.p., 1817), Mercer Family Papers, section 39, VHS.

2. Caspar Morris, *Memoir of Miss Margaret Mercer* (Philadelphia: Lindsay and Blackiston, 1848), 16.

3. Thomas Talley, *Negro Folk Rhymes (Wise and Otherwise)* (New York: Macmillan, 1922); Charles K. Wolfe, *Thomas W. Talley's Negro Folk Rhymes* (Knoxville: University of Tennessee Press, 1991), 21. Thanks to Tatiana van Riemsdijk for alternate stanzas.

4. Examples include Morris, *Margaret Mercer*, where unintended levity is confined to the first few pages; L. Minor Blackford, *Mine Eyes Have Seen the Glory: The Story of a Virginia Lady Mary Berkeley Minor Blackford, 1802–1896, Who Taught Her Sons to Hate Slavery and to Love the Union* (Cambridge, Mass.: Harvard University Press, 1954); and C. W. Andrews, *Memoir of Ann R. Page* (Philadelphia: Herman Hooker, 1844). Deborah Lee, in "'Life Is a Solemn Trust': Ann R. Page and the Antislavery Movement in the Upper South" (Ph.D. diss., George Mason University, 2002), 132, has suggested that, given women's lack of access to public forums and print media, the biographies, which included verbatim letters, diaries, and prayers, were a way of preserving and disseminating their views on public issues.

5. The number of Virginia women active and visible in African colonization probably numbered under fifty. The number of those who joined auxiliaries, donated money, wrote letters, made clothing, informally circulated periodicals, or otherwise participated is elusive—and their commitment is harder to gauge—but it probably totals more than four hundred in forty years.

6. The extent to which southern women supported or objected to slavery was the subject of a generation of debate after Anne Firor Scott's *The Southern Lady: From Pedestal to Politics, 1830–1930* (Chicago: University of Chicago Press, 1970). Scott argued that there was much antislavery sentiment among such women; Elizabeth Fox-Genovese, *Within the Plantation Household: Black and White Women of the Old South* (Chapel Hill: University of North Carolina Press, 1988), and Catherine Clinton, *The Plantation Mistress: Women's World in the Old South* (New York: Pantheon Books, 1982), found most southern women to be complacent about slavery, at best. Abundant scholarship has responded to this initial dichotomy by considering urban and town women, farm wives and small planters, and regional and temporal differences among southern women. For my purposes, the most useful works are Elizabeth Varon, *"We Mean to Be Counted": White Women and Politics in Antebellum Virginia* (Chapel Hill: University of North Carolina Press, 1998); Suzanne Lebsock, *The Free Women of Petersburg: Status and Culture in a Southern Town, 1784–1860* (New York: W. W. Norton, 1984); and the core text on southern evangelical women, Donald Mathews, *Religion in the Old South* (Chicago: University of Chicago Press, 1977). I have benefited greatly from two recent dissertations: Tatiana van Riemsdijk, "Time and Property from Heaven: Wealth, Religion, and Reform in Chesapeake Society,

1790–1832" (Ph.D. diss., University of California at San Diego, 1999); and Lee, "Life Is a Solemn Trust." See also Brenda Stephenson, *Life in Black and White* (New York: Oxford University Press, 1996).

7. Studies such as Kathleen Brown, *Good Wives, Nasty Wenches, and Anxious Patriarchs: Gender, Race, and Power in Colonial Virginia* (Chapel Hill: University of North Carolina Press, 1996), trace the connection between race and gender that created the patriarchal structure that was well established by the Revolutionary Era. For comparison with grassroots activists in the North, see Julie Roy Jeffrey, *The Great Silent Army of Abolitionism* (Chapel Hill: University of North Carolina Press, 1998).

8. Charles Wesley Andrews, "Obituary" for Ann R. Page, *AR* 14 (April 1838): 123–27, in Lee, "Life Is a Solemn Trust," 111–12.

9. The literature on evangelical identity formation among women is substantial and constantly evolving. Useful here are Anne Firor Scott, *Natural Allies: Women's Associations in American History* (Urbana: University of Illinois Press, 1991), 26, who notes that benevolent societies both made women conscious of themselves as women and reinforced class and kin ties; and Lee, "Life Is a Solemn Trust," who treats African colonization in Virginia as a social movement with attendant possibilities for recasting identity.

10. Diana Scott, "Louisa Maxwell Holmes Cocke, 1788–1843," in *Bulletin: The Publication of the Fluvanna County Historical Society* 53 (Spring 1992): 1.

11. Morris, *Margaret Mercer*, 14–15.

12. Margaret Mercer to Maria Hunter Garnett, May 5, 1821, and Margaret Mercer to Mrs. James M. Garnett, July 3, 1821, and December 21, 1821, in box 19, Hunter Family Papers, 1766–1918, VHS. I am grateful to Tatiana van Riemsdijk for copies of these letters. An account of the Liberian Society set up within Mrs. Garnett's school can be found in *The Eighth Annual Report of the American Society for Colonizing the Free People of Colour of the United States* (Washington, D.C.: James H. Dunn, 1825), 26–29.

13. Philip Staudenraus, *The African Colonization Movement, 1816–1865* (New York: Columbia University Press, 1961), 110; Morris, *Margaret Mercer*, 84.

14. Margaret Mercer to Miss Garnett, June 15, 1829, Robert M. T. Hunter Papers (microform), 1817–1887, reel 2of, VHS.

15. Diary of Mary Ann Custis Lee, 1852–58, May 20, 1855, Lee Family Papers, LVA.

16. Ann Randolph Page to Mary Lee Fitzhugh Custis, n.d., Mary Lee Fitzhugh Custis Papers, 1818–1902, VHS.

17. Andrews, *Ann R. Page*, 16–17.

18. J. H. B. Latrobe to R. R. Gurley, January 1829, reel 5, RACS.

19. Mary Minor Blackford to R. R. Gurley, January 31, 1829, reel 5, RACS; Blackford, *Mine Eyes*, 44–45; Susan B. Terrell to R. R. Gurley, July 24, 1832, in Patricia Hickin, "Antislavery in Virginia" (Ph.D. diss., University of Virginia, 1968), 269–70; *ACS Eighth Annual Report* (Washington, D.C.: James H. Dunn, 1825), 29.

20. *ACS Eighth Annual Report*, 29.

21. Margaret Mercer to Anna Mercer Harrison, April 17, 1833, Byrd Family Papers, 1791–1867, VHS.

22. *ACS Eighth Annual Report*, 26–29.

23. "Report of the Female Colonization Society of Richmond and Manchester," *AR* 5 (February 1830): 577.

24. Maria Minor, *Launcelot Minor: Pioneer Missionary in Liberia* (New York: National Council of Episcopal Church, 1960), 1, 7, 8; Blackford, *Mine Eyes*, 3–7.

25. S. J. Quinn, *History of Fredericksburg, Virginia* (Richmond: Hermitage, 1908), 226.

26. William Blackford to R. R. Gurley, October 21, 1829, reel 6, RACS.

27. Mary Carter (Wellford) Carmichael, Fredericksburg, Va., to Jane (Wellford) Corbin, King and Queen County, February 18, 1833, VHS.

28. Mary Blackford to R. R. Gurley, May 12, 1829, reel 5, RACS.

29. Benjamin Brand to Lott Cary, January 17, 1826, Benjamin Brand Papers, Section 7, VHS.

30. "To the Colonists of Liberia," *AR* 7 (March 1831): 24–25, reprinted from *Religious Herald* of February 1831.

31. Mary Blackford to R. R. Gurley, November 4, 1830, reel 10, RACS.

32. *AR* 9 (1833): 149.

33. *AR* 10 (1834): 314–15.

34. Quoted in Blackford, *Mine Eyes*, 24; *AR* 10 (1834): 252–53.

35. Colston Waring and Elijah Johnson, "To the Ladies of Richmond and Manchester Colonization Society," *AR* 7 (June 1831): 115–16.

36. See Evelyn Brooks Higginbotham, "African American Women's History and the Metalanguage of Race," *Signs: Journal of Women in History* 17, no. 2 (Winter 1992): 261–63.

37. Patrick H. Breen, "The Female Antislavery Campaign of 1831," *VMHB* 110, no. 3 (2002): 377–98, quote on 394; Virginia Randolph Cary, *Letters on Female Character, Addressed to a Young Lady, On the Death of Her Mother* (Richmond: A. Works, 1828). Cary, not an advocate of colonization, shared the grievances of Virginia women of her class in regard to slavery. See Elizabeth Varon, *We Mean to Be Counted: White Women and Politics in Antebellum Virginia* (Chapel Hill: University of North Carolina Press, 1998), 41–43.

38. Margaret Mercer to Maria Hunter Garnett, June 18, 1830, box 19, Byrd Family Papers, Section 6, VHS; Kitty Slater in *The Spur*, n.d., and "The Rambler," *Washington Post*, December 22, 1918, both in "Belmont Construction Chronology," Traceries Architectural History Research Firm, 1606 Twentieth Street, Washington, D.C. (1986); Catherine Mildred Lee Childe to Mary Ann Randolph Custis, West River, Md., November 1829, Lee Family Papers, VHS.

39. Margaret Mercer to Maria H. Garnett, March 25, 1837, Hunter Family Papers, VHS; Morris, *Margaret Mercer*, 104–5, 116–18; "Rambler," in "Belmont Construction Chronology."

40. Margaret Mercer to Margaret Fenton Hunter, November 12, 1835, box 22, Hunter Family Papers, VHS.

41. Margaret Mercer to Gerrit Smith, in Morris, *Margaret Mercer*, 131–32.

42. Gerda Lerner, *The Grimké Sisters from South Carolina* (New York: Shocken Books, 1971), 13–58.

43. Angelina Grimké to Catharine Beecher, July 20, 1837, in *The Public Years of Sarah and Angelina Grimké: Selected Writings, 1835–1839*, ed. Larry Ceplair (New York: Columbia University Press, 1991), 164–66.

44. Angelina Grimké, "Appeal to the Christian Women of the South," 1836, in Ceplair, *Selected Writings*, 77–79, 149.

45. Ann R. Page to R. R. Gurley, April 4, 1831. A version of this letter appeared in *AR* 7, no. 4 (April 1831): 58–59. Thanks to Deborah Lee for a copy of this letter.

46. Ann R. Page to Gerrit Smith, August 13, 1834, Special Collections, Syracuse University Library. Thanks to Deborah Lee for a copy of this letter. There was general agreement that citizenship meant masculine and white. See David Roediger, *Wages of Whiteness: Race and the Making of the American Working Class* (New York: Verso, 1991), 13; James Oliver Horton and Lois E. Horton, *In Hope of Liberty: Culture, Community, and Protest among Northern Free Blacks, 1700–1860* (New York: Oxford University Press, 1997), 166–67.

47. John Randolph to Betsy Coalter, December 25, 1828, John Randolph Papers, UVA, in Clinton, *The Plantation Mistress*, 161.

48. Blackford, *Mine Eyes*, 54.

49. John Hartwell Cocke to George Fitzhugh (1853), n.d., in Scott, *Southern Lady*, 20.

50. Ruth Coder Fitzgerald, *A Different Story: A Black History of Fredericksburg, Stafford, and Spotsylvania, Virginia* (Fredericksburg: Unicorn Press, 1979), 85; William Lee Miller, *Arguing about Slavery: The Great Battle in the United States Congress* (New York: Knopf, 1996), 225–30.

51. On the development of proslavery theology in the South, see Mitchell Snay, *Gospel of Disunion: Religion and Separatism in the Antebellum South* (Chapel Hill: University of North Carolina Press, 1993), esp. 20–28; and Drew Gilpin Faust, *The Ideology of Slavery: Proslavery Thought in the Antebellum South, 1830–1860* (Baton Rouge: Louisiana State University Press, 1981).

52. Blackford, *Mine Eyes*, 55, 11; Andrews, *Memoir*, 26.

53. The manner in which Virginia women used African colonization to nurture and emancipate persons known to them supports Suzanne Lebsock's assessment that race relations in Petersburg were grounded in the personal daily interactions between white women and African Americans. Suzanne Lebsock, *The Free Women of Petersburg: Status and Culture in a Southern Town* (New York: W. W. Norton, 1985).

54. Cynthia Wolff, "'Masculinity' in Uncle Tom's Cabin," *American Quarterly* 47, no. 4 (December 1995): 598–601. Wolff, among others, argues that, in the United States in this era, the definition of masculinity was more aggressive and self-aggrandizing, at the expense of communal ideals and leadership. Northern reform movements were engaged in a radical redefinition of masculinity away from such standards and back toward men of civic and domestic virtue. Virginia colonization women appear to have had similar goals.

55. Elizabeth Varon, *Southern Lady, Yankee Spy: The True Story of Elizabeth Van Lew, a Union Agent in the Heart of the Confederacy* (New York: Oxford University Press, 2003), 28–31.

56. Elizabeth Van Lew to Anthony Williams, September 10, 1859, reel 84, RACS.

57. Fitzgerald, *A Different Story*, 80.

58. Blackford, *Mine Eyes*, 61; Mary Blackford to William McLain, October 11, 1843, reel 43, RACS.

59. Blackford to Rev. McLain, May 17, 1844, and June 6, 1844, reel 44, RACS.

60. Mary B. Blackford to William McLain, August 10, 1844, reel 45, RACS.

61. Alphabetical index of emigrants on 3-by-5-inch cards in metal file box, SHC, temporarily stored and not yet accessioned at Archive of Traditional Arts, University of Indiana, Bloomington; VEL.

62. Anne Rice to William McLain, March 29, 1848, reel 55, RACS.

63. Anne Rice to William McLain, April 2, 1848, reel 55, and December 18, 1847, reel 54, RACS.

64. Letters do not reveal whether these marriages were done by a minister or whether any long-term relationship, seen as a marriage by both parties, was sufficient to be honored. Rice to McLain, December 18, 1847, reel 53; Rice to McLain, April 2, 1848, reel 55, RACS.

65. Elizabeth Varon, *We Mean to Be Counted*, 103–5; Carroll Smith-Rosenberg, "(Dis)Covering the Subject of the 'Great Constitutional Discussion,' 1786–1789," *Journal of American History* 79 (December 1992): 841–73; and Linda Kerber, "The Republican Mother: Women and the Enlightenment—An American Perspective," in *Toward an Intellectual History of Women* (Chapel Hill: University of North Carolina Press, 1997), 41–62.

66. The probate inventory of her property after her death valued the library at $200 and a "chemical apparatus" at $250, the highest assessments given. A silver teapot, at $15, was the highest individual item. Probate Inventory of Belmont Estate, Loudoun County Will Book 2D, 197–98 (February 9, 1847).

67. Varon, *We Mean to Be Counted*, 105–6, 206n8.

68. *AR* 16 (August 1840): 248–49.

69. Harriet Beecher Stowe, *Uncle Tom's Cabin*, 1851–52 (reprint, New York: Bantam Books, 1981), 429–33.

70. Varon, *We Mean to Be Counted*, 105–7, 115.

71. Ibid., 112–13, 107–11.

72. Ibid., 5, 6, 73, 91–92, 117–18, 127, 210n.

73. Mary Price Coulling, *Margaret Junkin Preston: A Biography* (Winston-Salem, N.C.: John F. Blair, 1993), 52–53, 62–65.

74. Mary Blackford to "My Dear Friend," April 1861, reel 91, RACS.

75. Mary Minor Blackford to James Monroe Minor, July 24, 1866, in Fitzgerald, *Different Story*, 86.

Chapter Six

1. Jesse Burton Harrison, "The Prospects of Letters and Taste in Virginia: A Discourse Pronounced before the Literary and Philosophical Society of Hampden-Sydney College, at Their Fourth Anniversary, in Sept., 1827," reprinted in Fairfax Harrison, ed., *Aris Sonis Focisque: Being a Memoir of an American Family, the Harrisons*

of Skimino (privately printed, 1910), 272, 275, in Rare Books, Alderman Library, UVA; emphasis in original.

2. Thomas R. Dew, "Abolition of Negro Slavery," *American Quarterly Review* 12 (September 1832): 189–265, reprinted in *The Ideology of Slavery: Proslavery Thought in the Antebellum South, 1830–1860,* ed. Drew Gilpin Faust (Baton Rouge: Louisiana State University Press, 1981), 21–77; Joseph Dorfman, *The Economic Mind in American Civilization, 1606–1865* (New York: Viking Press, 1946), 2:903–6.

3. Jesse Burton Harrison, "The Slave Question in Virginia," *American Quarterly Review* (December 1832), in Harrison, *Ars Sonis Focisque,* 337–38, 342, 349, 352, 385.

4. See, for the interconnection of sectional and economic issues with slavery, William A. Link, *Roots of Secession: Slavery and Politics in Antebellum Virginia* (Chapel Hill: University of North Carolina Press, 2003); and William G. Shade, *Democratizing the Old Dominion: Virginia and the Second Party System, 1824–1861* (Charlottesville: University Press of Virginia, 1996). See Alison G. Freehling, *Drift toward Dissolution: The Virginia Slavery Debates of 1832* (Baton Rouge: Louisiana State University Press, 1982), for the pointed exchanges that inspired Harrison and Dew.

5. The earliest visions of Virginia, from the Hakluyts and John Smith forward, are reviewed in Hugh Honour, *The New Golden Land: European Images of America from the Discoveries to the Present Time* (New York: Pantheon, 1975); and Lewis P. Simpson, *The Dispossessed Garden: Pastoral and History in Southern Literature* (Athens: University of Georgia Press, 1975).

6. Vernon L. Parrington, *The Romantic Revolution in America, 1800–1860,* vol. 2 of *Main Currents in American Thought,* 1928 (reprint, New York: Harcourt, Brace and World, 1954), 28; Jane Tompkins, *Sensational Designs: The Cultural Work of American Fiction, 1790–1860* (New York: Oxford University Press, 1985), xi–xiii; Jan Nederveen Pietersee, *White on Black: Images of America from the Discoveries to the Present Time* (New Haven: Yale University Press, 1992); David S. Reynolds, *Beneath the American Renaissance: The Subversive Imagination in the Age of Emerson and Melville* (New York: Knopf, 1988).

7. William Byrd to John Perceval, July 12, 1736, *Correspondence,* 2:487–88, in Mechal Sobel, *The World They Made Together: Black and White Values in Eighteenth-Century Virginia* (Princeton: Princeton University Press, 1988), 88.

8. Philip Hamilton, *The Making and Unmaking of a Revolutionary Family: The Tuckers of Virginia, 1752–1830* (Charlottesville: University of Virginia Press, 2003), 132–34, 146–55, 199–200. See Hamilton for an assessment of the Tucker family, whose declining fortunes caused them to embrace a paternalistic model of slavery. George Tucker, *The Valley of the Shenandoah or, Memoirs of the Graysons,* ed. Donald Noble, Southern Literary Classics Series (Chapel Hill: University of North Carolina Press, 1970); George Tucker, *A Century Hence, or, A Romance of 1941,* ed. Donald Noble (Charlottesville: University Press of Virginia, 1977), xii–xiii; William L. Van Deburg, "Slave Imagery in the Literature of the Early Republic," *Mississippi Quarterly* 36, no. 1 (Winter 1982–83): 65, 67.

9. George Tucker, *The Progress of the United States in Population and Wealth in Fifty*

Years, as Exhibited by the Decennial Census (Boston: Little, Brown, 1843), quotations on 117–18, 108–18, 68–75; Dorfman, *Economic Mind*, 2:886–87.

10. Richard Beale Davis, *Intellectual Life in Jefferson's Virginia* (Chapel Hill: University of North Carolina Press, 1964), 312–13; James Ewell Heath, *Whigs and Democrats; or, Love of No Politics: A Comedy in Three Acts* (Richmond: T. W. White, 1839), Special Collections, UVA; Agnes Bondurant, *Poe's Richmond*, 1942 (reprint, Richmond: Poe Associates, 1978), 100, 152, 185; Susan J. Tracy, *In the Master's Eye: Representations of Women, Blacks, and Poor Whites in Antebellum Southern Literature* (Amherst: University of Massachusetts Press, 1995), 49.

11. John Pendleton Kennedy, *Swallow Barn; or, A Sojourn in the Old Dominion*, 1832, 1851 (reprint, Baton Rouge: Louisiana State University Press, 1986), 452–53.

12. William R. Taylor, *Cavalier and Yankee: The Old South and American National Character*, 1961 (reprint, New York: Harper Torchbooks, 1969), 203–18; Jay Hubbell, *Virginia Life in Fiction* (New York: Columbia University Press, 1922), 8, 13–14, 23.

13. David A. Rawson, "The Publishing World of *Poe's Richmond*, or Thomas Willis White and the Southern Periodical Trade," paper given at International Poe Conference, Richmond, Va., October 1999; copy in possession of author. "H" in *Southern Literary Messenger* (August 1834), in David K. Jackson, *Poe and the Southern Literary Messenger* (New York: Haskell House, 1970), 23.

14. Candy Gunter Brown, *The Word in the World: Evangelical Writing, Publishing, and Reading in America, 1789–1980* (Chapel Hill: University of North Carolina Press, 2004), 154; Jonathan Daniel Wells, *The Origins of the Southern Middle Class, 1800–1861* (Chapel Hill: University of North Carolina Press, 2005), 79, 314.

15. Jesse Burton Harrison address to ACS, "Eleventh Annual Report of the ACS, 1828," in *AR* 8 (1832): 16–17.

16. Douglas Egerton, "Averting a Crisis: The Proslavery Critique of the American Colonization Society," in *Rebels, Reformers, and Revolutionaries: Collected Essays and Second Thoughts* (New York: Routledge, 2002), 147–60.

17. Beverley Tucker, *The Partisan Leader: A Tale of the Future*, 1836 (reprint of 1861 edition, Upper Saddle River, N.J.: Gregg Press, 1968), 97–99, 100, 123; Robert Brugger, *Beverley Tucker: Heart over Head in the Old South* (Baltimore: Johns Hopkins University Press, 1978), 202–3, 120–27, 123.

18. David Allmendinger, *Ruffin: Family and Reform in the Old South* (New York: Oxford University Press, 1990), 140–51. For the black response to claims of inferiority, see Patrick Rael, *Black Identity and Black Protest in the Antebellum North* (Chapel Hill: University of North Carolina Press, 2002), 237–61; George Frederickson, *The Black Image in the White Mind: The Debate on African American Character and Destiny, 1817–1914* (New York: Harper and Row, 1971), 27–42; Bruce Dain, *"A Hideous Monster of the Mind": American Race Theory in the Early Republic* (Cambridge, Mass.: Harvard University Press, 2002), vii–ix, 16–24, 81–83, 150–51.

19. Allmendinger, *Ruffin*, 140–51; Betty Mitchell, *Edmund Ruffin, A Biography* (Bloomington: Indiana University Press, 1981), 113–14.

20. Edmund Ruffin, *African Colonization Unveiled* (Washington, D.C.: Lemuel Towers, 1859), 32.

21. W. S. Morton to Edmund Ruffin, Cumberland, box marked "1959" [1859], Edmund Ruffin Papers, VHS.

22. Douglas E. Pielmeier, "Arlington House: The Evolution of a Nineteenth-Century Virginia Plantation," unpublished manuscript at Arlington House National Historic Site, Robert E. Lee Memorial, Arlington, Va., 63–64, 69–70.

23. Horace Binney, *Bushrod Washington* (Philadelphia: C. Sherman, 1858), 9; Ben Perley Poore, *Perley's Reminiscences of Sixty Years in the National Metropolis*, 2 vols. (Philadelphia: Hubbard, 1886), 1:86; Bushrod Washington to Editor, *Niles' Weekly Register*, September 18, 1821, in Philip Staudenraus, *The African Colonization Movement, 1816–1865* (New York: Columbia University Press, 1961), 173; Diary (January 21–October 7) of John Brazier Cannon, Manager, Mount Vernon, Mount Vernon Archives, Mount Vernon, Va.

24. Staudenraus, *African Colonization Movement*, 128; Bushrod Washington to R. R. Gurley, Washington, D.C., March 15, 1828, reel 3, RACS.

25. Originally published in *Baltimore Morning Chronicle* (August 25, 1821) and republished in *Niles' Weekly Register* (September 1, 1821). My copy from *Woodstock Observer*, Woodstock, Vt. (September 25, 1821). Thanks to Scott Casper for original sources.

26. Bushrod Washington, Jefferson County, Va., to Editor, *Niles' Weekly Register* (September 29, 1821); Charles Poland, *From Frontier to Suburbia* (Marcelline, Mo.: Walsworth, 1976), 143n; *Philadelphia Union* (July 29, 1822).

27. Jean B. Lee, "Historical Memory, Sectional Strife, and the American Mecca: Mount Vernon, 1783–1853," *VMHB* 109, no. 3 (2001): 257–58, 260–61.

28. Washington Custis to Charles Fenton Mercer, n.p., February 17, 1832, ser. I, file 1, George Washington Parke Custis Papers, 1832–56, Manuscripts and Rare Books, Swem Library, College of William and Mary, Williamsburg, Va. <http://ead.ib.virginia.edu/servlets> or <http://www.swem.wm.edu/SpColl/index.html>.

29. Lee, "Historical Memory," 256–58, 271–72.

30. Ibid., 281–83; *Daily National Intelligencer*, quoted in *Baltimore Patriot and Commercial Gazette*, June 15, 1853, in ibid., 292–93. See the post–Civil War account in Maria Diederich, *Love across Color Lines* (New York: Hill and Wang, 1999), 284. "At Mount Vernon she [Ottilie Assing], accompanied by the children of Frederick Douglass, encountered a black gardener who claimed to have been a teenager at Washington's death. Assing took a close look and felt that [was] rather far-fetched, but she decided that a man who had endured slavery had every right to make a little money by fooling a few credulous whites."

31. John W. Wayland, *The Washingtons and Their Homes*, 1943 (reprint, Berryville: Virginia Book Co., 1973), 293; Bushrod Washington married Anne Blackburn of Rippon Lodge, Fairfax County, Va. Bushrod's nephews, John Augustine and Bushrod C. Washington, married sisters, Jane Charlotte and Thomasina Blackburn.

32. Judith M. Blackburn to R. R. Gurley, October 1830 and March 29, 1831, reel 10, RACS.

33. *AR* 8 (November 1832): 280–82.

34. U.S. Senate, Roll of Emigrants That Have Been Sent to the Colony of Liberia, West Africa, 28th Cong., 2nd sess., 1844, S.Doc. 150, 105–414; Property Records for Monrovia, SHC.

35. Pielmeier, "Arlington House," 98; Clippings in Master Data File Books 1 (1805–11) and 2 (1811–23), Arlington House National Historic Site, Robert E. Lee Memorial, Arlington, Va.

36. Jay B. Hubbell, "The Smith-Pocahontas Story in Literature," *VMHB* 65, no. 3 (July 1957): 294.

37. ACS, *Fourteenth Annual Report* (Georgetown, D.C.: James C. Dunn, 1831), 22–23.

38. Samuel Janney, *Memoirs of Samuel M. Janney* (Philadelphia: Friends Book Association, 1881), 28–29.

39. ACS, *Eleventh Annual Report* (Georgetown, D.C.: James C. Dunn, 1828), 16–17.

40. Robert E. Lee, Fort Brown, Texas, to Mary Randolph Lee, Arlington, December 27, 1856, Lee Family Papers, VHS.

41. Diary of Mary Randolph Lee, 1852–58, ibid.

42. Bell Wiley, ed., *Slaves No More: Letters from Liberia, 1833–1869* (Lexington: University of Kentucky Press, 1980), 188.

43. Rosabella Burke to Mary Custis Lee, Clay-Ashland, Liberia, August 21, 1854, in ibid., 192.

44. Rosabella Burke to Mary C. Lee, Clay-Ashland, Liberia, February 20, 1859, in ibid., 207. Wiley identifies the women referenced as Lee family members, but National Park Service staff at Arlington House National Historic Site, Robert E. Lee Memorial, Arlington, Va., have identified them as sisters to William Burke. "An Inventory of the Slaves, at Arlington belonging to the Estate of G. W. P. Custis, taken January 1st, 1858."

45. William C. Burke to R. R. Gurley, Clay-Ashland, Liberia, June 27, 1856, in Wiley, *Slaves No More*, 193.

46. Pielmeier, "Arlington House," 91–92.

47. Blanche Berurd to "Mother," Pelham Priory, April 18, 1856. Typescript copy in Arlington House Internal Training Manual, Arlington House National Historic Site, Robert E. Lee Memorial, Arlington, Va.

48. Gillian Brown, *Domestic Individualism: Imagining Self in Nineteenth-Century America* (Berkeley: University of California Press, 1992), 13, 16; Lucinda H. MacKethan, "Domesticity in Dixie: The Plantation Novel and Uncle Tom's Cabin," in *Haunted Bodies: Gender and Southern Texts*, ed. Anne Goodwyn Jones and Susan V. Donaldson (Charlottesville: University Press of Virginia, 1997), 223–42.

49. Daniel Meaders, *Advertisements for Runaway Slaves in Virginia, 1801–1820* (New York: Garland, 1997), 190–91.

50. Dr. John Ker, the most prominent colonizationist in Mississippi, related this story to Gurley, hoping for a denial. Gurley could only deny any knowledge of the exact whereabouts of the family whose cause he represented to the planter. Dr. John Ker, Natchez, to R. R. Gurley, April 13, 1831, in Franklin L. Reilly, "A Contribution to the History of the Colonization Movement in Mississippi," *Pub-*

lications of the Mississippi Historical Society 9 (Jackson, Miss., 1908): 344–47, 353–56.

51. Washington Custis Will and Inventory and Estate Settlement (Alexandria City), Will Book 7, 1855–60, 267–68; Will Book 7, Estate of GWP Custis, July 15, 1859, 485–92.

52. Mary Randolph Lee to Anne Carter Lee, [month illegible] 10, 1860, Lee Family Papers, VHS.

53. Pielmeier, "Arlington House," 116–17, 119–20, 155–56, notes a persistent oral tradition among African American families that has lived on for two hundred years in the District of Columbia, Arlington, and Alexandria. An 1865 land claims case by the Syphax family and the legal record of emancipations by Custis supports this idea. Archivists at Mount Vernon and Arlington House support the conjecture with such notations as "Judy appears to have had at least two children, possibly by GWPC." Slave Families File, Mount Vernon Archives, Alexandria, Va., 23–24. See also pp. 28, 36–37, in Slave Files. For "shadow families" among generations of Custises, see, among others, Philip Morgan, "Interracial Sex in the Chesapeake and the Atlantic World, c. 1700–1820," in *Sally Hemings and Thomas Jefferson: History, Memory, and Civic Culture*, ed. Jan Ellen Lewis and Peter S. Onuf (Charlottesville: University Press of Virginia, 1999), 52–55.

54. "Citizen" to the Editor of the *New York Daily Tribune*, June 24, 1859, from clipping in Arlington House datebook, in Pielmeier, "Arlington House," 154–55.

55. Richard Bushman, *The Refinement of America: Persons, Houses, Cities* (New York: Knopf, 1992), xiv, 98–99.

56. Mary Randolph Lee to W. G. Webster, Arlington, February 17, 1858, Lee Family Papers, LVA.

57. William Burke to R. R. Gurley, Clay-Ashland, Liberia, January 29, 1858, in Wiley, *Slaves No More*, 199.

58. William Burke to Mary Custis Lee, Clay-Ashland, Liberia, February 20, 1859, in ibid., 203.

59. William Burke to R. R. Gurley, Clay-Ashland, Liberia, September 29, 1863, in ibid., 213.

Chapter Seven

1. The family histories in this chapter are based on both research and informed speculation. Relationships among antebellum black family members traveling to Liberia are not recorded, although they are sometimes apparent. In some cases, the surname is one of temporary convenience for the enumerators or represents a farm or plantation group emancipated and traveling together. For the most part, I have focused on individuals for whom more than one source of information is available. Information in the VEL is supplemented with letters, real estate records, court records, and cemetery markers. For the Coopers, see Palm Grove Cemetery inscriptions, SHC, and "Applicants for Passage to Liberia for Apr. 1853," reel 306, RACS.

2. *AR* 43 (1867): 109–17; William Duglass (variant spelling) to "Friend," [Dr.

James Minor], James Hunter Terrell Letters, Special Collections, UVA. Found at Electronic Text Center: <http://etext.lib.virginia.edu/rbs/98>; *AR* 41 (1865): 362–65. Dr. James Minor was the executor for emancipator James Terrell of Albemarle County.

3. Floyd Miller, *The Search for a Black Nationality: Black Emigration and Colonization, 1787–1863* (Urbana: University of Illinois Press, 1975), 49, 59–68; Samuel Wilkinson, *A Concise History . . . of the Colonies in Liberia* (Washington, D.C.: Madisonian Office, 1839), 3–4.

4. Warren L. D'Azevado, "A Tribal Reaction to Nationalism," *LSJ* 1, no. 2 (Spring 1969): 1–21; Tom Shick, *Behold the Promised Land: A History of Afro-American Settler Society in Nineteenth-Century Liberia* (Baltimore: Johns Hopkins University Press, 1980), 20–25, 28–30; Mahammad Alpha Beh, "The History of Liberia before 1820," in *History and Culture Study Seminar on Liberia, Sierra Leone, Senegal,* ed. James Tarpeh (Monrovia: U.S. Department of Education and U.S. Educational and Cultural Foundation of Liberia, 1985), 47–51, SHC; T. E. Besolow, "Zulu Dumah, or King Peter: The Napoleon of Liberia," *Liberian Churchman* 2, no. 4 (April 1924): 3–8, SHC.

5. Lott Cary to Corresponding Secretary, Baptist Board, March 13, 1821, in *The Latter-Day Luminary: By a Committee of the Baptist Board of Foreign Missions for the United States,* vol. 2, 1820–21 (Philadelphia: Anderson and Mehany, 1821), 398.

6. Charles H. Huberich, *The Political and Legislative History of Liberia,* 2 vols. (New York: Central Book Company, 1947), 1:213, 295; James Wesley Smith, *Sojourners in Search of Freedom: The Settlement of Liberia by Black Americans* (Lanham, Md.: University Press of America, 1991), 44.

7. Shick, *Behold,* 38, 86, 91; Miller, *Search for a Black Nationality,* 72–74; Smith, *Sojourners,* 45–47; *Constitution, Government, and Digest of the Laws of Liberia . . . May 23, 1825* (Washington City: Way and Gideon, 1825), Toner Collection, LC.

8. George Brooks Jr., ed., "A. A. Adee's Journal of a Visit to Liberia in 1827," *LSJ* 1, no. 1 (1968): 67: "Dined at the Governor's House with Mrs. Thompson, Mrs. Williams, and Mr. Prout, all black." At his death, Ashmun left bequests to five Liberians. He left his Monrovia warehouse to housekeeper Martha Thompson, with the requirement that she give his "beloved and adopted child Sally Goss" a Christian education. The other bequests were to Anthony D. Williams, Colston Waring, William L. Weaver, and "Mrs. James, my housekeeper at Caldwell." "Last Will and Testament of Jehudi Ashmun," District of Columbia, Washington County, to wit Orphan's Court, October 11, 1828, copy in SHC; Smith, *Sojourners,* 56.

9. Smith, *Sojourners,* 64, 67.

10. VEL; Benjamin Brand to Lott Cary, February 3, 1827, and January 15, 1829, Benjamin Brand Papers, Section 4, VHS; "Rev. J. D. Paxton, D.D.," *AR* 47 (1871): 213–15.

11. Benjamin Brand to Lott Cary, January 15, 1829, Benjamin Brand Papers, Section 4, VHS; Smith, *Sojourners,* 65; Charles, Patrick, and David Bullock to Col. Bullock to Benjamin Brand, enclosed in Benjamin Brand to R. R. Gurley, June 10, 1828, reel 4, RACS.

12. Richard Strong, ed., *The African Republic of Liberia and the Belgian Congo* (Cambridge, Mass.: Harvard University Press, 1930), 30; Smith, *Sojourners*, 61; Shick, *Behold*, 26–27; Claude A. Clegg, *The Price of Liberty: African Americans and the Making of Liberia* (Chapel Hill: University of North Carolina Press, 2004), 79–80.

13. W. E. B. Du Bois, *Suppression of the African Slave Trade to the United States of America, 1638–1870*, 1896 (reprint, Baton Rouge: Louisiana State University Press, 1970), 128–29; Smith, *Sojourners*, 63–66.

14. Brooks, "A. A. Adee," 60.

15. Simon Fraser Blunt Journal, July 5, 1845, Section 3: "Extracts From the Private Journal," Simon Fraser Blunt Papers, 1833–1921, VHS; D. Elwood Dunn, Amos Beyan, and Carl Patrick Burrowes, eds., *Historical Dictionary of Liberia*, 2nd ed. (Lanham, Md.: Scarecrow Press, 2001), 82–83; Debra L. Newman, "The Emergence of Liberian Women in the Nineteenth Century" (Ph.D. diss., Howard University, 1984), 165; Lott Cary to Benjamin Brand, August 12, 1826, Benjamin Brand Papers, Section 4, VHS.

16. J. Mechlin Jr. to R. R. Gurley, April 22, 1829, reel 5, RACS; *AR* 5 (June 1829): 122–23.

17. Frederick Lewis to ACS, May 6, 1829, reel 5, RACS; J. Mechlin Jr. to R. R. Gurley, August 1829, in *AR* 5 (1829): 282–84.

18. *Richmond Whig*, January 5, 1828, in Henley Index and Online Database, LVA.

19. J. Mechlin to R. R. Gurley, April 22, 1829, reel 5, RACS.

20. *AR* 43 (1867): 110–17; Smith, *Sojourners*, 109.

21. *AR* 43 (1867): 110–17; VEL; John W. McPhail to R. R. Gurley, November 27, 1831, in Thomas C. Parramore, *Southampton County, Virginia* (Charlottesville: University Press of Virginia, published for the Southampton County Historical Society), 111–15; Smith, *Sojourners*, 110, 118–19.

22. William Broaddus to R. R. Gurley, November 2, 1833, reel 19, RACS; Walker Hawes to Gurley, December 16, 1833, reel 19, RACS; *AR* 10 (1834): 286.

23. Shick, *Behold*, 99, 73.

24. William S. White, *The African Preacher: An Authentic Narrative*, 1849 (reprint, Freeport, N.Y.: Books for Libraries Press, 1972), 107, 111, 119–20, 122–25; VEL; Fox, *American Colonization Society*, 96–98.

25. Smith, *Sojourners*, 137–44.

26. Eric Burin, "The Peculiar Solution: The ACS and Antislavery Sentiment in the South, 1820–1860" (Ph.D. diss., University of Illinois, 1999), cites a letter from Pennsylvania colonizationist Elliot Cresson, suggesting in late 1835 that Jones send out a "selection" as "pioneers." Elliot Cresson to Dr. James Jones, October 2, 1835, Watson Family Papers, LVA, in ibid., 87n41. Clegg, in *Price of Liberty*, 154, cites a letter from Cresson to Louis Sheridan in mid-1836, asking Sheridan to lead a company of emigrants to Bassa Cove. See also Eric Burin, *Slavery and the Peculiar Solution: A History of the American Colonization Society* (Gainesville: University Press of Florida, 2005), 82–89.

27. Eli Seifman, "The United Colonization Societies of New-York and Pennsylvania and the Establishment of the African Colony of Bassa Cove," *Pennsylvania Maga-*

zine of History and Biography 35, no. 1 (January 1968): 23–43; C. Abayomi Cassell, *Liberia: A History of the First African Republic* (New York: Fountainhead Publishers, 1970), 107; Smith, *Sojourners*, 137, 143–44, 148–49; VEL; Shick, *Behold*, 33.

28. *Virginia Colonizationist* (May 1852), LVA; Early Lee Fox, *The African Colonization Society, 1817–1840* (Baltimore: Johns Hopkins University Press, 1919), 102; "Virginia in Africa," *AR* 19 (1845): 270–71; Clegg, *Price of Liberty*, 214; Edmund Ruffin, *African Colonization Unveiled* (Washington, D.C.: Lemuel Towers, 1859), 26.

29. There is no indication in the VCS records that the 1837 suggestion to fund a colony was ever adopted. Yet the colony existed by 1846, and letters published in the *African Repository* mention it briefly. See *AR* 29 (1853): 232–33, where it is called "the worst off of any." By 1870, it is described as the depot for the Mandingo cloth trade from Boporu, although the "Virginians" are not traders but "supply the produce and vegetable markets of Monrovia"; *AR* 46 (1870): 313. Shick, *Behold*: page 33 for Mississippi, page 34 for Maryland, and page 75 for Virginia. *AR* 43 (April 1867) puts the total receipts of the ACS from 1817 to 1866 at $2,141,507.77. The total receipts for the Maryland Colonization Society were $309,759.33, and the New York City and Pennsylvania societies, "during their independent condition," were $95,640.00. The Mississippi Colonization Society received $12,000, and the Virginia Colonization Society failed to report its income.

30. Henry and Milly Franklin to Dr. James Hunter Minor, January 27, 1858, James Hunter Terrell Letters, Special Collections, UVA; Mars Lucas to Townsend Heaton, March 12, 1830, in Marie Tyler-McGraw, ed., "The Prize of Liberty: A Loudoun County Family in Liberia," *VMHB* 97, no. 3 (July 1989): 364.

31. Mars Lucas to Townsend Heaton, June 19, 1830, 368, and Jesse Lucas to Friends, 373–74, in ibid.

32. George Todsen to R. R. Gurley, April 25, 1834, reel 153, ACS Records, SHC.

33. Svend E. Holsoe, "Land Records and Treaties," box 11, SHC.

34. Tom W. Shick, "Emigrants to Liberia, 1820–1843: An Alphabetical Listing" (Liberian Studies Working Paper Number 2, Department of Anthropology, University of Delaware, Newark, Del., for Liberian Studies Association, 1971); VEL.

35. Mary H. Moran, *Civilized Women: Gender and Prestige in Southeastern Liberia* (Ithaca: Cornell University Press, 1990), 41–44; Sampson Ceasar to David S. Haselden, February 7, 1834, in Ceasar Letters, Special Collections, Electronic Text Center, UVA <http://etext.lib.Virginia.edu/subjects/liberia> (accessed August 2002); Philip Barrett, *Gilbert Hunt, the City Blacksmith* (Richmond: James Woodhouse, 1859), 29–30.

36. Barrett, *Gilbert Hunt*, 29–30; Staudenraus, *African Colonization Movement*, 189.

37. Joseph Shiphard, Monrovia to ACS, n.d., printed in *AR* 6 (1830): 245–46; Abraham Blackford to Susan Wheeler, in Bell Wiley, ed., *Slaves No More: Letters from Liberia, 1833–69* (Lexington: University Press of Kentucky, 1980), 8–9; Henry J. Roberts to ACS, August 24, 1852, SHC.

38. Sampson Ceasar to Henry Westfall, April 1, 1834, in Ceasar Letters, Special Collections, Electronic Text Center, UVA.

39. Ibid.; J. B. Pinney to R. R. Gurley, March 12, 1835, in *AR* 11 (1835): 173; Peyton Skipwith to John Hartwell Cocke, in Wiley, *Slaves No More*, 4; Dunn et al., *Historical Dictionary of Liberia*, 99.

40. William Duglass (variant spelling) to "Dear Friend," January 29, 1866, James Hunter Terrell Letters, Special Collections, UVA.

41. Adaline Southall to James H. Minor, ibid.

42. Postscript to letter, Davey Scott to John H. Minor, January 28, 1858, ibid.

43. Tibey Scott to Dr. Minor, January 8, 1858, ibid.

44. George Walker to James H. Minor, January 27, 1858, ibid.

45. Desserline T. Harris to "Dear Sir," April 19, 1850, reel 154, ACS Records, SHC.

46. George Walker to James H. Minor, January 27, 1858, James Hunter Terrell Letters, Special Collections, UVA.

47. Adaline Southall to James H. Minor, ibid.

48. Benjamin Brand to Lott Cary, January 18, 1825, Benjamin Brand Papers, Section 4, VHS.

49. Young Barrett to James H. Minor, March 3, 1857, James Hunter Terrell Letters, Special Collections, UVA.

50. Desserline T. Harris to "Dear Sir," April 19, 1850, reel 154, ACS Records, SHC.

51. Tibey Scott to Dr. Minor, January 8, 1858, James Hunter Terrell Letters, Special Collections, UVA.

52. Ruth Coder Fitzgerald, *A Different Story: A Black History of Fredericksburg, Stafford, and Spotsylvania, Virginia* (Fredericksburg, Va.: Unicorn Press, 1979), 81.

53. L. T. Walker to McLain, September 1, 1841, in Hickin, "Antislavery in Virginia," 305. The "Harris" in Walker's letter may be the highly successful Zion Harris, formerly of east Tennessee. Zion Harris is one of two Liberians that Edmund Ruffin cites in "Colonization Unveiled" as exceptions that prove the rule of black incompetence. Ruffin's awareness of Harris likely stems from this visit or the one in 1848. Dixon Brown, originally from Richmond, was an officeholder in Liberia and may have been the Brown who returned to visit Virginia in 1841. T. J. Shepherd to McLain, July 31, 1841, and Steven Taylor to Wilkinson, September 17, 1841, in Hickin, "Antislavery in Virginia," 305.

54. Benjamin Brand to R. R. Gurley, September 19, 1833, Benjamin Brand Papers, Section 4, VHS.

55. Desserline T. Harris to "Dear Sir," [agent at Norfolk], April 19, 1850, SHC.

56. Thanks to Leila Boyer for this documentation on the Henrys. Important sources include Washington and Lee Trustee's Papers, Special Collections, Washington and Lee University, Lexington, Va.; John V. Henry for Patrick Henry to Thomas Jefferson, Lexington, Va., April 27, 1819, in Thomas Jefferson Collection, Massachusetts Historical Society, Boston, Mass.; Will of Patrick Henry, Rockbridge County Will Book G:340–41, Lexington, Va.; Westmoreland County Deed and Will Book 22:217 and 2:178, County Clerk's Office, Montross, Va.; 1840 Rockbridge County Black Schedule, in possession of Leila Boyer, 199.

57. Desserline T. Harris to J. W. Lugenbeel, February 27, 1853, and to William McLain, February 27, 1853, SHC.

58. VEL; John Kennedy, Norfolk, to Gurley, November 5 and 26, 1830, reel 10, RACS; Anthony W. Gardner to ACS, November 28, 1877, SHC. Gardner refers to Dr. Washington W. Davis, 1825 emigrant from Southampton County, as "my learned cousin" and to his parents as freeborn.

59. Washington Davis to ACS Board of Managers, May 12, 1835, reel 22B, and Anthony W. Gardner to ACS, November 28, 1877, reel 163, ACS Records, SHC; Parramore, *Southampton County*, 6; Clegg, *Price of Liberty*, 153–58.

60. For Curtis as an American Indian, see Canot's description of him, in Svend Holsoe, "Theodore Canot at Cape Mount, 1841–47," *LSJ* 4, no. 2 (1971–72): 167.

61. All the people involved appear to be from Petersburg, including the chronicler of this story. Caroline Shiphard Lundy to Benjamin Brand, November 26, 1831, Benjamin Brand Papers, VHS.

62. VEL.

63. Ibid.

64. In Southampton County, from which this Rix/Ricks family came, Bob Ricks escaped from slavery in 1824 and formed a band of fugitives who preyed upon travelers along the Virginia–North Carolina border. Parramore, *Southampton*, 70.

65. Holsoe, "Theodore Canot at Cape Mount, 1841–47," *LSJ* 4, no. 2 (1971–72): 167.

66. Ibid., 166–73, 36n; Newman, "The Emergence of Liberian Women," quotes Joseph J. Roberts's statement that Curtis was the only emigrant he knew who became a slave trader (236, 342).

Chapter Eight

1. Charles W. Thomas, *Adventures and Observations on the West Coast of Africa and Its Islands* (New York: Derby and Jackson, 1860), in Tom Shick, *Behold the Promised Land: A History of Afro-American Settler Society in Nineteenth-Century Liberia* (Baltimore: Johns Hopkins University Press, 1980), 43. Travel literature of this era had its own narrative imperatives, and Shick notes that eyewitness accounts of Liberia tended to exaggerate either the achievements or the failings of the colony in order to make larger political points.

2. Debra L. Newman, "The Emergence of Liberian Women in the Nineteenth Century" (Ph.D. diss., Howard University, 1984), 162–64, 166, quote on 246. George E. Brooks Jr., ed., "A. A. Adee's Journal of a Visit to Liberia in 1827," *LSJ* 1, no. 1 (1968): 56–72; Edward Shippen, *Thirty Years at Sea*, 1879 (reprint, New York: Arno Press, 1979), 84–85.

3. John Day to Arch Thomas, November 22, 1848, John Day Missionary Correspondence, Southern Baptist Foreign Mission Board, Southern Baptist Historical Library and Archives, Nashville, Tenn. My thanks to Jane Leigh Carter for letter copies.

4. Newman, "Emergence of Liberian Women," 169; "J.W.L." to ACS, June 19, 1848, reel 154, ACS Records, SHC.

5. James Wesley Smith, *Sojourners in Search of Freedom: The Settlement of Liberia by Black Americans* (Lanham, Md.: University Press of America, 1991), 60; Shick, *Behold*, 44–50, 102. See also Katherine Harris, *Africa and American Values: Liberia and West Africa* (New York: University Press of America, 1985).

6. Newman, "Emergence of Liberian Women," 73; Shick, *Behold*, 44, 53.

7. Smith, *Sojourners*, 61.

8. Luther Porter Jackson, *Free Negro Labor and Property-Holding in Virginia* (New York: D. Appleton/Century Company, 1942), 147; Joseph Roberts to Sarah Colson, January 1, 1836, and N. H. Elebeck to Sarah N. Colson, June 15, 1836, in Colson Collection, Virginia State University Archives, Petersburg, Va.; Luther Porter Jackson, "Free Negroes of Petersburg, Virginia," *JNH* 12, no. 3 (July 1927): 373–75; Smith, *Sojourners*, 45; Desserline Harris to "Dear Sir," April 19, 1850, reel 154, RACS.

9. Harriet D. Waring to R. R. Gurley, Monrovia, July 18, 1836, reel 25, ACS Records, SHC.

10. VEL.

11. Floyd Miller, *The Search for a Black Nationality: Black Emigration and Colonization, 1787–1863* (Urbana: University of Illinois Press, 1975), 84–89; Wilson J. Moses, ed., *Liberian Dreams: Back-to-Africa Narratives from the 1850s* (University Park: Pennsylvania State University Press, 1998), xix, xxiii.

12. Mia Bay, *The White Image in the Black Mind: African American Ideas about White People, 1830–1925* (New York: Oxford University Press, 2000), 26, 36, 33–35, 44–45, 28.

13. Smith, *Sojourners*, 57–59, 61.

14. Ibid., 87–89, 147.

15. Ibid., 136; J. B. Pinney to ACS, January 7, 1835, SHC.

16. "The Late Hilary Teage of Liberia," *AR* 29 (1853): 316–17.

17. Smith, *Sojourners*, 146, 151.

18. John Russwurm to R. R. Gurley, May 5, 1854, and George Todsen to R. R. Gurley, Monrovia, April 25, 1834, reel 153, SHC.

19. Martin Delany, *The Report of the Niger Valley Exploring Party*, 1859 (reprint, ed. Howard Bell, Ann Arbor: University of Michigan Press, 1971), 58–59; Bernard L. Herman, "Settler Houses," *A Land and Life Remembered: Americo-Liberian Folk Architecture* (Athens: University of Georgia Press, 1988), 99–107.

20. John Day to Rev. James B. Taylor, April 10, 1854, John Day Letters; Newman, "Emergence of Liberian Women," 242.

21. Charles H. Huberich, *The Political and Legislative History of Liberia* (New York: Central Book Company), 1947, 638–39, 641, 647n2.

22. Smith, *Sojourners*, 170–72.

23. Ibid., 173–74.

24. Warren S. Howard, *American Slavers and the Federal Law, 1837–62* (Berkeley: University of California Press, 1963), 40–41; W. E. B. Du Bois, *The Suppression of the African Slave Trade to the United States of America, 1638–1870*, 1896 (reprint, Baton Rouge: Louisiana State University Press, 1970), 108–11, 118–23, 126–29, 140–67; Hugh G. Soulsby, *The Right of Search and the Slave Trade in Anglo American Relations,*

Johns Hopkins University Studies in Historical and Political Science, series 51, no. 2 (Baltimore: Johns Hopkins University Press, 1933), 8–11.

25. Simon Fraser Blunt Papers, 1833–1921, section 2, p. 8, VHS; D. Elwood Dunn, Amos J. Beyan, and Carl Patrick Burrowes, *Historical Dictionary of Liberia*, 2nd ed. (Lanham, Md.: Scarecrow Press, 2001), 82.

26. James Mason Hoppin, *Life of Andrew Hull Foote: Rear Admiral of the United States Navy* (New York: Harper, 1874).

27. Shick, *Behold*, 61; quote in F. Devany, J. Lewis, J. B. Russwurm, W. L. Weaver, A. Curtis to [ACS] Board of Managers and their auxiliaries, n.d., approximately September 17, 1830, Benjamin Brand Papers, Section 10, VHS; Newman, "Emergence of Liberian Women," 152–53.

28. Theophile Conneau (Theodore Canot), *Adventures of an African Slaver, Being a True Account of the Life of Theodore Canot, Trader in Gold, Ivory & Slaves on the Coast of Guinea: His Own Story as Told in the Year 1854 to Brantz Mayer & Now Edited with an Introduction by Malcolm Cowley* (New York: Albert and Charles Boni, 1928), 28–31, 62, 70–77, 135–36, 310–12, 324, 334, 356–59.

29. Thomas Buchanan to ACS in Newman, "Emergence of Liberian Women," 237; "Monrovia Lot Histories" file, in "Land Records and Treaties," box 11, SVH; Rosaline Canot gravestone engraving in SVH.

30. Shick, *Behold*, 92, 99; Newman, "Emergence of Liberian Women," 75, 152–53; *AR* 5 (1829): 155; Smith, *Sojourners*, 173–74.

31. Shick, *Behold*, 103; *AR* 23 (1847): 15–19, 81–82.

32. The frequent assertion that the Constitution was written by Samuel Greenleaf of Harvard is based on the only surviving source, fragments of the notes taken by U.S. Agent J. W. Lugenbeel, a somewhat hostile observer. They are likely in error. See the version of Constitution-making in Charles Henry Huberich, *The Political and Legislative History of Liberia* (New York: Central Publishing Company, 1947), 1:822–27; and D. Elwood Dunn, Amos J. Beyan, and Carl Patrick Burrowes, *Historical Dictionary of Liberia*, 2nd ed. (Lanham, Md.: Scarecrow Press, 2001), 84–86, for a context for the writing of the Liberian Constitution.

33. "The Late Hilary Teage of Liberia," *AR* 29 (1853): 316–17; Hilary Teage to William Fergusson, Monrovia, September 16, 1841, and William Fergusson to Hilary Teage, Sierra Leone, October 6, 1841, both enclosed in letter of William Fergusson to Lord John Russell, Sierra Leone, October 8, 1841, SHC.

34. Huberich, *Political and Legislative History of Liberia*, 2:1029–30, 1014–15; Shick, *Behold*, 46–51.

35. Shick, *Behold*, 104–5; John N. Lewis to Rev. William McLain, April 5, 1848, reel 154, ACS Records, SHC.

36. *AR* 10 (1834): 158–59, for his return on the *Jupiter*; Smith, *Sojourners*, 125; *AR* 24 (1848): 259.

37. "Citizens of Liberia in United States," *AR* 24 (1848): 259–60.

38. Shick, *Behold*, 107; *Petersburg Daily Democrat* (June 5, 1856): 2, from newspaper file index, Petersburg Main Library, Petersburg, Va.

39. Martin R. Delany, "Introduction," to William Nesbit, *Four Months in Liberia; or African Colonization Exposed*, reprinted in *Liberian Dreams: Back-to-Africa Narratives*

from the 1850s, ed. Wilson Jeremiah Moses (University Park: Pennsylvania State University Press, 1998), 83.

40. Robert S. Levine, ed., *Martin R. Delaney: A Documentary Reader* (Chapel Hill: University of North Carolina Press, 2003), 1–2; Martin Delany, *Condition, Elevation, Emigration and Destiny of the Colored People . . .* , 209–15, in Moses, *Liberian Dreams*, xxvii.

41. Delany, "Introduction," in Moses, *Liberian Dreams*, 81–86.

42. Moses, *Liberian Dreams*, xxxi–xxxii.

43. Delany, *Niger Valley Report*, in ibid., 52–67; Levine, *Martin R. Delaney*, 11–12.

44. President J. J. Roberts, Government House, Monrovia, to Capt. A. H. Foote, United States Navy, New Haven, Conn., July 10, 1855, in Joseph Roberts Family Collection box, RACS.

45. John N. Lewis to Rev. William McLain, Monrovia, January 7, 1848, reel 154, RACS.

46. Desserline T. Harris to "Dear Sir," Pleasant View, Clay-Ashland, Liberia, February 27, 1853, reel 156, ACS Records, SHC.

47. Hilary Teage to J. B. Pinney, Monrovia, August 27, 1851, in *AR* 29 (January 1853): 17–18.

48. Stanley A. Davis, *This Is Liberia* (New York: William Frederick Press, 1953), 93.

49. Newman, "Emergence of Liberian Women," 214–16.

50. Ibid., 233. The material used was a product of the cotton silk tree, native to Liberia, interwoven with cotton, according to Kyra Hicks, "Martha Erskine Ricks, Nineteenth-Century Quiltmaker," <http://anyonecanflyfoundation.org/library/Hick_on_Ricks_essay.html>, 6 (accessed September 10, 2006).

51. See Hollis Lynch, *Edward Wilmot Blyden: Pan Negro Patriot, 1832–1912* (London: Oxford University Press, 1967), for a biography; but the journal literature is wide-ranging and useful.

52. Joseph Roberts's first inaugural address, January 3, 1848, printed in Wilson Armistead, *Calumny Refuted by Facts from Liberia . . . presented to the Boston Anti-Slavery Bazaar, U.S.* (London: Charles Gilpin, 1848), in box 31, "Miscellaneous Papers," SHC. Claude A. Clegg, in *The Price of Liberty: African Americans and the Making of Liberia* (Chapel Hill: University of North Carolina Press, 2004), has a brief and excellent assessment of the manipulation and elasticity of Liberian national identity, on pp. 239–41.

Chapter Nine

1. Daniel P. Mannix and Malcolm Cowley, *Black Cargoes: A History of the Atlantic Slave Trade, 1518–1865* (New York: Viking Compass, 1965), 230–31, 235–37.

2. *Liberator*, "Letter from Bishop Meade—Characteristic and Satanic," August 26, 1853; *Petersburg Democrat*, May 1856, in Jasper Johns, *A Memoir of the Life of the Right Reverend William Meade* (Baltimore: Innes, 1867), 473–76. Thanks to Deborah Lee for citations.

3. Tom Shick, *Behold the Promised Land: A History of Afro-American Settler Society in Nineteenth-Century Liberia* (Baltimore: Johns Hopkins University Press, 1980), 123–

24, 128–29; Eli Seifman, "The Passing of the American Colonization Society," *LSJ* 2, no. 1 (1969): 1–6; Gus Liebenow, *The Quest for Democracy* (Bloomington: Indiana University Press, 1987), 123–31.

4. See conclusion to chapter 4 for Washington Copeland; William Douglass to "Friend" [Dr. James Minor], James Hunter Terrell Papers, Special Collections, UVA <http://etext.lib.virginia.edu/rbs/98> (accessed September 17, 1998); *AR* 42 (1866): 119; Debra L. Newman, "The Emergence of Liberian Women in the Nineteenth Century" (Ph.D. diss., Howard University, 1984), 29.

5. See Kenneth C. Barnes, *Journey of Hope: The Back-to-Africa Movement in Arkansas in the Late 1800s* (Chapel Hill: University of North Carolina Press, 2004); and Edwin Redkey, *Black Exodus: Black Nationalist and Back-to-Africa Movements, 1890–1916* (New Haven: Yale University Press, 1969).

6. Jane Dailey, *Before Jim Crow: The Politics of Race in Postemancipation Virginia* (Chapel Hill: University of North Carolina Press, 2000), 1–14, 160–65.

7. *AR* 45 (1869): 103–17; *Petersburg Index and Appeal*, February 13, 1869, 3, and February 15, 1869, 3, in newspaper file index, Petersburg Main Library, Petersburg, Va. Although the story is summarized in the index, the referenced MIC reel 128 with the citations in fact lacked the Roberts story.

8. *Petersburg Index and Appeal*, October 1, 1873, Editorial, 2, newspaper file index, Petersburg Main Library, Petersburg, Va.

9. Elizabeth Varon, *Southern Lady, Yankee Spy: The True Story of Elizabeth Van Lew, a Union Agent in the Heart of the Confederacy* (New York: Oxford University Press, 2005), 165–68.

10. "Richmonia Richards," *Anglo-African*, New York City, October 7, 1865, p. 2. Thanks to Marianne E. Julienne and Sarah Bearss of LVA for finding this item and bringing it to my attention. Richards later taught school in Reconstruction South Carolina, where she married before disappearing from the historical record.

11. Shick, *Behold*, 110–11, 120; D. Elwood Dunn, Amos J. Beyan, and Carl Patrick Burrowes, eds., *Historical Dictionary of Liberia*, 2nd ed. (Lanham, Md.: Scarecrow Press, 2001), 204.

12. Dunn et al., *Historical Dictionary of Liberia*, 284.

13. Shick, *Behold*, 118–19.

14. Robert W. Rydell, ed., *The Reason Why the Colored American Is Not in the World's Columbian Exhibition* (Urbana: University of Illinois Press, 1999), xi–xiii; Christopher Robert Reed, *"All the World Is Here": The Black Presence at the White City* (Bloomington: Indiana University Press, 2000), x–xvii, xxii–xxx, 182–91.

15. Miles Orvell, *The Real Thing: Imitation and Authenticity in American Culture, 1880–1940* (Chapel Hill: University of North Carolina Press, 1989), 34–35, 59; Robert W. Rydell, *All the World's a Fair: Visions of Empire at American International Expositions, 1876–1916* (Chicago: University of Chicago Press, 1984), 60, 64.

16. The fair promoted not just ethnographic and anthropological racial categories but also the new science of eugenics. English scientist and eugenics founder Francis Galton used the fair to test his theory that photographs revealed essential racial and ethnic composite types, anticipating the racial purity theories of the twentieth century; Orvell, *Real Thing*, 34–35, 58.

17. Rydell, *All the World's a Fair*, 60, 63–64, 67; Curtis M. Hinsley, "The World as Marketplace: Commodification of the Exotic at the World's Columbian Exhibition, Chicago, 1893," in *Exhibiting Cultures: The Poetics and Politics of Museum Display*, ed. Ivan S. Karp and Steven D. Levine (Washington, D.C.: Smithsonian Institution Press, 1991), 344–65; Ida B. Wells, Frederick Douglass, Irvine Garland Penn, and Ferdinand L. Barnett, *The Reason Why the Colored American Is Not in the World's Columbian Exposition*, ed. Robert W. Rydell (Urbana: University of Illinois Press, 1999).

18. Reed, *"All the World Is Here,"* 114–15.

19. One explanation is that Bishop Turner asked Martha Ricks to make a second quilt for the Atlanta Exposition three years later. Given that it took more than twenty years for Mrs. Ricks to make the first one, this seems a quick turnaround. Kyra Hicks telephone interview, February 1, 2006. See also Kyra Hicks, *Black Threads: An African American Sourcebook* (Jefferson, N.C.: McFarland, 2003).

20. Reed, *"All the World Is Here,"* 79.

21. Claude A. Clegg, *The Price of Liberty: African Americans and the Making of Liberia* (Chapel Hill: University of North Carolina Press, 2004), 266–67.

22. See Shick, *Behold*, chaps. 8 and 9, for a recounting of these factors.

23. Howard Temperley, "African American Aspirations and the Settlement of Liberia," *Slavery and Abolition* 21, no. 2 (2000): 86–87.

24. Benjamin Brawley to Dr. E. C. Sage, president, New York State Colonization Society, New York City, May 15, 1920, reel 309, RACS.

25. *AR* 3 (1828): 325.

Bibliographical Essay

1. John H. B. Latrobe, *Maryland in Liberia: A History of the Colony Planted by the Maryland Colonization Society* . . . Maryland Historical Society Fund Publications, no. 21 (Baltimore: John Murphy, 1885); David W. Blight, *Race and Reunion: The Civil War in American Memory* (Cambridge, Mass.: Belknap Press of Harvard University Press, 2001), esp. 381–97.

2. The monograph was a dissertation published as Early Lee Fox, *The African Colonization Society* (Baltimore: Johns Hopkins University Press, 1919). Essays from this era by Frederick Bancroft were not published until 1957, in Jacob E. Cooke, *Frederick Bancroft, Historian: With an Introduction by Allan Nevins and Three Hitherto Unpublished Essays on the Colonization of American Negroes from 1801 to 1865 by Frederick Bancroft* (Norman: University of Oklahoma Press, 1957). Other essays were Henry Noble Sherwood, "Paul Cuffee and His Contributions to the American Colonization Society," *Proceedings of the Mississippi Valley Historical Association for the Year 1912–1913* 6: 370–402; "Early Negro Deportation Projects," *Mississippi Valley Historical Review* 2 (March 1916): 484–508; "The Formation of the American Colonization Society," *JNH* 2 (July 1917): 209–28; "Paul Cuffee," *JNH* 8 (April 1923): 169–93; Walter Fleming, "Deportation and Colonization, an Attempted Solution to the Race Problem," *Studies in Southern History and Politics Inscribed to William Archibald Dunning* (New York: Columbia University Press, 1914); Louis R. Mehlinger, "The Attitude of the Free Negro toward African Colonization," *JNH* 1 (July 1916): 276–301; and Miles Mark Fisher, "Lott Cary, the Colonizing Missionary," *JNH* 7 (1922):

340–418. For black scholarship on race as more "modern" than white scholarship in the early decades of the twentieth century, see Gunnar Myrdal, quoted in Mia Bay, *The White Image in the Black Mind: African American Ideas about White People, 1830–1925* (New York: Oxford University Press, 2000), 187.

3. Bay, *White Image*, 187–202; Brian William Thompson, "Racism and Racial Classification: A Case Study of the Virginia Racial Integrity Legislation" (Ph.D. diss., University of California, Riverside, 1978), 169–71; Ethel Wolfskill Hedlin, "Earnest Cox and Colonization: A White Racist's Response to Black Repatriation, 1923–1966" (Ph.D. diss., Duke University, 1974); Scope and Content Note, in "A Guide to the Earnest Sevier Cox Papers, 1821–1973," Rare Book, Manuscript, and Special Collections Library, Duke University, Durham, N.C. Thanks to Laura Feller for the references.

4. Carter G. Woodson selected African American letters to the ACS and published them as part of *The Mind of the Negro as Reflected in Letters Written during the Crisis, 1800–1860* (Washington, D.C.: Association for the Study of Negro Life and History, 1926). The letters were also published in a series in *JNH*. John Hope Franklin, *From Slavery to Freedom* (New York: Knopf, 1967), 237–41; Philip Staudenraus, *The African Colonization Movement, 1816–1865* (New York: Columbia University Press, 1961); Penelope Campbell, *Maryland in Africa, 1831–57* (Urbana: University of Illinois Press, 1971). Staudenraus fit the ACS into the benevolent empire and focused on the connection between African colonization and American national politics. Campbell extended J. H. B. Latrobe's account of the Maryland colony and concluded that Latrobe and other leaders were genuinely philanthropic but that the motives of the general membership could never be known. Louis Filler, in *The Crusade against Slavery, 1830–1860* (New York: Harper and Row, 1960), 20–22, represented the ACS as a sincere, although unsuccessful, effort to remove a barrier to emancipation. Charles I. Foster, "The Colonization of Free Negroes in Liberia, 1816–1835," *JNH* 38 (January 1953): 41–66, was the most critical of the ACS.

5. Merton Dillon, *Benjamin Lundy and the Struggle for Negro Freedom* (Urbana: University of Illinois Press, 1966), 25–26, 75; Dwight Dumond, *Antislavery: The Crusade for Freedom in America* (Ann Arbor: University of Michigan Press, 1961), 128.

6. Winthrop Jordan, *White over Black: American Attitudes toward the Negro, 1550–1812* (Chapel Hill: University of North Carolina Press, 1968), 546–69; David Brion Davis, *The Problem of Slavery in the Age of Revolution*, 1966 (rev. ed., Cambridge: Oxford University Press, 1988); David Brion Davis, *Slavery and Human Progress* (Cambridge: Oxford University Press, 1984); George Fredrickson, *The Black Image in the White Mind: The Debate on Afro-American Character and Destiny, 1817–1914* (New York: Harper and Row, 1972); second quote in Duncan Rice, *The Rise and Fall of Black Slavery* (New York: Harper and Row, 1975), 242; Donald Robinson, *Slavery in the Structure of American Politics, 1765–1820* (New York: Harcourt, Brace, Jovanovich, 1971); Howard Temperley, "Capitalism, Slavery and Ideology," *Past and Present* (1977): 94–118; Thomas Haskell, "Capitalism and the Origins of the Humanitarian Sensibility," *American Historical Review* 90, no. 3–4 (April and June 1985).

7. Edmund Morgan, *American Slavery, American Freedom: The Ordeal of Colonial Virginia* (New York: W. W. Norton, 1975), 381–83; Carl Degler, *The Other South:*

Southern Dissenters in the Nineteenth Century, 1974 (reprint, Gainesville: University Press of Florida, 2000), 22–46; William Freehling, *Secessionists at Bay*, vol. 1 of *The Road to Disunion* (New York: Oxford University Press, 1990), esp. 190–96; William Freehling, "Absurd Issues: Colonization as a Test Case," in *The Reintegration of American History: Slavery and the Civil War* (New York: Oxford University Press, 1994).

8. Herbert Aptheker's and Benjamin Quarles's work on antislavery is foundational for those topics, especially Herbert Aptheker, *American Negro Slave Revolts* (New York: Columbia University Press, 1943); Herbert Aptheker, *Abolitionism: A Revolutionary Movement* (Boston: Twayne Publishers, 1989); and Benjamin Quarles, *Black Abolitionists* (New York: Oxford University Press, 1969). Examples of recent scholarship that explore a connection between the ACS and social control are Douglas Egerton, *Charles Fenton Mercer and the Trial of National Conservatism* (Oxford: University of Mississippi Press, 1989); and Larry Tise, *Proslavery: A History of the Defense of Slavery in America, 1701–1740* (Athens: University of Georgia Press, 1986).

9. William Lloyd Garrison, *Thoughts on African Colonization*, 1832 (reprint, New York: Arno Press, 1968); Douglas Egerton, "It's Origin Is Not a Little Curious: A New Look at the American Colonization Society," *Journal of the Early Republic* 5 (Fall 1985): 465–80; Lawrence Friedman, "Purifying the White Man's Country," *Societas* 6, no. 1 (Winter 1976): 1–24; Paul Goodman, *Of One Blood: Abolitionism and the Origins of Racial Equality* (Berkeley: University of California Press, 1998).

10. Peter Ripley et al., eds., *The Black Abolitionist Papers*, vol. 3 (Chapel Hill: University of North Carolina Press, 1991), 6; James Wesley Smith, *Sojourners in Search of Freedom* (Lanham, Md.: University Press of America, 1991), 86. Other recent examples include John Stauffer, *The Black Hearts of Men: Radical Abolitionists and the Transformation of Race* (Cambridge, Mass.: Harvard University Press, 2002); Stanley Harrold, *Subversives: Antislavery Community in Washington, D.C.* (Baton Rouge: Louisiana State University Press, 2003); Ellen Eslinger, "The Brief Career of Rufus W. Bailey, American Colonization Society Agent in Virginia," *JSH* 71, no. 1 (February 2005): 39–74.

11. Randall Miller, *"Dear Master": Letters of a Slave Family*, 1978 (reprint, Athens: University of Georgia Press, 1990); Tom Shick, *Behold the Promised Land: A History of Afro-American Settler Society in Nineteenth-Century Liberia* (Baltimore: Johns Hopkins University Press, 1980); J. Gus Liebenow, *Liberia: The Evolution of Privilege* (Ithaca, N.Y.: Cornell University Press, 1969); J. Gus Liebenow, *Liberia: The Quest for Democracy* (Bloomington: Indiana University Press, 1987); Amos Beyan, *The American Colonization Society and the Creation of the Liberian State: A Historical Perspective, 1822–1900* (Lanham, Md.: University Press of America, 1991); Smith, *Sojourners*; Antonio McDaniel, *Swing Low, Sweet Chariot: The Mortality Cost of Colonizing Liberia in the Nineteenth Century* (Chicago: University of Chicago Press, 1995).

12. Earl Lewis, "To Turn as on a Pivot: Writing African Americans into a History of Overlapping Diasporas," *American Historical Review* (June 1995): 765–87; Ira Berlin, "Time, Space and the Evolution of African American Society," *American Historical Review* 85 (February 80): 44–78; Floyd Miller, *The Search for a Black Nationality: Black Emigration and Colonization, 1787–1863* (Urbana: University of Illinois

Press, 1975); Richard S. Newman, *The Transformation of American Abolitionism: Fighting Slavery in the Early Republic* (Chapel Hill: University of North Carolina Press, 2002), 96–98, 110–11.

13. Patrick Rael, *Black Identity and Black Protest in the Antebellum North* (Chapel Hill: University of North Carolina Press, 2002), 209–13; Dickson D. Bruce Jr., "National Identity and African American Colonization, 1773–1817," *Historian* 58 (Autumn 1995): 15–28; Dickson D. Bruce Jr., *The Origins of African American Literature, 1680–1865* (Charlottesville: University Press of Virginia, 2000), 146–47; Bruce Dain, *A Hideous Monster of the Mind: American Race Theory in the Early Republic* (Cambridge, Mass.: Harvard University Press, 2002), 103–5.

14. William G. Shade, *Democratizing the Old Dominion: Virginia and the Second Party System, 1824–1861* (Charlottesville: University Press of Virginia, 1996), 191, 194.

15. Claude A. Clegg, *The Price of Liberty: African Americans and the Making of Liberia* (Chapel Hill: University of North Carolina Press, 2004); Kenneth Barnes, *Journey of Hope: The Back-to-Africa Movement in Arkansas in the late 1800s* (Chapel Hill: University of North Carolina Press, 2004); Michele Mitchell, *Righteous Propagation: African Americans and the Politics of Racial Destiny after Reconstruction* (Chapel Hill: University of North Carolina Press, 2004); Alan Huffman, *Mississippi in Africa: The Saga of the Slaves of Prospect Hill Plantation and Their Legacy in Liberia Today* (New York: Gotham Books, 2004); Richard Hall, *On Afric's Shore: A History of Maryland in Liberia, 1834–1857* (Baltimore: Maryland Historical Society, 2003); Eric Burin, *Slavery and the Peculiar Solution: A History of the American Colonization Society* (Gainesville: University Press of Florida, 2005).

Except for addresses given at reunions of abolition or benevolent societies, or per-haps the postbellum annual meetings of the American Colonization Society (ACS) itself, the ACS received scant attention from the historically inclined for fifty years after the Civil War ended. The only significant publication was a participant's ac-count of the Maryland Colonization Society by J. H. B. Latrobe, written in 1885. This general disinterest was to be expected, as the people who were once active in abolitionism or colonization reminisced, while another generation of white Ameri-cans, weary of the question of race, generally considered the issue closed with the end of Reconstruction. In post-Reconstruction politics and society, North-South reunion sentiment was dominant everywhere at the expense of attention to any aspect of the black experience.[1]

In the second and third decades of the twentieth century, deep into the age of Jim Crow segregation and lynching commonly regarded as the nadir of race relations, some members of a generation of university-trained American historians turned their attention to early colonization schemes. A series of articles written be-tween 1913 and 1926 investigated the origins and founding of the ACS and brought renewed attention to questions of race and citizenship. The only monograph pub-lished on the topic in this period, deeply influenced by Lost Cause and Dunning school perspectives, examined the early years of the ACS and suggested that the society might have prevented the Civil War, had it not been for the abolitionists. By contrast, the *Journal of Negro History* began publication in 1916 and was a hospitable site for a more complex interpretation of this topic, publishing most of the scholarly articles produced on African colonization in these years, many by black scholars.[2]

The early twentieth century was a time in which popularized scientific racism and racial eugenics purported to prove the inferiority of the African American even as social and biological sciences moved toward a new environmentalism. White supremacist groups in the 1920s and 1930s evoked Liberia as they sought to introduce congressional bills that would provide financial aid to blacks emigrating to Africa. They sought–successfully–rapprochement with black nationalist move-ments, especially that of Marcus Garvey. The ACS had become simply a channel for missionary and educational bequests to Liberia by the 1920s, and the almost-moribund society did not respond to overtures by the white racial supremacists, who essentially co-opted the history and existence of Liberia for their own pur-poses. Although in decline through much of the 1930s and 1940s, advocates of racial separation received new energy after *Brown v. Board of Education*. The 1954 Supreme Court decision that declared racial segregation inherently unequal both fueled white supremacist efforts and powered a civil rights movement of almost two decades. For scholars beginning their careers in the 1950s with the twentieth-century civil rights movement, this was part of the intellectual baggage that accom-panied a consideration of African colonization.[3]

The mid-1950s, when the black civil rights movement became visible to the larger world, marked a pronounced shift toward an interest in African American history and, ultimately, the ACS. African American historians had already explored much of this ground, but their work did not find outlets in the major historical journals until the 1950s. Most of the researchers of that period stressed the impracticality of the ACS, not its racism, and very few saw the ACS as central to their research. Only two monographs directly related to African colonization were published in the 1960s and early 1970s—one examined the institutional and political history of the American Colonization Society and one did the same for the Maryland Colonization Society.[4]

Research on African American topics grew exponentially in the 1960s and 1970s and included a new interest in the abolitionists and the history of antislavery. Among scholars examining these topics in the 1960s was Benjamin Quarles, who gave black abolitionists their central place in antislavery history. Merton Dillon, in an influential judgment that would echo through the decades, said that the ACS wanted to expunge blacks from the historical record through emancipation and emigration to Africa. But, he believed, the sin of slavery must be acknowledged and retribution made to African Americans. And Dwight Dumond spoke for many scholars when he wrote that colonization was "either an attempt to remove from society an element in the population believed to be incapable of progress, or an attempt to avoid the expense and effort of compensating, by special devotion to the task, for the years of soul-destroying oppression." The purpose of the ACS, he believed, was to strengthen slavery and make it more secure.[5] These and other scholars urged compensation within America for the moral evil of slavery and described African colonization as the polar opposite of grappling with racism.

Studies that considered the ACS as an idea, rather than a national political strategy, approached the topic differently. In his classic *White over Black*, also published in the 1960s, Winthrop Jordan titled his review of early colonization proposals "Toward a White Man's Country" and saw the ACS as cautiously antislavery in the interest of the white republic. Because Jordan believed African colonization to be impossible as an answer to the dilemmas of race, he suggested that its persistence was due to "a compelling fantasy" and that it was particularly compelling in Virginia. Foundational historians of ideas writing in the 1960s and 1970s, such as Jordan, David Brion Davis, and George Frederickson, described the society as initially based on eighteenth-century environmentalism and as promoting gradual emancipation as part of the general growth of benevolence. These historians agreed that the ACS did not describe blacks as inherently inferior but characterized them as "degraded" by a prejudice that almost all whites shared. Other historians of the same period, examining African colonization in its larger Atlantic setting, saw the ACS as a "legitimate agency through which one aspect of the benevolence of America's philanthropic community was channeled."[6]

On related topics, Edmund Morgan did not address the ACS directly when he concluded, in *American Slavery, American Freedom*, that slavery acted as a powerful basis for republicanism in Virginia, but his conclusion is important for understanding the "compelling" aspects of African colonization in Virginia. Carl Degler usefully divided antislavery white Southerners into two camps, those who feared for the white republic and those who cared for the fates of blacks, although the two were not mutually exclusive. In several publications, William W. Freehling pointed out the great reluctance of Virginians, of any political persuasion, to give up the concept of eventual and conditional termination of slavery and noted that, to nineteenth-century Americans in the midst of many migrations and even deportations, it did not seem that unreal or unreasonable that the ACS should seek support for emigration or deportation.[7]

Three approaches to the ACS emerged in the 1970s and 1980s: one from the history of American antislavery, especially abolitionism; one from histories of Liberia; and one, broadly speaking, from the history of American ideas and literature. Divisions have never been tidy, but broad differences in approach and assessment are reasonably clear.

In the first group, historians of antislavery and the abolitionist struggle, building on Herbert Aptheker, as well as Quarles, Dillon, and Dumond, emphasized nineteenth-century black resistance in slavery and black agency in antislavery, correcting a history in which African Americans had frequently been portrayed as passive. For many scholars, the ACS program of racial separation was the exact reverse of the freedom struggle for civil rights waged by nineteenth- and twentieth-century African Americans and their allies, and that made it difficult for them to see beyond William Lloyd Garrison's journalistic jeremiads. Historians' jaundiced view of the ACS can be understood when Garrison's righteous, if occasionally overwrought, prose is contrasted with the equivocations and glaring inconsistencies in the ACS rhetoric. Specious, disingenuous, and maddeningly patronizing are reasonable descriptions of much of the public ACS argument. It was then easy, especially since the ACS was only a minor theme in many studies of slavery, to categorize it as a stark example of American intellectual dishonesty, social control, and racism, despite the fact that its contradictory rhetoric never achieved a unified voice or a hegemonic position in the nation.[8]

Scholars of slavery and antislavery have routinely cited the same sources when referencing the ACS. Reliance on secondary sources encouraged reductionist assessments of the society and minimized its role in race and national identity formation in the decades between the American Revolution and the Civil War. Most frequently cited, in my unofficial tabulation, are William Lloyd Garrison, the 1919 Fox monograph, and the two institutional studies of Staudenraus and Campbell previously cited, as well as an article on the founding of the ACS by Douglas Egerton and one by Lawrence Friedman on the manner in which ACS language portrayed America as a white body being purified of black excrescence. More recently, Paul Goodman's *Of One Blood* has been added to the citations.[9]

Goodman's belief that the actual deportationist functions of the ACS were hidden beneath a false profession of concern is a common one. The introduction to one volume of the collected papers of black abolitionists says, "Black leaders stripped away the facade of [ACS] philanthropy, revealing that the movement had no antislavery goals, no sincere concern for the condition of free blacks, and no serious commitment to Christian missions in Africa." Against his own evidence, another researcher argues in a book about Liberian emigration that "the Board's object was to rid the nation of its unwanted free blacks. Consequently, it mattered little to its members as to whether the emigrants lived or died upon their arrival in the colony."

Certainly these assessments of the ACS are contrary to the record, but there is a second part to this argument that has legitimacy. Northern free blacks did do serious damage to the ACS by attacking it directly and carrying off its white antislavery evangelical sympathizers, especially Garrison. Many of the most prominent reformers in the early ACS had a conversion experience, based on the African American critique of American republicanism, and an egalitarian biracial antislavery movement was created. But the claim of an uncaring deportationist Board of Managers and agents is not supported by the records of the ACS. In their commendable efforts to emphasize black agency and to find examples of interracial cooperation toward the goal of black liberation, these scholars and others tend to consign the ACS to an overt or inadvertent proslavery "otherness."[10]

Scholarly studies of emigration to Liberia and of the history of the country began in the late 1960s. This approach placed Liberia primarily in Atlantic and African American history. Randall Miller's excellent edited study of the Skipwith family letters from Liberia is grounded in the Skipwiths' American perspective. In contrast, Tom Shick's important early study of nineteenth-century Liberia is centered in the West African settlement. Most academic studies that are centered in Liberian history, starting with Gus Liebenow in 1969, have been quite critical of the settler elite and their attitudes as "frozen" in time. Settler unwillingness or inability to extend civil rights and education to the majority ethnic groups, especially in the twentieth century, is blamed for the disastrous course of Liberian history since 1980. These studies, sympathetic to the ordinary emigrants who suffered most, include Liebenow, Amos Beyan, James Wesley Smith, and Antonio McDaniel. They blame both the ACS and the settler elite for suppressing the true death rate in Liberia, providing inadequate provisions, and failing to modify American tastes and values. Of these historians, Liebenow provides the strongest argument.[11]

Most scholars agree that African American identity developed from many overlapping sets of relations and contingencies. Recent works on intellectual history and the history of African American literature have been open to considering African colonization as a central part of antebellum racial formation and identity construction, but the focus has been almost entirely upon northern free blacks. Studies by Floyd Miller, *The Search for a Black Nationality*, and Richard Newman, *The Transformation of American Abolitionism*, some thirty years apart, stand out for their portrayal of African colonization as a pivotal part of black identity formation and as the gradual emancipation base of abolitionism. Newman particularly notes the dynamic reshaping of antislavery reform with the addition of women and African Americans.[12]

Patrick Rael, in *Black Identity and Black Protest in the Antebellum North*, argues that the black nationalism in formation in the early nineteenth century was the product of urban northern black leadership that sought to establish an African identity as legitimate but not as the sole identity of African Americans. Rael suggests that discourse about nationality is central to its construction and that, for that reason, it could not take place among the enslaved. But the evidence offered in this study suggests that Virginia enslaved and free blacks were able to communicate with each other about African colonization and to assess the extent to which emigration and an African identity were advantageous or disastrous for them. Since their access to publication was usually limited to white-edited religious journals and ACS publications, this evidence must be found in private letters, church records, and the actions of free and enslaved blacks.

Bruce and Dain point out the ways in which discussion of African colonization by the ACS contributed to a sense of black national identity within the United States. The ACS understood the necessity of relying on black voices in order to promote colonization. The *African Repository and Colonial Journal* published the letters, essays, and travel accounts of black emigrants to Liberia and also took up the theme of ancient black African civilizations, the first publication to support the claim of the primacy of African civilization. Bruce suggests that, because the ACS was an organization of paternalist or racist white men, the earlier construction of race and colonization by African Americans was not part of its history. Again evidence from the letters of Virginia free blacks and other events chronicled in the ACS records suggest that a discourse about race and identity arose in some form whenever African colonization was a topic in Virginia. Such men as Lott Cary and John Day carried a black construction of racial identity to Africa even as northern African Americans charted a different course.[13]

Slavery was the central and insoluble issue. The defense of slavery began in the 1820s, and Virginia took a more aggressively proslavery stand in the 1840s and 1850s while clinging to its Unionism. Conservative and proslavery Virginians who saw themselves as descendants of Cavaliers and called themselves "the Chivalry" dominated the Old Dominion's democracy after 1844, despite the fact that Virginia finally entered the nineteenth century with the Constitution of 1851. William Shade writes that "after three-quarters of a century, the feasibility of colonization lay at the center of the controversy over slavery in the Old Dominion" and that no politician could discuss slavery openly. But historians have generally conflated the political ACS leadership in Virginia, which revived after a long slumber to become deportationist, proslavery, and antiblack, with all the membership.[14]

Currently, a growing number of scholars are reexamining the ACS and emigration to Liberia. These recent and valuable studies mark a new interest in the ACS from a variety of perspectives and demonstrate the richness of the ACS resources for interpreting American history. A characteristic of most of this work is to give equal weight to both the American and the African experiences. In *The Price of Liberty*, Claude Clegg used North Carolina emigrants to convey a deeper context for the colonization movement as it played out on two continents. Two studies examine post-Reconstruction interest in Liberia on the part of African Americans, who assessed their lives and conditions as growing more desperate every year. Kenneth Barnes, in *Journey of Hope*, traces the aspirations and frustrations of freedmen in Arkansas. Michele Mitchell, in *Righteous Propagation*, uses late-nineteenth-century emigration to Liberia to chart evolving theories of racial destiny. Alan Huffman, in

Mississippi in Africa, follows one Mississippi plantation family to Liberia and seeks to find their descendants in that currently war-ravaged country. Richard Hall, in *On Afric's Shore*, did a massive study of Maryland in Liberia and concluded that the early settlers were as intrepid and clever as any group in such circumstances has ever been. Finally, Eric Burin's *Slavery and the Peculiar Solution* has taken on the daunting task of quantifying all of the ACS-sponsored emigration to Liberia and assessing whether or not the society was antislavery. He concludes that African colonization disturbed and disrupted slavery whenever emancipation took place.[15]

The ACS is most useful viewed as a multifaceted perspective on the construction of race, nation, and gender in the nineteenth-century United States. This is especially so in Virginia, where it is an important source for examining African American thought and activity, women's advocacy of public policies, and antebellum politics and an example of the widespread communication among Chesapeake African Americans before emancipation. African colonization and Liberia were a constant undercurrent in the construction of American self-identity for much of the nineteenth century, as the Virginia experience suggests.

American Baptist, 87

American Colonization Society:
goals of, 1, 24, 27, 42, 51, 52,
56, 131, 228, 229–30; formation
of, 1–2, 31, 35; financial support
for, 2, 3, 4, 27, 28, 153, 160; and
republicanism, 2, 176; regional
agenda in state societies, 3; and
Liberian agents, 3, 129, 157, 159;
and authority in Liberia, 3, 132;
free blacks' critiques of, 5, 26, 27,
230; northern blacks' hostility
toward, 5, 26, 166, 167; Fairfax's
plan compared to, 17; as political
organization, 27; and slavery issue,
27, 28, 53–54, 228, 230, 231; and
emancipation, 27, 42, 51, 52, 56,
228; Charles Fenton Mercer as
founder of, 28, 32, 35, 40, 83, 87,
115, 171; Jefferson quoted by, 35;
reputation as abolition society, 42;
Dew's attack on, 47, 105, 111; crises
of, 53–54; Virginia free blacks'
distrust of, 56–57, 65–66, 77–78,
79–80; white women's participation
in, 86; factionalism of, 88; white
women's donations and bequests
to, 89; Ruffin's attack on, 111–12;
and Bushrod Washington, 113–14,
115; and treatment of emigrants
to Liberia, 143; construction of
Africa's past, 152–53; and Liberian
politics, 159, 164, 165, 168, 179;
Roberts's address to, 173; scholarly
interest in, 223 (n. 4), 227, 228–32;
inconsistencies in rhetoric of, 229;
deportation function of, 229, 231.
See also Auxiliaries of American
Colonization Society

American Indian ancestry of
mulattoes, 67, 69

American Quarterly Review, 47, 105

American Revolution: Gabriel's
rebellion associated with, 10, 14,
186 (n. 4); principles of, 10, 29, 60,

81, 86, 113; and Virginia's slavery
laws, 13

American Society for Colonizing the
Free People of Colour, 20

Andrews, Charles Wesley, 53

Anglo-African, 174

Anti-immigrant tensions, 33, 80

Aptheker, Herbert, 229

Arkansas, 173

Arlington House, 112, 113, 118, 119,
120, 121, 122, 123

Ashmun, Jehudi, 131–32, 155, 157,
213 (n. 8)

Assing, Ottilie, 210 (n. 30)

Atkinson, William Mayo, 46, 47, 55

Atlanta Exposition of 1896, 177, 222
(n. 19)

Auxiliaries of American Colonization
Society: in Virginia, 3, 4, 39–42,
44, 56, 60; funds raised by, 3,
28; organization of, 31–32, 40;
leaders of, 39, 40, 41; and petitions
for federal funding, 42, 43; and
emancipation, 42, 43, 44, 45, 51, 60;
and antislavery statements, 42–43;
and slavery issue, 45, 48; and family
divisions over emigration, 79; white
women's involvement in, 86, 88,
89, 90, 97, 101, 203 (n. 5); and
narrative of progress, 133

Bagot, Charles, 83

Bailey, Rufus, 55, 56, 57, 58–59, 76

Balch, T. B., 54

Baltimore Morning Chronicle, 114

Banshee, 127

Baptist Board of Foreign Missions, 41,
63, 64, 131

Baptist Church, 15, 19, 40–41, 48, 63

Baptist Davenport Church, 15–16

Barbour, Agnes, 131, 145

Barbour, James, 145, 157, 200 (n. 26)

Barbour, John J., 145

Barbour, John W., 145

Barbour, Robert, 145

Barbour, William, 145

Barker, John, 59

Barnes, Kenneth, 231

Bassa Cove, Liberia, 74, 137, 138, 139, 164

Bassa peoples, 130, 137, 138, 142, 152, 163

Benevolent societies: place of American Colonization Society in, 3, 27, 30, 228; and white women's visions of national reform, 86–87, 204 (n. 9); and auxiliaries, 88

Benevolent Society of Alexandria, 52

Benning, Thomas, 55

Beyan, Amos, 230

Black achievement: restricted by embedded white prejudice, 1; lack of recognition of, 70; in Liberia, 111, 112, 174, 177, 179; Ruffin on, 111–12

Blackburn, Christian, 116–17, 118

Blackburn, Judith, 116, 118

Blackburn, Samuel, 201 (n. 35)

Black churches, 15

Black conventions, 5–6, 47

Black family, 5, 90, 94–95, 100, 117

Blackford, Abraham, 99, 141

Blackford, Mary Berkeley Minor, 75, 89–90, 91, 92, 96, 98, 99, 103

Blackford, William, 75, 89–90, 96

Black identity: role of Africa in, 6; and Christianity, 15; effect of systematic oppression in U.S. on, 26; role of African colonization in, 26, 156, 230–31

Black inferiority: Jefferson on, 13; and Cooper's hereditary racial traits theory, 35; Ruffin's theory of, 111–12; proslavery arguments of, 156; and eugenics, 227

Black preachers, 46, 48

Black Republicans, 61

Black women: education of, 5, 90–91, 98; and class differences, 92, 152; lack of social or legal protection for,

97; and white men's sexual license, 122–23; in Liberia, 152, 154–55, 159, 165, 169–70

Blair, James, 41

Blyden, Edward, 169, 170, 179

Board of Commissioners for Foreign Missions, 87

Botetourt County Auxiliary, 55

Brand, Benjamin, 41, 42, 46, 54, 77, 133, 144, 145

Brander, Albert, 155

Brander, Charles, 155

Brander, Harriet Waring, 155

Brander, James, 155–56

Brander, Nathaniel, 63–64, 130, 131, 138, 155, 157

Brawley, Benjamin, 182

Brazil, 174

Brisbane, John (Jack), 79

Britain: and slave trade, 2, 13, 162; antislavery movement in, 14; and trade with Liberia, 164, 168, 174; and politics in Liberia, 164–65, 169; Roberts's treaty with, 166

British African Association and African Institution, 24

Brodnax, William, 46

Brown, Anderson, 100

Brown, Ann, 148

Brown, Burwell, 148

Brown, Dixon, 216 (n. 53)

Brown, Kathleen, 204 (n. 7)

Brown v. Board of Education (1954), 227

Bruce, Dickson D., Jr., 185 (n. 10), 231

Buchanan, Thomas, 159–60, 163, 164

Bullock, David, 78, 132, 133

Bullock family, 132–33

Burgess, Ebenezer, 27

Burin, Eric, 184 (n. 1), 185 (n. 6), 214 (n. 26), 232

Burke, Rosabella, 120–21, 124

Burke, William, 120, 124–25, 211 (n. 44)

Burr, David, 41, 72, 79
Bushman, Richard, 123
Bushrod Island, 132
Byrd, Agnes, 77
Byrd, William, II, 108
Byrd, William, III, 15

Cabell, Joseph, 34, 35
Cain, George, 148
Caldwell, Elias B., 20
Caldwell, Liberia, 133, 158
Calhoun, John C., 53
Campbell, Penelope, 223 (n. 4), 229
Campbell, Robert, 167
Canada: as settlement site, 79, 122
Canot, Theodore, 148, 149, 162–63
Cape Mesurado, 130, 131, 151
Careysburg, Liberia, 129, 173
Carroll, Lydia, 117, 118
Caruthers, Alexander: *The Cavaliers of Virginia*, 109
Cary, Lott: in Richmond-Manchester Auxiliary, 41; and trade, 42, 153–54; emigration to Liberia, 47, 63, 66, 81, 130, 145; funding of, 64; as missionary, 64; as promoter of Liberia, 66, 69–70, 200 (n. 25); death of, 70, 135, 155; on emancipation, 81; and American Colonization Society, 131; and revolt against Ashmun, 131–32; and recaptured Africans, 135; and provisions, 144; and Liberia's patriotic narrative, 153; as vice agent, 157; correspondence of, 185 (n. 9); and black identity, 231
Cary, Virginia Randolph, 93, 205 (n. 37)
Catholicism, 80
Ceasar, Sampson, 140, 141, 142
Cheeseman, Abraham, 155
Cheeseman, John, 142
Christianity: and Liberia's ties to U.S., 3; and black identity, 15; emancipation based on ideals of, 19; and goal of American

Colonization Society, 24; African missions spreading, 64; Cuffe's interest in, 124. *See also* Protestant evangelicalism; *and specific churches*
Citizenship in republic: meaning of, 1; and homogeneity, 2; white Americans' attitudes toward, 4, 17; African colonization's effect on, 5; free blacks' views on, 6; Liberian citizenship standard, 6, 165, 179; free blacks' seeking of, 11; and status of free blacks, 11, 16, 17–18, 67, 106; and American Colonization Society, 27; Charles Fenton Mercer on, 33, 191 (n. 27); and mulattoes, 67; and idealized republican mother, 86
Civil rights movement, 227–28
Clark, Harris, 69
Clark, Lemuel, 69, 140
Clark, Matilda, 140
Clark, Nancy, 140
Clark, Page, 69
Clark family, 131
Clay, Henry, 29, 33, 42, 53, 60, 184 (n. 5)
Clay-Ashland, Liberia, 17
Cleaveland, Johnson, 50
Clegg, Claude, 214 (n. 6), 231
Cocke, John Hartwell, 74–75, 87, 92–93, 97, 201 (n. 35)
Cocke, Louisa, 74
Coghill, Benjamin C., 52
Color: and imperfect connection of free blacks with full citizenship, 2, 35, 67; lifetime indenture associated with, 12; and emigrants to Liberia, 152; and Liberian politics, 175; and hierarchy of White City, 176
Colson, William N., 154
Colston, Edward, 200 (n. 27)
Columbus, Christopher, 176
Compromise of 1850, 55–56
Congress on Africa, 178
Conneau, Elisa McKinley, 171

Conneau, Henri, 171

Conneau, Theophile, 171–72; *Memoirs of a Slave Trader*, 171

Connecticut, 3, 16, 42

Cooper, Charles, 127

Cooper, Hilary, 127

Cooper, Thomas, 34–35

Copeland, Washington, 80–81, 173

Cowling, Jack, 77

Cowling, Willis, 77

Crane, William, 41, 47–48, 63, 64, 66, 91

Crenshaw, Nathaniel, 52

Cresson, Elliot[t], 74, 214 (n. 26)

Cromwell, John, 201 (n. 31)

Cuba, 174

Cub Creek black congregation, 15

Cuffe, Paul, 2, 6, 20, 24, 26, 27, 63, 130

Cultural assimilation: as Liberian citizenship standard, 6, 165, 179

Curtis, Augustus, 147, 148–49

Curtis, Edward, 147–48

Curtis, Mary, 147–48

Curtis, Minerva, 147

Custis, George Washington Parke, 42, 112, 116, 118–19, 122–25, 212 (n. 53); *Pocahontas*, 119

Custis, Mary Lee Randolph (Molly), 30, 32, 88, 118, 119, 120, 123, 124

Custis family, 113, 118

Cyrus, 69, 131, 145, 155, 168

Cyrus, Rosaline, 163

Dabney, George, 58

Dailey and Russwurm, 154

Dain, Bruce, 231

Davis, Alan, 146

Davis, Amanda, 146

Davis, Charles, 147

Davis, David Brion, 228

Davis, Eliza, 147

Davis, Elsie, 146

Davis, Martha, 146

Davis, Patrick, 147

Davis, Washington, 146, 147, 217 (n. 58)

Davis, William, 147

Day, John (Baptist minister), 68, 80, 81, 142, 152, 158–59, 185 (n. 9), 199 (n. 17), 231

Day, John (cabinetmaker), 68

Day, R., 68, 199 (n. 17)

Degler, Carl, 228–29

Delany, Martin, 166–67

Delaware, 42

Deportation, 46, 64, 70, 229, 231

Dew, Thomas R., 29, 47, 105–6, 107, 111

Dey peoples, 130, 131, 137

Dillon, Merton, 228, 229

Dissenting religions, 15, 18–19

Dongey, Reuben, 69, 164

Doris, 78, 132, 168

Douglass, Frederick, 166, 167, 176

Douglass, William, 129, 142

Draper, William, 144

Dueling, 36, 192–93 (n. 38)

Dumond, Dwight, 228, 229

Dunmore, Lord (John Murray), 14

Eastman, Mary, 102

Education: white women's advocacy of, 5, 46, 84, 87, 88, 90–91, 92, 98; of black women, 5, 90–91, 98; for free blacks intending to emigrate, 31; and republican virtues, 33, 191 (n. 25); and Charles Fenton Mercer, 33–34, 35, 191 (nn. 25, 27), 192 (n. 30); Samuel Janney on, 52; Sabbath schools for enslaved children, 87, 88, 90; of white women, 87, 93, 109; and Margaret Mercer, 93, 100, 101, 207 (n. 66); and emigrants to Liberia, 136, 152, 153; and Roye, 175; and expanded suffrage, 191 (n. 27)

Egerton, Douglas R., 186 (n. 4), 189 (n. 9), 192 (n. 30), 229

Elizabeth, 63, 128, 129–30, 168, 182

156; Lincoln's plan for, 172; in post–Civil War era, 172; Henry M. Turner's advocacy of, 175; and World's Columbian Exposition, 178–79; scholarly studies of, 230, 231

English rights of labor, 12

Enlightenment, 2, 24, 33, 74, 81, 138

Episcopal Church: evangelicalism in, 84, 188 (n. 26)

Essex County Society, 89

Eugenics, 175, 221 (n. 16), 227

Eugenie (empress of France), 171

Evans, Diego, 59, 76, 145

Fairfax, Ferdinando, 2, 17

Fairfax County Colonization Society, 43

Family Visitor, 87, 110

Fan Toro (Vai chief), 148, 149

Farmer's Register, 111

Federalists, 35, 36

Female Colonization Society of Richmond and Manchester, 91

Female Colonization Society of Virginia, 101

Fendall, Philip, 54

Fergusson, William, 164–65

Finley, Robert B., 20, 26

Fitzhugh, George, 97

Fitzhugh, William, 43

Fitzwhylson, William, 41

Fleet, Malvina, 147

Floyd, Governor, 46

Folk beliefs: science contrasted with, 23

Forbes, Robert, 191 (n. 25)

Force, Charles, 157

Forten, James, 81, 202 (n. 57)

Fox, Early Lee, 229

France: and African colonization, 24, 26; and Liberia, 164, 168

Frederick County Auxiliary Society, 32

Fredericksburg and Falmouth Female Auxiliary, 74, 90, 91, 92

Fredericksburg Political Arena, 75, 90

Frederickson, George, 228

Free blacks: resolution of problem of, 2; Virginia population of, 4, 5, 11; critiques of American Colonization Society, 5, 26, 27, 230; lack of interest in colonization, 5, 48, 54, 57, 58–60, 64, 65–66, 72–73, 81, 125, 167–68, 172; communication networks of, 5–6, 136, 231, 232; northern blacks contrasted with Virginia blacks, 6, 81; northern blacks contrasted with emigrants, 7; Maryland population of, 11; removal from Virginia, 11, 12; white Virginians' debate over status of, 11, 12–13, 14; citizenship status of, 11, 16, 17–18, 67, 106; laws restricting, 12, 68, 79, 80, 91, 128, 166; free papers of, 14; American Colonization Society's transmutation of, 24; Charles Fenton Mercer on, 33; Richmond Auxiliary managers' attitudes toward, 41–42; Tyler on, 44; proposals to expel, 56; kidnapping threats toward, 56, 79; as emigrants to Liberia, 63–64, 65, 72, 127–28, 131, 133, 136–37, 143, 155, 168, 201 (n. 31); preference for emigration within America, 64; fears of forced deportation, 64, 70; ambitions of, 67; mulattoes as, 67; and retaliation for Nat Turner's rebellion, 72; and manliness models, 76; distrust of motives of American Colonization Society, 77–78, 80; terms of freedom in America, 81; African colonization as resolution of problem of, 84, 102; and racial arguments, 156

Freedom's Journal, 156

Freehling, William W., 229

Freemasons, 10

Freetown, Sierra Leone, 14–15

French Revolution: Gabriel's rebellion associated with, 10, 186 (n. 4)

impulse of, 2; and Freetown settlement, 15; and antislavery movement, 18–19; and success with slaves, 24; and African colonization, 26, 74, 84, 110; and Meade, 30; and virtue, 33; and black preachers, 46; and idealized republican mothers, 86; and women's benevolent societies, 87
Providence Baptist Church, 63, 155
Public education, 33–34, 192 (n. 30)

Quakers: and abolitionism, 19; and American Colonization Society, 39, 60; in Loudoun County, 48, 49, 50, 51, 196 (n. 37); and African colonization, 50–51; antislavery views of, 50–52; Orthodox Friends versus Hicksite Friends, 51
Quarles, Benjamin, 228, 229

Race as category: meanings of, 1, 2, 26; African colonization's effects on, 5; and hereditary racial traits theories, 35; and concepts of racial origins, 156; and White City, 176, 221 (n. 16)
Racism: and American Colonization Society, 1, 228, 229, 231; scientific racism, 227
Rael, Patrick, 185 (n. 10), 230–31
Randolph, John, 32, 96
Reconstruction, 173, 227
Religious tract societies, 86–87, 90
Republicanism: and America as white republic, 2, 4, 176, 229; and rhetoric of American Colonization Society, 2, 176; and idealized republican mother, 4, 86, 100; Virginia's construction of, 5, 10; black critique of, 6, 230; and emigrants to Liberia, 7; emancipation based on, 19; and intermediate species of population, 27; slavery as corruption of, 84; George Washington as symbol of, 112

Republicans, 36, 37, 175
Rhode Island, 16
Rice, Anne, 99–100
Rice, John Holt, 15, 34, 35, 100, 110
Richards, Mary Jane, 98–99, 173–74, 221 (n. 10)
Richmond, 118
Richmond African Baptist Missionary Society, 63, 64, 69
Richmond Auxiliary, 32, 40–41, 43–45, 69, 77, 109, 144
Richmond Baptist Church, 66, 69
Richmond Enquirer, 42
Richmond-Manchester Auxiliary, 40–42, 47, 141, 194 (n. 8)
Richmond Temperance Society, 41
Richmond Whig, 42, 43
Ricks, Bob, 217 (n. 64)
Ricks, Henry, 169
Ricks, Martha Erskine Harris, 169, 177, 220 (n. 50), 222 (n. 19)
Rives, Judith Walker Page, 102
Roanoke County Auxiliary, 55
Roberts, Amelia, 71, 136
Roberts, Henry, 141
Roberts, Jane Rose Waring, 154, 155, 159, 165, 169
Roberts, Joseph Jenkins: emigration to Liberia, 71, 136; as president of Liberia, 152, 153, 155, 157, 166, 170, 175; and trade, 154; Victorian house of, 158–59; and slave trade, 159–60; as director of Public Works and Commercial Operations, 164; visits U.S., 165–66, 173; on U.S. recognition of Liberia, 167–68; death of, 175; correspondence of, 185 (n. 9)
Roberts, Colson, and Company, 154, 158
Robertsport, Liberia, 158
Rockbridge County Auxiliary, 55, 58, 59
Roper, David, 66
Ross, David, 67, 79

Smith, James Wesley, 230
Smith, William, 56
Smith, Willis, 78
Snyder, Jacob, 76
Southall, Adaline, 142–43
Southall, Henry, 142–43
Southall, Horace, 143
South Carolina: American Coloniza-
    tion Society auxiliaries in, 31; lack of
    support for colonization, 42, 45–46;
    and Nullification Controversy, 116;
    and emigration to Liberia, 173
Southern Literary Messenger, 41, 101,
    102, 109, 110
Sparks, Jared, 37
Sprigg, Nancy, 71
Starr, William, 59, 60–61, 77–78
States' rights: and Tallmadge
    Amendment debate, 37; and African
    colonization, 43; and Virginia
    Colonization Society, 45; and Dew,
    47; and Ruffin, 111; and burial site
    of George Washington, 116
Staudenraus, Philip, 223 (n. 4), 229
Stewart, Thomas, 68, 199–200 (n. 17)
Stockdell, James W., 201 (n. 35)
Stowe, Harriet Beecher: *Uncle Tom's
    Cabin*, 101, 102, 121
Stuart, Charles Augustus, 92–93

Tallmadge Amendment, 37
Tappan, Arthur, 190 (n. 18)
Tapscott, Martin, 146
Taylor, Francis, 154
Taylor, Jonathan, 51
Teage, Colin, 41, 63, 64, 66, 130, 140,
    157
Teage, Frances, 157
Teage, Hilary, 157, 159, 164–65
Temperance movement, 86–87
Texas, 173
Thompson, Martha, 132, 213 (n. 8)
True Whig Party, 175
Tucker, Beverley, 109, 110–11; *The
    Partisan Leader*, 111

Tucker, George, 16, 17, 42, 108–9,
    110, 121; *The Valley of the Shenandoah*,
    108
Tucker, St. George, 17, 108, 110
Turner, Henry M., 175, 177, 222
    (n. 19)
Turner, Joseph, 136
Turner, Nat, 46, 47, 60, 72, 92, 105,
    106–7, 128, 137, 146, 201 (n. 31)
Tyler, John, 44, 45, 48, 54, 102
Tyler, Julia Gardiner, 102
Tyranny: as effect of slavery, 84

U.S. Congress: lack of financial
    support for American Colonization
    Society, 2, 3, 27, 44, 60; petitioned
    by Charles Fenton Mercer for
    financial aid for asylum for free
    blacks, 20; Charles Fenton Mercer as
    advocate for American Colonization
    Society in, 27–29, 36; petitioned by
    auxiliaries of American Colonization
    Society, 42, 43; and Nullification
    Controversy, 116; and status of
    Liberian colony, 159
U.S. Constitution, 37
U.S. Supreme Court, 176–77, 227

Vai peoples, 130, 137, 148–49, 165,
    177
Valador, 72, 146–47
Van Lew, Elizabeth, 98, 173–74
Vermont Constitution of 1777, 16
Victoria (queen of England), 154, 169
Vine, 157, 168
Virginia: auxiliaries of American
    Colonization Society in, 3, 4, 39–42,
    44, 56, 60; support for American
    Colonization Society in, 3–4, 28, 39,
    190 (n. 10); free black population
    of, 4, 5, 11; debate on slavery in,
    4, 5, 16, 42–43, 45, 47, 49–51,
    54, 55–56, 60, 105–12, 231; and
    sectional dispute mediation, 4, 45;
    and construction of suitable past, 5;

Jamestown settlement narrative of, 6–7; constitution of, 13, 231; and antislavery laws, 16–17; abolition societies in, 19; and relocation of emancipated blacks, 21; economy of, 37, 39, 106, 107; secession from Union, 81, 111; British force slavery on, 105–6; utopian symbols of, 107, 111; and legality of visitors from Liberia, 144–45; post-Reconstruction politics in, 173

Virginia Argus, 10

Virginia Colonization Board, 59

Virginia Colonizationist, The, 56

Virginia Colonization Society: and gradual-emancipation tradition, 4; Marshall as president of, 29, 48, 139; Richmond-Manchester Auxiliary becomes, 44, 194 (n. 8); funding for, 45, 46–47, 54, 56, 57–58, 60; proslavery stance of, 51–52, 54, 56, 60, 64–65; meetings of, 52–53; reorganization of, 55–56, 60, 79, 101; funding of, for colony in Liberia, 57–58, 139, 215 (n. 29); attitude of, toward women's money-raising, 91; women's involvement in, 101, 103

Virginia colonization women: and vision of domestic utopia, 4–5, 88, 98; and Revolutionary ideals, 86; generational cohort of, 87, 103; and freedom from responsibilities of slaves, 88; and antislavery advocacy, 97; interest in emigrants to Liberia, 98; and slave marriages, 100, 207 (n. 64); later generation of, 101–3

Virginia Evangelical and Literary Magazine and Missionary Chronicle, 35, 110

Virginia General Assembly: and funding of Virginia Colonization Society, 4, 45, 46–47, 53, 57–58; and law restricting manumissions, 11, 13; and law ordering emancipated

slaves out of Virginia, 12; and Louisiana Purchase as site for removal of blacks, 12; Jefferson's secret correspondence with, 12, 19–20, 35, 37; and St. George Tucker's emancipation plan, 17; and law on assisting slaves' claims to freedom, 19; and national effort for relocation of emancipated and free blacks, 21; and funding of American Colonization Society, 44; and slavery, 46, 47, 56, 64–65; and funding of Liberian emigration, 47, 53, 56, 57–58, 59, 60, 61, 65, 73, 78, 139; and western Virginia efforts at constitutional change, 54–55; and laws restricting free blacks, 68; women's petitions to, 92–93

Virginia Manumission Act of 1782, 11, 13

Virginia Theological Seminary, 31

Virginia Whig Party, 90

Walker, David, 156, 200 (n. 25)

Walker, George, 142

Waring, Colston, 69, 92, 131, 132, 147, 154–55, 157, 200 (n. 26), 213 (n. 8)

Waring, Harriet Graves, 154, 155, 165

Warner, Jacob, 132

War of 1812, 19, 24, 36

Washington, Anne Blackburn, 113, 115

Washington, Bushrod, 28, 29–30, 49, 112, 113, 115, 122

Washington, George, 28, 29, 30, 102, 112, 113, 115, 116

Washington, Henry, 14

Washington, Jane Charlotte, 116

Washington, John Augustine, 29, 116

Washington, Martha, 113, 118

Washington, Walter, 117

Washington family, 5

Weaver, William, 138, 200 (n. 26), 213 (n. 8)

Wells, Ida B., 176

Westfall, Henry, 141

Whig Party, 175

White, Thomas Willis, 109

White City, 176

White men: and vision of domestic utopia, 4; and sexual license, 84, 122–23

White supremacists, 227

White Virginians: and republicanism, 4; and fear of slave rebellions, 10–11, 14, 20; on hiring-out practices, 11; debate over status of free blacks, 11, 12–13, 14; uneasiness with free black/slave relationship, 13; and antislavery laws, 16–17; free blacks' view of, 65–66, 81; and verbal and political assertiveness of black men, 75; and burden of slavery, 106, 120

White women: and vision of domestic utopia, 4–5, 84, 86, 90, 98; advocacy of education, 5, 46, 84, 87, 88, 90–91, 92, 98; and emancipated slaves sent to Liberia, 75; blacks' skepticism about intentions of, 83–84; commitment to African colonization, 84, 86, 100, 203 (n. 5); hagiographic biographies of, 84, 203 (n. 4); northern women compared to Virginia women, 86, 92, 97; antislavery advocacy of, 86, 92–96, 205 (n. 37); circulation of information among, 90; and class differences, 92, 97; and defense of slavery, 101–2. *See also* Virginia colonization women

Wilberforce, William, 31

Williams, Anthony D., 98, 149, 157, 213 (n. 8)

Wilson, Beverly R., 139, 166

Winchester Auxiliary, 55

Wise, Henry, 48

Wolff, Cynthia, 206 (n. 54)

Women. *See* Black women; White women

Woolfolk, Ben, 10

World's Columbian Exposition of 1893, 175–76

World War I, 182

Wynn, James, 73

Wythe, George, 67

Yates, Beverly Page, 71–72, 136

Young Men's Colonization Society of Pennsylvania, 74, 137

CPSIA information can be obtained
at www.ICGtesting.com
Printed in the USA
LVHW090045060619
620339LV00003B/323/P

9 781469 615189